Praise for

STOIC EMPATHY

"A radical approach to influence rooted in ethical strength. Kruse's synthesis of stoicism and empathy offers a road map for anyone navigating complex power dynamics. This book is a profound blend of philosophy, personal story, and actionable insights that will inspire readers to lead with both heart and mind."

— **Dr. Mike Dow**, *New York Times* best-selling author of *The Brain Fog Fix*

"Kruse encapsulates so many of the lessons that I teach my teenage children in this book. Two things can be true at the same time in that you can be both disciplined and tough and care for the people and the world around you. . . . A great example for us all to live by."

— **Pete Kadens**, co-founder and former CEO of Green Thumb Industries

"Shermin Kruse offers a master class of what Stoic Empathy is and how to harness this soft skill into something that translates across public and private sectors. . . . Kruse's book spoke to me as a leader, a woman, and a change agent. For those who lead people and value leading change, this is a must-read."

— **Amrith Aakre**, director of the U.S. Equal Employment Opportunity Commission's (EEOC) Chicago District

"Stoic Empathy might seem like a contradiction at first, but as you immerse yourself in Shermin Kruse's labor of love, the brilliance of her vision becomes clear. Epictetus, Seneca, and Stockdale would surely applaud this delightful and insightful book, masterfully crafted for the modern world."

— **Marie P. Anderson**, renowned modeling agent for Cindy Crawford, founder of Boss Babe Models, and former vice president of Elite/Chicago models

"A powerful reminder of what it truly means to be brave in the face of life's paradoxes. Stoic Empathy *is more than a book—it's a guide for navigating the complexities of modern life with resilience and an open heart. Shermin doesn't just teach you how to stay grounded amidst chaos; she shows you how to lean into your emotions with courage, grace, and intention."*

— **Dr. Neeta Bhushan**, author of *That Sucked. Now What?* and host of *The Brave Table podcast*

*"*Stoic Empathy *is as much a solution to the modern problem of chronic burnout as it is a title. Kruse cruises through a sweeping and compelling personal story rich in philosophy, ethics, and pragmatism. I could say that it borders on spirituality, but it might suffice to note that I would recommend this volume for its utile techniques of effective Method acting."*

— **Harry Lennix**, actor

"Teaching graduate students at Notre Dame, I often share 'life lessons' about managing influence and integrity. Shermin Kruse's Stoic Empathy *resonates with those teachings, offering a fresh and essential tool kit for anyone aiming to lead with both wisdom and empathy. . . .
This book is an indispensable resource for educators, leaders, and anyone committed to ethical self-leadership in an ever-changing world."*

— **Greg Hedges**, adjunct faculty, University of Notre Dame Mendoza School of Business, and president and CEO of the National Association of Corporate Directors Chicago Chapter

"In Stoic Empathy, *Shermin Kruse delivers a bold and practical guide for leaders who know that real influence starts with real connection. Her blend of stoicism and empathy isn't just compelling—it's actionable. As someone committed to empowering young people, I was blown away by how Kruse breaks down complex ideas into strategies you can use immediately to foster trust, build resilience, and create meaningful change. Whether you're mentoring, leading a team, or working with at-risk youth as I do, this book gives you the tools and mindset to make a meaningful impact."*

— **Josh Shipp**, youth advocate and best-selling author of *The Grown-Up's Guide to Teenage Humans*

"Shermin Kruse brings ethics to life in a way that's both practical and powerful. Kruse's clear and relatable approach shows how empathy and strength can work together to make a real difference in your life and the world around you. Stoic Empathy *weaves timeless wisdom with real-world examples to help anyone lead with integrity and purpose.
This is an essential guide for anyone who wants to be a change-maker, not as a tyrant, but with heart and courage."*

— **David Ambroz**, best-selling author of *A Place Called Home*

STOIC EMPATHY

STOIC EMPATHY

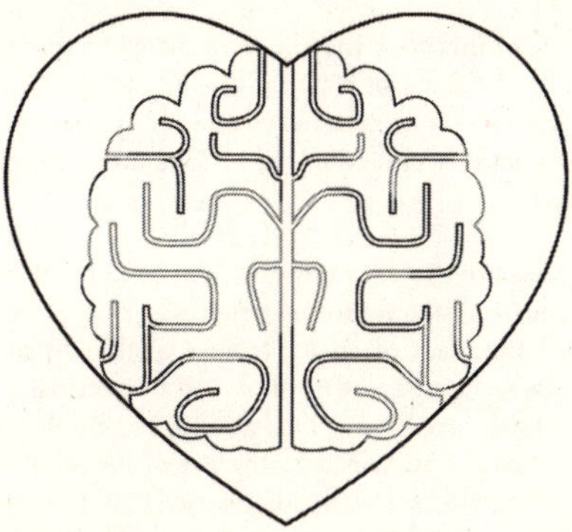

The ROAD MAP to a LIFE of INFLUENCE, SELF-LEADERSHIP, and INTEGRITY

SHERMIN KRUSE

HAY HOUSE INDIA
New Delhi • London • Sydney
Carlsbad, California • New York City

Hay House Publishers (India) Pvt Ltd
Muskaan Complex, Plot No. 3, B-2, Vasant Kunj, New Delhi – 110070, India

Hay House LLC, P.O. Box 5100, Carlsbad, CA 92018-5100, USA
Hay House UK Ltd, 1st Floor, Crawford Corner, 91-93 Baker Street, London W1U 6QQ, UK
Hay House Australia Publishing Pty Ltd, 18/36 Ralph St., Alexandria NSW 2015, Australia

Email: contact@hayhouse.co.in
Website: www.hayhouse.co.in

Cover design: Jo Obarowski • *Interior design:* Nick C. Welch
Interior photos/illustrations: Rachel Lara
Indexer: Shapiro Indexing Services

First published by Hay House India, 2025
10 9 8 7 6 5 4 3 2 1

ISBN 978-93-6611-748-5

Printed at Thomson Press

MIX
Paper | Supporting responsible forestry
FSC www.fsc.org
FSC® C010615

Hay House is committed to a sustainable future for our business, our readers and our planet. This book is made from Forest Stewardship Council® certified paper.

To my Zeeba, Pierce, Amara, and Cole, with unwavering love and commitment. May you always find the strength within your hearts and the power of your minds, knowing that these virtues shine brightest when united in purpose.

CONTENTS

PREFACE

I'm not afraid of storms, for I'm learning how to sail my ship.

— Louisa May Alcott, *Little Women*

Stoic Empathy might seem like a paradox—combining the rigidity of stoicism with the compassion of empathy. However, through my experiences and research, I've discovered that they're not opposing forces but symbiotic companions on the journey of self-discovery and influence. From childhood oppression and war to teenage bullying and climbing the corporate ladder, I've unearthed the profound synergy between stoicism and empathy. These aren't mere concepts to understand intellectually but guiding principles that, when embraced fully, become the bedrock of personal empowerment and societal change.

With this book, I serve as your navigator through the confluence of ancient Stoic wisdom and empathic connection, presenting a structured process that increases your power while deepening your relationships. With each chapter, I hope you'll not only be informed but also transformed as you explore the nuances of empathy, the discipline of stoicism, and the application of these timeless concepts in the modern world. As you progress along the path of Stoic Empathy, the book will draw on personal stories, influential figures and events, and expert research to explore its complex beauty. My goal is to provide you with a practical road map for navigating life's challenges with grace, resilience, and compassion while effecting meaningful change in the world.

The first chapter explores the nuanced interplay between external forces that shape our lives and the personal power we possess to navigate and influence these dynamics. It sets out the benefits of Stoic Empathy, which combines the fortitude and inner control espoused by Stoic philosophy with the deep understanding fostered by empathy to offer a transformative framework for wielding influence. Chapters 2 through 4 detangle the concept of empathy, and then 5 through 8 dig deep into stoicism.

Specifically, Chapters 2, 3, and 4 elaborate on the two primary types of empathy, Cognitive and Emotional, and set the foundation for their practical application through what I call *strategic empathy*. Together, these chapters draw out five essential tools to advance our empathic skills, including Affect Labeling, Silence, Active Listening, Mirroring and Repeating, and Probing Questions, to facilitate a deeper connection and trust between people, enhance rapport, and provide pathways to insights and clarity. Going far beyond trendy euphemisms, these chapters lay out scientific grounding behind the tools, provide techniques for empathetic engagement, and create a comprehensive framework for understanding and connecting with others in a more meaningful and empathic manner.

Chapters 5, 6, 7, and 8 shift focus to the principles of stoicism, grounding ancient wisdom in contemporary understanding and practical application. Together, these chapters update Greco-Roman philosophy to fit the modern era, highlight neuroscience breakthroughs that corroborate ancient teachings, distinguish emotional regulation from emotional denial (controlling our emotions isn't repressing them), and outline multiple emotional regulation exercises to unravel the mechanisms behind our ability to consciously manage our emotions. Significantly, just as the strategic empathy chapters earlier in the book present five empathy tools, the stoicism chapters in this part of the book set out five concrete methods of stoic self-regulation (updated with modern methodologies) to help you discern what is and is not in your control, modulate your emotions whenever possible, and act ethically at all times. These five techniques are Dichotomy of Control, Discomfort Embracing, Habituation, Memento Mori, and Moral Courage. Together, these chapters on stoicism equip you with the means to foster resilience, shape your character through consistent practice, and underscore the importance of living ethically and embracing life's impermanence, which can profoundly affect empathetic interactions.

Once we've explored the collaborative capabilities of stoicism and empathy, the last portion of the book shows how deliberately and purposefully employing Stoic Empathy equips us to navigate the complex dance of geopolitical issues with both compassion and strategic insight, enabling us to gain power while remaining true to our own ethics and values. With our newfound powers of persuasion and self-control, we must also embrace the duty to wield that power responsibly.

This book is more than a guide—it's an invitation to transform. It equips you with the knowledge to navigate life's complexities through an empathic lens enhanced by stoic clarity. By blending rigorous scientific research with philosophical depth, it challenges you to apply ancient principles in ways that are both strategically effective and profoundly ethical. As you move toward the concluding chapters, prepare to be empowered by a synthesis of stoic and empathetic mastery, ready to face the world with resilience, understanding, and virtue. Here you'll find actions, philosophies, tools, and stories to ethically influence and shape your environment and yourself, fostering a world where power is exercised wisely and with a deep awareness of its far-reaching implications.

Welcome to the journey.

CHAPTER 1

MY LIFE, POWER, AND APPLYING STOIC EMPATHY

The most common way people give up their power
is by thinking they don't have any.

— ALICE WALKER

I remember the evening vividly, like a painting come to life in my mind—vibrant, poignant, and bursting with energy. Our home in Iran buzzed with the excitement of the night's gathering. For me at 11 years old, these events offered a glimpse into a captivating yet mystifying world. The air was rich with the scents of cardamom and saffron, and sad songs softly colored the background as my mother danced through her cooking. Soon, the music shifted to livelier tunes as guests began arriving, each bringing stories of daily struggles. The living room, filled with relatives and friends, echoed with laughter and the murmur of deep conversations, while children darted in and out with games of hide-and-seek. As the night grew, so did the energy, transforming our space into a display of resilience underscored by the forbidden voices of Iranian exiles and Western rock—each melody a whisper of hope amid adversity. The very air we breathed was alive with our spirit. At the center of it all was Lily, who danced with a grace that seemed untouched by the years of political upheaval that had scarred our homeland. Unlike the other, more traditional aunts, Lily insisted we call her by her first name alone, discarding the "aunt" title and its aging formality. Her dance was more than an art—it was an act of resistance and self-preservation.

Lily's movements were fluid, each gesture weaving a narrative of resilience and quiet rebellion. With every step and turn, she seemed to cast off the world's burdens, embodying a profound Stoic Empathy. Here was a woman who had endured the betrayal of a revolution yet found strength, not in the overt displays of defiance, but in the subtlety of her dance. She showed us that true fortitude lies in maintaining one's essence in the face of misfortune, a lesson in emotional control and understanding deeply aligned with the principles of Stoicism.

Her dance reflected the stoic acceptance of her reality—acknowledging the pain but not being overcome by it—paired with a profound empathy, seen in the way her performance resonated with all who watched, mirroring their collective sorrow and optimism. This was Stoic Empathy in motion: the balance of enduring strength and visceral connection, setting the stage for us to explore how these forces aren't just compatible but synergistic.

Beneath the veneer of festivity and brightness of hope, though, there lay a palpable tension. As the music faded and conversations about politics and war filled the room, I was left to ponder the juxtaposition of our external chaos against the lively spirit that danced through our gatherings. Though I didn't always understand, I could listen and experience the fear, hope, and stoic acceptance of the turmoil that enveloped our country. As the evening waned and guests departed, I lay in bed, the echoes of laughter and somber conversations replaying in my mind. I closed my eyes and allowed Lily's silent protests against the chains that sought to bind her spirit, a powerful lesson in navigating life's complexities with both stoic wisdom and empathetic grace, lull me to sleep.

From my early childhood, it was stoicism, with its aspects of emotional regulation, and empathy, with its awareness of others, that got me through a time marked by revolution and war. It was 1979 and I was only two years old (my twin sisters were recently born) when Iran underwent a seismic shift in governance and culture. Revolution, transformation, and turmoil defined us as we transitioned into an

Islamic theocracy that redefined the fabric of our society. These years were further complicated by the outbreak of a devastating conflict with Iraq, a war that spanned a decade and etched the realities of fear, loss, and resilience deep into my psyche. In Tehran, where we lived, the war wasn't a distant concept relayed through news reports; it was our lived reality. Missile attacks shattered our tranquility in civilian areas, and the threat of violence loomed large, forcing us into bomb shelters and away from the normalcy of school and childhood play. My education during these formative years unfolded in the shadow of conflict, with state-sponsored math and reading programs on TV replacing traditional schooling and with the scarcity of essentials defining our daily lives.

But my real education was watching the adults around me, particularly my parents. During this tumultuous period, the conditions of our existence forced them to inhabit dual realities—a bifurcation of self that was as much a survival strategy as it was a silent rebellion. Outwardly, they presented a facade meticulously crafted to align with the expectations of the morality police, who enforced strict Islamic codes of behavior and dress through intimidation and public punishment, and the conservative ethos that now enveloped our everyday interactions. This external persona was a carefully orchestrated performance designed to navigate the scrutinizing gaze of a society keen on uniformity and adherence to its newly imposed norms. Survival required malleability to every situation, which meant awareness of who was around us at any time, what they were thinking, what they were feeling, and how they would respond to what we did—and, in turn, it required us to control our emotional experiences and expressions in response to the empathic read.

I exercised what I saw. The space for intellectual exploration within the confines of our home helped with my practice. There were always books around, constant poetry games, art in every meal, and best of all, heated debate about everything from politics to religions. This internal life was a testament to the human spirit's resilience, an assertion of identity in the face of systemic erasure. Navigating these divergent worlds from a tender age instilled in me an acute sense of awareness and adaptability. I learned not just to read a room but to embody its expectations, discerning the values and morals of those around me. This skill was constantly accompanied by my parents' ideals of equality, their faith in me that I could be *anything* the world around me allowed, and their refusal to *ever* resort to brutality, injustice, and exploitation. I watched as my mother seemingly controlled the very streets upon which she walked, while extending a helping hand to whoever needed it. I watched as my father practiced daily Transcendental Meditation, reciting a mantra a monk gave him when he was a teenager (a mantra he hasn't revealed to the family to this day). We maneuvered our way around the government and legal systems to get us permission to exit the country at a time when no other country would take an Iranian, without ever selling out a friend or taking advantage of a colleague to get what we wanted.

These teachings became my compass, allowing me to maneuver through the intricate labyrinths of social interactions and the challenges they presented. It was a dance of conformity and resistance played out on Tehran's shifting sands, where survival hinged on the ability to be a chameleon amid the stark black-and-white contrasts of our reality.

Stoic Empathy, in essence, is the delicate balance of strength and sensitivity, resilience and understanding. It's the quiet resolve to confront life's adversities with unwavering fortitude, coupled with strategic empathy that serves us as well as others. Through this synthesis, I've not only found solace and serenity within myself but also unlocked the potential to effect meaningful change in the world around me. With the union of stoicism and empathy, anyone can transcend the confines of our individual existence, contribute to the collective tapestry of human experience, and forge a more compassionate, resilient, and harmonious world—a world that honors the inherent dignity and worth of every person and sows the seeds of positive transformation.

A Power Approach to Life: Navigating Complex Power Dynamics with Stoic Empathy

As I reflect on my life, I recognize that the journey to embracing Stoic Empathy has been ongoing, a continuous evolution marked by moments of clarity and revelation. It's shaped my worldview, informed my advocacy, and imbued my words with a resonance born from lived experience.

The first of these insights is that, as I write these paragraphs today, I gratefully do so with the rather remarkable comfort to say and write as I wish without reprisal from the government. Yet, a sense of complete freedom eludes me. Others, you see, intrude upon my power.

I sometimes come across assertions like: "the only power others have over you is the power you give them" or "our reality is ours to manifest" or "nothing is beyond our control." They're frequently cited in various contexts, especially in discussions focusing on personal empowerment and self-determination. Reflecting on my childhood juxtaposed against my current life, one might argue these sayings find validation. Yet, these overly simplistic notions, rampant in self-help and motivational realms, aren't merely misleading but inherently dangerous. My childhood taught me (and adulthood confirmed) that every society is full of power dynamics that exist external to our individual selves. These entrenched dynamics extend from local communities to global interactions and cut across all imaginable divides: racial, cultural, political, economic, ethnic, and gender. Common platitudes of personal will overcoming all, therefore, overlook systemic inequalities that silently dictate aspects of our lives, often without our consent or knowledge.

Consider, for example:

- A corporate CEO can hold sway over his employees' livelihoods, impacting their access to healthcare, housing, and nutrition, balancing these interests with shareholder concerns.
- Stopped at a traffic light, a driver is suddenly approached by an armed person who demands they exit the car, ultimately driving away with it.
- A young lawyer up for a partnership he deserves is passed over again and again due to office politics and hidden agendas.

- A public health official navigates the complexities of managing a public health crisis, such as a pandemic, where decisions impact the health and safety of millions.

There is, in fact, a world external to us, with many other human minds—billions of them—influencing us and one another. Suggesting that people can simply override every power dynamic they're entrenched in dismisses the real and complex challenges that those under the yoke of oppression or discrimination face. It also carries the serious risk of misplaced responsibility, dangerously shifts blame onto victims (suggesting that if they suffer, it's by their own doing), and undermines the imperative for systemic change by overstating the role of personal agency.

But . . .

While it's essential to grasp the influence of external power dynamics, it's equally important to recognize the role of personal responsibility and agency. Phrases like "circumstances make men" or "show me your friends and I'll show you your future," while correctly highlighting the impact of environmental factors, oversimplify the complex interplay between individual agency and external influences. They risk undermining the importance of personal responsibility and willpower in shaping our lives and are complicit in hope-crushing feelings of learned helplessness that disempower people from all places and walks of life.

The reality, inherently more complex and enriching, transcends the limitations of simplistic maxims.

Acknowledging personal responsibility alongside external constraints doesn't deny the impact of societal, political, cultural, and economic forces on our lives. Instead, it cultivates a nuanced perspective that appreciates how our internal decisions significantly influence our life's direction. This balance isn't about denying the existence of external power dynamics; rather, it's about recognizing our capacity to navigate and respond to these forces with intention and resilience. While we *are* influenced by our social, political, cultural, and economic surroundings, we're also capable of self-determination and control over our responses to these influences.

In other words, understanding the complexity of power within a well-thought-out and meaningful framework doesn't give us total control of our lives, but neither does it mean that we are powerless. Rather:

The very existence of external influence demonstrates that we have some power over others, and furthermore, the impact of others on us does not render us powerless.

Our power over others?

That's best exercised through empathy.

Our power over ourselves?

That's the core of Stoic philosophy.

Therefore, the pages of this book will flesh out a power approach to life: Stoic Empathy, the application of empathic awareness and Stoic principles as tools to understand and navigate power dynamics constructively.

In this paradigm, we strategically use empathy, which in essence is information we've gathered about the mental and emotional states of another person, to navigate power dynamics and positively impact our environments and the people within them. Concurrently, the capacity for self-determination and control over our responses to external circumstances is rooted in the principles of ancient Stoicism, which teaches that while we may not have total control over external events, we can steer our reactions to them. Stoicism empowers us to recognize our agency in choosing our responses, thereby retaining a sense of control and self-efficacy. It also is a reminder that some matters are simply *beyond* our sphere of influence.

Stoic Empathy in Action: A Framework for Human Connection

Stoic Empathy integrates ethical considerations with strategies for influence, offering a path to impact our world while staying true to our values. This approach combines strategic empathy and Stoic principles into a framework for understanding and navigating human interactions effectively.

Let's look at a few examples of how these two perspectives come together in public, professional, and private life.

Public Health Official During a Pandemic

In the throes of a global health crisis, a public health official stands at the forefront, steering the response to a pandemic that threatens the health and safety of millions. This role involves not only the management of medical resources and the implementation of health policies but also the navigation of sociopolitical landscapes that influence societal behavior and perception.

- *Impact of Strategic Empathy:* In the midst of a pandemic, a public health official's strategic empathy becomes crucial, employing a nuanced understanding of the public and healthcare workers' fears, frustrations, and needs. By acknowledging the anxiety of families, the exhaustion of frontline workers, and the skepticism fueled by misinformation, the official crafts empathetic communication strategies that resonate personally, fostering trust and encouraging adherence to health guidelines. This approach enhances community health campaigns' effectiveness and addresses the pandemic's mental health impacts, ensuring interventions are tailored to the diverse cultural and socioeconomic contexts of communities, thereby promoting equitable access to resources and support.
- *Stoic Perspective:* Adopting a stoic perspective alongside empathy, the public health official recognizes the enormity of pandemic challenges and the limitations of control, facing the unpredictable virus mutations and variable public health measure compliance. Instead of yielding to despair, the official focuses on controllable aspects: spreading clear information; mobilizing resources for testing, treatment, and vaccination; and applying evidence-based measures to lessen the pandemic's effects. This stoic approach also equips the official to handle ethical dilemmas and difficult decisions like prioritizing vaccine distribution

and imposing health-protective restrictions, underscoring resilience and the importance of a rational, clear-headed approach to problem-solving and decision-making.

Employees and the Workplace Bully

An employee is working for an unreasonable supervisor who has significant control over their lives, including their benefits, time off, and even job security. However, the employee possesses power in their professional development, adaptability, and the pursuit of opportunities inside or outside the company. They can also find empowerment in advocating for workplace rights and engaging in collective action.

- *Impact of Strategic Empathy:* Employees using empathy strategically can better understand the challenges and pressures faced by leadership and their specific boss. This insight can lead to more effective communication and advocacy within the company, potentially influencing the supervisor's policies and practices. Empathetic employees can also create a more supportive and collaborative work setting, which can improve overall morale and productivity, indirectly influencing the supervisor's decisions and company direction.
- *Stoic Perspective:* The employee focuses on what they can control—their skills, their adaptability, and their response to change, understanding that their worth is not determined solely by their employment status.

The Inconsiderate Spouse

A person's spouse constantly makes them late, resulting in trouble at work. This repeated action creates stress and tension in their personal and professional life.

- *Impact of Strategic Empathy:* By employing strategic empathy, the person seeks to understand the underlying reasons behind their spouse's behavior. They engage in open, empathetic conversations to explore any issues or challenges their spouse might be facing. This approach can help identify potential solutions, such as better time-management practices or mutual agreements on schedules, fostering a more cooperative and understanding relationship. Additionally, the individual can express how the behavior impacts their work, appealing to their spouse's empathy and encouraging change.
- *Stoic Perspective:* Adopting a stoic perspective, the individual focuses on what they can control—their reactions and their efforts to mitigate the impact of their spouse's conduct. They might set up contingencies, such as leaving earlier to accommodate potential delays or finding alternative transportation. By maintaining a calm and rational mindset, they can manage their stress and frustration, ensuring that their professional responsibilities aren't compromised by personal challenges.

The essence of this work lies in its holistic view, providing tools for deep comprehension of others and morally sound actions. Supported by scientific evidence and illustrative stories, this concept bridges ancient philosophy with modern challenges, showing how timeless principles apply today. By updating ancient teachings with contemporary ethical thought, Stoic Empathy emerges as a transformative method, empowering us to wield influence, master the complexities of relationships, and ensure our actions are both impactful and aligned with our moral compass.

Applying Stoic Empathy: Enhancing Negotiations, Relationships, and Personal Resilience

Stoic Empathy, a potent fusion of understanding and emotional resilience, not only enriches our lives but fundamentally transforms our interactions and decisions. By allowing us to connect deeply with others' perspectives, needs, and emotions, it extends our influence and enhances our effectiveness in negotiations, relationships, and even personal growth. This dual capacity to empathize and maintain emotional balance empowers us to navigate complex social dynamics with grace and strategic insight, leading to more meaningful and constructive outcomes in both personal and professional realms.

For instance:

- *Negotiations:* Strategic empathy enables us to understand and resonate with the perspectives, needs, and emotions of the other party, allowing us to extend our radius of influence, control, and power while fostering an environment of mutual respect and open communication. Stoicism allows us to approach negotiations with a clear, calm mindset so we can focus on objective outcomes rather than be swayed by emotional responses. This dual approach not only aids in reaching more favorable outcomes as well as amicable and effective agreements, but also in maintaining positive alliances post negotiation, a key aspect often overlooked in the heat of the moment. With a balance between emotional insight and rational thought, we can steer negotiations in a way that is beneficial for all parties involved, fostering trust and respect and positioning us as effective, fair negotiators, enhancing our influence in both personal and professional spheres.
- *Personal Relationships and Workplace Dynamics:* Empathy, when strategically utilized, allows you to understand and connect with the feelings of others, enhancing your personal and professional bonds. You can facilitate more collaborative and understanding

home and work environments, essential for teamwork and management of both. Stoicism provides a framework for managing your own emotions, which can prevent overreactions during even the most heated moments and lead to healthier and more stable relationships. This balance enhances the depth and quality of our personal connections. It also furthers our abilities and success as current or would-be leaders, because leaders who embody these traits are often more respected and effective. This not only enhances our personal power but also contributes to a more productive and positive organizational dynamic and a greater sense of achievement and satisfaction.

- *Stress Management and Conflict Resolution:* With empathy, we can understand others' perspectives, significantly reducing conflict and the stress that comes with it. This paves the way for resolution and swaying hearts and minds, even sometimes when it didn't seem possible at first. The ability to remain composed and objective in stressful situations, combined with the foresight of knowing what you can and can't change—while also considering the emotional aspects of conflicts—make experts into conflict and stress navigators. The ability to remain calm and empathetic under pressure is a rare and valuable asset in today's fast-paced and often high-pressure environments.
- *Personal Growth:* Empathy contributes to developing emotional intelligence, critical for both personal betterment and professional advancement. Stoicism, on the other hand, fosters self-reflection and resilience. The practice of Stoic Empathy enhances these qualities, helping us understand and influence the world around us. By continually honing these skills, we adapt better, understand others more deeply, and maintain emotional stability, giving us a significant advantage in navigating the ever-changing power dynamics of our world.

- *Communication Skills and Problem Solving:* Empathy improves your ability to listen and respond effectively, improving communication. Communicating clearly and without emotional bias, which stoicism helps you do—while also being receptive to others' emotions and perspectives—is crucial in building strong, influential relationships. It lets you not only solve problems, but also innovate in new realms that you thought you couldn't before. This skill is invaluable in all aspects of life, from personal interactions to professional engagements.
- *Mental Health and Coping with Change:* With strategic empathy, we gain sway in our world while still enhancing the long-term social bonds that are good for our mental health and overall well-being. Practicing stoicism can yield equal if not more mental health, minimizing suffering, expanding joy, and leading us to a more contented life by focusing on what we can and can't control. Better mental health significantly increases our power to achieve our goals and enjoy the very essence of life itself.

Beyond Borders and Barriers: From Iran to Interconnected

My work with Stoic Empathy followed me far beyond my early childhood in Iran that I described at the start of this chapter. In 1988, when I was 11, we packed it all up to move: Canada was waiting for us. In so many ways, it felt like the "happily ever after" part of the fairy tale—the struggle was over, and we'd won. My child self believed (much more than hoped) that immigrating to a new country would be a panacea for all the troubles we faced. In my youthful innocence, I imagined that the world beyond the reach of air raids and oppressive regimes, the place where freedom and opportunities were abundant, would be entirely problem-free.

Upon immigrating, I was, indeed, free of rockets. Went to a real school and played in the park with my sisters, wearing whatever I wanted. I had a much more open future ahead of me. And yet we left behind our family, our money, and our socioeconomic status; our photo albums, our silver, our Lily—and our very soil. What's more, I came face-to-face with the multifaceted challenges posed by my financial insecurity, gender, and national origin. These aspects of my identity, which I carried with me across borders, were significant barriers in my quest to establish myself in a world that often seemed indifferent, if not hostile, to my aspirations. The realization that my journey toward empowerment and success would be an uphill battle and fraught with its own unique set of obstacles, even in a Western, democratic country, was a sobering awakening from my childhood dreams.

I quickly learned that even in a society as open and democratic as Canada's, power dynamics and systemic barriers persist, subtly shaping the experiences of immigrants, people of color, women, and other marginalized groups. I was a fish out of water if you'd ever seen one, without any preparation for adaptation into this new culture, without even the ability to speak to the other fish—since I had no English-language skills before immigrating. I was severely bullied in lower and middle school, a kind of suffering that sometimes made my young mind wonder whether I'd have been better off with rockets and morality police (I wouldn't have). While I learned English within six months of immigration, it took me until my junior year of high school to find my voice again, to adapt fully to this new world and navigate through it to pursue my goals.

Interestingly, it was debate class that opened my eyes to my ability to craft an emotional and logical argument. Learning that, when presented with a captive audience, I could *argue* my way into and out of anything, was a revelation—and more importantly, realizing that the more I knew my audience, the more convincing I'd be. I'd been reading rooms and people since I was a toddler. So, I went back to my old tool kit: asking myself, "What are they thinking?" or "What are they feeling?" I kept calm, creating space in my mind to evaluate and think, always holding true to what I believed was right, refusing to take advantage of others' weakness, and holding compassion as much as I could. There were many failures. But as time passed, I succeeded more and more.

In university, I continued my climb into the world of persuasion. Fascinated by self-discovery and intellectual rigor, I studied neuropsychology and philosophy at the University of Toronto. My work in philosophy emphasized logic and argument as well as metaphysics, beginning with Greco-Roman Stoics and continuing from there all the way to 20th-century thought. At the same time, my neuropsychology research fed my appetite for exploring human nature through evidence-based studies, learning about psychological thought of all kinds, and using cognitive-behavioral psychology as a means of personal control and growth. I didn't realize it at the time, but looking back, I can see that I've been immersed in the study of understanding human beings, including myself, since I was a child.

After graduation, law school and opportunities in the United States seemed like excellent next moves. So I moved a little south, finding myself within the halls of Michigan Law School. But in the U.S., land of opportunity and diversity, I found echoes of the same power dynamics I'd experienced in Canada. Eventually, though with a mountain of law-school debt and no family connections to get me started in the corporate world, I began to see a path of power that was different from the others. My ability to relate to and influence others using psychology and logic, combined with my increasing study of controlling my own emotions during moments of intense stress, fueled a 20-year legal practice in the realm of international multinational corporations (primarily in the fashion sector and the Louis Vuitton Moet Hennessy (LVMH) group of companies, but including others such as Shell Oil and Volkswagen). I could navigate my way through an intimidating courtroom, representing clients in nine-figure cases despite often being the youngest, only woman, or only person of color in the room. I formed alliances within my firm's partnership, recruited my own major corporate clients (such as Walmart and Google) into the firm, and forged meaningful relationships with my colleagues, many of whom I'm friends with to this day. My legal career also gave me the gift of financial security, and with it, a host of new freedoms.

I found love. We had kids. Four of them.

Meanwhile, I entrenched myself more and more in the study of influence, control, and resilience. Eventually, this led me to teaching negotiation and persuasion using empathy at Northwestern University Pritzker School of Law, changing the world of ideas by giving and producing TED and TEDx talks (over 80 of them), and contributing to literature with as much writing as I could—including this book.

My nearly half century of living and studying Stoic Empathy has therefore become the ultimate integration of control. It can be for you as well. This is because with Stoic Empathy, we engage in the dual process of gaining power and influence by controlling the world around us (using empathy) and the world within us (using stoicism). With core stoic internalized strength, we can slow down the time between stimulus and response, essentially gaining us greater access to a calm stillness and rationality regardless of the power dynamics around us. Mastery over our reactions provides a solid foundation for clear thinking and deliberate action, allowing us to navigate life's challenges with poise and resilience. Simultaneously, by practicing strategic empathy, we cultivate the capacity to understand and connect with others on a profound level. This empathetic reach empowers us to influence and transform the dynamics around us, fostering relationships and environments that reflect our values and intentions. By harmonizing stoic self-control with empathetic outreach, we enhance our internal fortitude and external influence. This powerful combination allows us to exert control over our inner world through stoicism and extend our reach into the external world through empathy.

Chapter 1 Takeaways

In this chapter, we've explored the following key concepts:

- Understand power dynamics within our complex social structures to find free will amid determinism.
- Apply Stoic Empathy in various contexts including negotiation, relationships, and personal resilience.

CHAPTER 2

COGNITIVE VERSUS EMOTIONAL EMPATHY

Language shows us that naming an experience doesn't give the experience more power, it gives us the power of understanding and meaning.

— Brené Brown

Joel Braunold is a public policy entrepreneur. These folks work with foreign and domestic policymakers to implement entrepreneurial strategies that can shift the status quo of entire governmental systems. Joel's specialization is in how to finance peacebuilding within international conflict resolution. Believe it or not, financing war is much easier than financing peace. For the last decade and a half, Joel's primary work has been in the Middle East. For many years, he was the CEO of the largest trade association of Israeli-Palestinian and Jewish-Arab peace groups in the world. As the executive director of the Alliance for Middle East Peace, he was instrumental in passing domestic legislation, authorizing a quarter-of-a-billion-dollar peacebuilding fund for the organizations he was serving. He's now the head of a private think tank, working with leaders in the Middle East and North Africa to find and implement macro and micro peace possibilities. Joel and I are both former fellows of the Chicago Council on Global Affairs and still friends. I know him and his family on a personal, "our kids play together" level and can assuredly say that Joel is one of the most compassionate and caring humans I know. And yet, I've never seen him become emotionally involved, or take an emotional or political position, in Middle East politics. I've watched as Joel, an Orthodox Jew who wears the kippah, works with Palestinian, Arab, and Muslim leaders to facilitate backdoor meetings that many times avoided tragedy or at least permitted communication, balancing that with his Jewish faith without ever displaying an allegiance to either side.

When it comes to contentious issues such as Mideast conflicts and policies, many are steadfast that there is only the *right* side and the *wrong* side. Sometimes such passions are held by advocates fighting for their people. Other times, they're espoused by politicians looking for reelection. For many, which "side" to support isn't complicated at all but a very simple fact that is observable and discernable by anyone who cares to really look. But if you're Joel, a peace advocate with the arduous work of directing policy development or facilitating dialogue to end or at least reduce conflict, looking at both sides simultaneously is necessary to do your job. In Joel's case and that of many other aid and peace workers, without the acceptance and trust of *both* sides, there would be no dialogue. As horrible as the situation is, it *would* get even worse. Simultaneously, as a peace worker, you see, hear, and feel the atrocities directly and routinely. You're viscerally bombarded—usually not in the same way as affected populations (although sometimes in this way as well, given the scale of the conflict), but more so than the average news consumer or distant politician.

"These conflicts are some of the most emotive conflicts on our planet," says Joel, "and there are very few people who can truly empathize with both sides, because most people believe that empathy would be a form of alignment and solidarity. In addition, these conflicts suffer from the fact that while there's an asymmetry of power, there's a symmetry of fear and mistrust. And very few people have had the opportunity or the interest to get to know and understand *both* sides without judgment or alignment. But I couldn't do my job unless I figured out a way to do that. It's *not* an easy task. But I don't have a choice." Joel is only human. How can he keep emotionally distant while gathering enough about each side to facilitate the objectives of his organization and assist in building peace resilience and dialogue even when it seems impossible? Because that's what his job as a peacebuilder essentially is: the very difficult task of *understanding* the perspective of the various people he's bringing together *without feeling* what they're feeling.

Far too often we focus only on the emotional connections that empathy can foster while ignoring the cognitive aspects. But those cognitive elements not only give us leverage; they also keep us emotionally grounded, allowing room for greater compassion without allowing our capacity for empathy to collapse. This need for emotional distance might seem obvious if we're discussing the life of someone in a role like Joel's, but how about:

- a trauma counselor;
- a lawyer advocating for a client who's a teen sexual-violence victim or an innocent criminal defendant;
- the owner of a family-owned business who poured her heart into her work for dozens of years before her accountant embezzled her life savings;
- a corporate CEO whose success will determine the employment status of hundreds of thousands of people while balancing consumer safety concerns and the environmental impact of their factories;
- a parent managing her teen's emotional turmoil;
- a salesperson who faces a quota on one hand and a client who's a single mom on a budget on the other hand; or
- the average couple struggling with conflict resolution?

It's essential for those seeking greater influence, power, or impact in the economic, social, domestic, political, and corporate spheres to distinguish between cognitive and emotional empathy, regardless of their particular social, economic, or political role in our society, and learn to modulate between the two given a particular situation. The reality is that, in the majority of negotiations, there's no clear "good guy" or "bad guy." Real life is complicated and full of gray and ambiguous spaces.

This chapter will explore what empathy is, what factors distinguish cognitive from emotional empathy, how cognitive empathy can help you avoid not only emotional alignment but also empathy collapse, why you should learn to oscillate between the two depending on the circumstances at hand, and how to tactically utilize your knowledge of the "other" and the situation to gain leverage. Most significantly, since there's already an understanding of *emotional* empathy in our culture and a wealth of literature on it, we'll spend more time here presenting you with the second, equally significant and hardly explored half of the empathy spectrum: cognitive empathy.

Empathy Versus Sympathy Versus Compassion

I'm very close with my father-in-law, Joseph, which some people find surprising given how different we are in terms of our political and sometimes even our global ideologies. This is a man whose dad worked the steel mills of Pittsburgh until he died and whose mom ran moonshine and fed the family on potatoes for months to make ends meet when the mill workers went on strike. As a child, he was beaten by the nuns at school if he did the wrong thing, lost friends to the random accidents that involved train tracks or lack of seat belts, and learned to like duck-blood soup because that's what you ate sometimes if you were a poor Polish Catholic living in a steel-mill town in the 1940s. Joseph pulled himself out of hunger and poverty with a combination of grit, street smarts, and outstanding basketball skills. He graduated Virginia Military Institute with a chemistry degree and a great jump shot, only to be enlisted as an officer in one of the most tragic wars in American history. They gave him an artillery unit and a hundred men. He kept all 100 alive, holding their minds and spirits intact by building a basketball court in the middle of the jungle using artillery boxes. Joseph earned a Bronze Star and a number of buried memories I've never heard him discuss. He came back to the wife he married shortly before he left and the son he barely knew, adjusted quickly, took up sales and made his way into the top one percent of income earners in this country. He was thus able to pay for his son's college, so his progeny didn't need to join the military or fight a war just to afford an education, and is now spending a very happy retirement traveling (going-to-the-South-Pole-in-his-late-70s kind of traveling). We might vote for opposite parties at the ballot box, but I adore this man nevertheless, which is saying something in these divided times.

I mention Joseph because he's the perfect example of how difficult it is to understand the concept of empathy. A few years after we met, the family was sitting around in the kitchen and chatting, and Joseph admitted he didn't know what empathy was. I mean, literally didn't know what it meant. We all had a good laugh. "Oh, of course *you* don't know what empathy is, Joe! They don't teach that at military school!" That night, though, no one could *really* explain empathy to Joseph. We *tried*, but not with much success. He was asking really good questions: "How's that different from compassion?" or "Isn't that sympathy?" and "So when you feel bad for someone, that's empathy?"

It's not just my military father-in-law; Joseph isn't alone. Most of us, when discussing emotions and responses to the experiences of others, tend to inadvertently interchange the terms *sympathy*, *compassion*, and *empathy*. This overlap, while understandable given the blurred lines in the realm of emotional responses, underscores a fundamental distinction in how we relate to and understand the experiences of those around us. The night of our conversation, Joseph concluded the evening by deciding that empathy wasn't necessary at all and that it duplicated a number of other actions and emotions. This is *not* where any of us wanted Joseph to end up that night!

We circled back to the conversation a few times after that in talks that really helped *me* understand and frame a very clear definition of empathy as distinct from sympathy and compassion. Let's discuss it.

- *Sympathy:* "Please accept my deepest condolences." Sympathy is an external expression, often manifesting as a recognition of another's misfortune. It's characterized by feelings of pity or sorrow for someone else's situation. When someone endures a hardship or a loss, we might offer words of consolation or send a sympathy card. Such gestures act as an acknowledgment of their pain, signaling, "I see your suffering." While sympathy holds its own importance and provides a way to express concern, it maintains a level of emotional distance. The one extending sympathy remains somewhat removed, acting more as an observer of the pain or discomfort being experienced by someone else.

- *Compassion:* "I'm sorry about your struggle. I'm here to do whatever I can to make things easier for you. Can I bring dinner for the family tomorrow?" Compassion goes a step further than sympathy. It's not only an expression of sorrow or pity for the pain of another person, but also the desire to help alleviate their suffering. Compassion often involves an element of action or a motivation to act based on concern for the well-being of others.
- *Empathy:* "Your pain in my heart" or "I can see that you're really excited about this!" In contrast to sympathy, empathy transcends mere acknowledgment. It represents an attempt to truly understand another person's emotions and perspective. Rather than standing at the periphery, empathy involves a closer approach—striving to grasp the intricacies of another's emotional landscape. In essence, while sympathy offers a kind gesture from a distance, empathy, in its various forms, seeks a deeper closeness and appreciation, enabling us to navigate the intricate web of human emotions and alliances more adeptly. It's further distinct from compassion because empathy isn't necessarily action oriented; in fact, some may feel absolutely frozen by it.

In sum, while sympathy provides a comforting recognition from afar and empathy fosters a deep, shared understanding of another's feelings, compassion bridges these with the impetus to take tangible steps to ease someone else's suffering. Each of these emotional responses plays a unique role in human connection, illustrating the varied ways we can respond to the emotions and experiences of those around us. With those general definitions in mind, let's dig much deeper into empathy.

The Two Facets of Empathy

This profound connection of empathy further branches into two distinct types: emotional and cognitive. **Emotional empathy** (or "affective" empathy) represents our innate response to others' states of mind. It's that instinctual mirroring of emotions when we witness someone experiencing joy, pain, or any other emotion. It's not calculated; it's a spontaneous and heartfelt reaction where we find ourselves feeling along with someone as if their emotions resonate within us. It's spontaneous and yet something we can cultivate. **Cognitive empathy** (or "evaluative" empathy), on the other hand, is a more deliberate form of insight. It doesn't necessarily involve the feeling of another's emotions, focusing instead on comprehending another's feelings and perspectives. It's akin to studying someone's narrative, discerning their challenges and emotions, and subsequently being able to predict or respond to their needs without being emotionally entangled.*

1. Emotional Empathy

Picture you're watching TV and seeing your favorite character, whom you've spent an entire season getting to know and relate to, driving a car. They're happy in this moment—everything is going great for Jordan, upbeat music is playing in the background, the sun is shining, and the trees are a vibrant green. Suddenly, a *ding* sounds, indicating a text message. Jordan scrambles to retrieve the phone, eyes

---

* Some researchers also identify a third type of empathy they call *compassionate empathy*, and others divide up empathy completely differently between *embodied empathy* and *mental empathy*. For purposes of clarity, we consider only the most researched, studied, and confirmed type of empathic divide: that between *emotional* and *cognitive*.

darting to the urgent message, and you can feel the tension mounting. Just as you anticipate, the distraction proves disastrous. Another car comes out of nowhere, colliding violently with Jordan's side in a deafening crash. The world inside the car whirls chaotically—everything spinning, glass shattering, the frame of the car grotesquely twisting. The phone flies out of Jordan's hand, symbolizing the sudden loss of control.

Your own reaction is visceral and immediate: You find yourself physically recoiling, gasping, or turning your head away from the screen. In this moment, you experience emotions that mirror Jordan's feelings. Of course, you don't feel the sharp sting of the glass cutting Jordan's face or the brutal jolt of the impact as he jerks back. Nothing bad has happened to you at all. Jordan isn't real—he's a fictional character. Yet his distress is your distress.

Emotional empathy goes beyond mirroring the emotional state of a fictional character during a dramatic television moment. As it pertains to some shows and movies, such as the dramatic film *Black Swan*, your brain can mirror the neural state of the fictional character's brain. *Black Swan* is a psychological thriller centered around Nina, a committed ballerina played by Natalie Portman. The film explores Nina's intense psychological journey in the competitive world of ballet, where her quest for perfection leads to a blurring of the lines between reality and fantasy, culminating in a descent into madness.

The climax of the film occurs during a crucial performance of *Swan Lake*, where Nina's transformation reaches its peak. Onstage, her passionate dance, combined with powerful emotions and vivid visual effects, fully immerses the audience in her experience. This moment is not just a display of her dance prowess but a representation of her psychological unraveling into full-blown schizophrenia. What does the audience undergo during this scene?

Astoundingly, according to Prof. Talma Hendler (Tel Aviv University's Sackler Faculty of Medicine, Sagol School of Neuroscience, and School of Psychological Sciences), audiences watching the dramatic scene have brain activity resembling that observed in many schizophrenics. At an event sponsored by the Academy of Motion Picture Arts and Sciences, Prof. Hendler said, "As Nina is getting crazier and crazier, the audience experiences something like schizophrenia."

We're drawn into the world of Nina; every pirouette, every stolen glance, each layer of makeup serves to weave the intricate tapestry of Nina's evolving psyche. With each scene, she becomes more tumultuous and her reality increasingly blurred, immersing the audience in Nina's descent into madness. The line between her world and the viewers' begins to waver. Thus, quite literally, viewers' brain patterns during the film's climax and Nina's descent into schizophrenia actually mimic the patterns of schizophrenic people.

The power of storytelling is undeniable and far-reaching, truly demonstrating the depths of emotional empathy. The strength of emotional empathy (affective in nature) lies in its universality. It doesn't discriminate between real and reel. When we watch characters on-screen, we don't just observe their behaviors; we live them, feel them, and are often profoundly affected by them. This is the quintessence of emotional empathy—feeling another's emotion as if it were our own. But while great cinema has a profound capacity to evoke emotional empathy, the impact of witnessing real emotions in real people can be even more striking. In real-life scenarios, the immediacy and authenticity of the emotions displayed carry a much higher weight than when watching a movie. When we observe the emotions of a real person, the connection isn't just with a character but with a fellow human being. We interact with experiences and reactions that aren't the product of a writer's imagination but the genuine article of human experience (sometimes within the context of meaningful and long-term relationships). This personal proximity means that when we empathize with someone in real life, it's often a reflection of our own experiences and understanding of the world, making the emotional impact more profound and personal.

Consider, for example:

- *Comforting a Friend:* When a friend shares that they are going through a tough time and you feel a sense of sadness or distress because you can sense their pain, that's emotional empathy in action.
- *Sports Fans' Reactions:* Experiencing a sense of personal defeat or exhilaration in response to the outcome of a

sports game, especially if you feel strongly connected to the team.

- *Parental Instinct:* A parent feeling distress when they hear their baby crying, driven by an innate response to soothe and comfort their child.
- *Hearing Good News:* Feeling a rush of happiness when a friend tells you about their promotion or other good news as if the success were your own.
- *Public-Speaking Sympathy:* Feeling nervous or experiencing secondhand embarrassment when watching someone struggle during a public speaking event, imagining how you would feel in their place.

To better understand this remarkable phenomenon, let's go back a few decades to the early 1990s, when a group of Italian researchers made a groundbreaking discovery in the realm of neuroscience. While studying the brains of macaque monkeys, they stumbled upon a type of neuron that activated *both* when a monkey performed an action (raised his arm) *and* when it merely *observed* the same action being performed by another (watched his friend raise her arm). This type of neuron, later dubbed the *mirror neuron*, presented a novel way of understanding neural processing.

Mirror neurons don't quite work the same way with humans, but since the early 2000s, researchers have been isolating what they've termed a *mirror neuron system* (MNS) in human brains.[1] The MNS is a group of specialized neurons in the brain helping us understand the actions and intentions of others. This system enables us to mirror or simulate the actions and emotions of others, essentially creating a form of internal imitation. It's like the brain is "mirroring" the actions it observes. It's what underpins our ability to learn through observation, navigate social interactions, and even have fun at the movie.[2]

In 2016, scientists created a map of the neural connections in the brain, called the *connectome*. The lead researcher in this area, Selen Atasoy, applied mathematical concepts to the connectome to see the brain's activity not as a series of isolated regions lighting up in response to specific stimuli (like single instruments playing at the same time but unrelated to one another), but as a *network* of interconnected regions resonating in harmony (like an orchestra harmonizing a symphony).[3] With this new research, we gained new perspective on how brain regions communicate. Rather than with discrete, linear communication, these regions interact in a highly synchronized, wavelike manner. These harmonics then shape our experiences, thoughts, and emotions. This explains why I and my husband can have different experiences watching the same movie or why we react or *feel* differently in response to our home team winning the championships or our child falling off a bike. To say the least, Atasoy and her team's findings push us to reconsider our perception of brain functionality. Instead of being collections of discrete processors, our brains are producing harmonies that shape our very essence. This research underscores the profound depth of emotional empathy, suggesting that our brains experience emotions individually *and* in harmony with others' emotional states.

2. Cognitive Empathy

Cognitive empathy (also known as *evaluative empathy*) revolves around the art of comprehending—a cerebral approach to understanding another person's emotional and mental state—*without* being immersed in those feelings ourselves. To arm our grasp of cognitive empathy, it helps to discuss the different regions of the brain activated during cognitive versus emotional empathy.

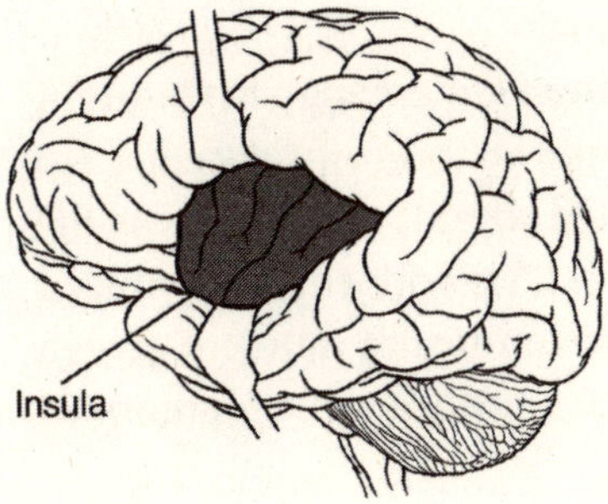

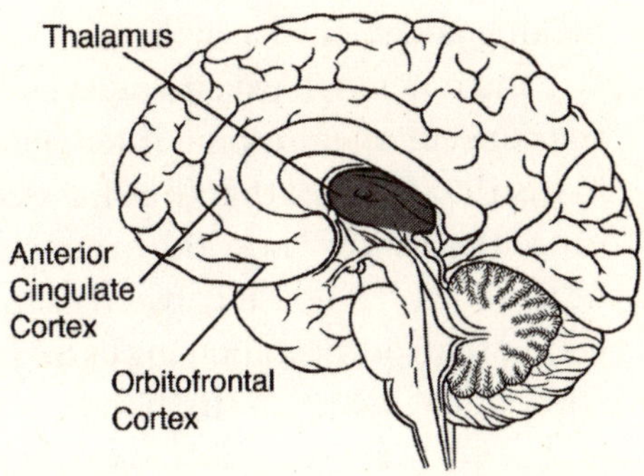

Emotional empathy, which entails sharing and appreciating others' emotions, activates:

- the right dorsal anterior cingulate cortex (involved in emotion processing and regulation);
- the right anterior insula (crucial for emotional state awareness and bodily sensations);
- the left anterior insula (with similar roles but perhaps more cognitive functions); and
- the right dorsomedial thalamus and the midbrain (both key in processing emotions and autonomic responses).

Conversely, cognitive empathy, focused on understanding and evaluating others' thoughts and emotions, engages different areas:

- the left orbitofrontal cortex (essential for decision-making and evaluating outcomes);
- the left anterior midcingulate cortex (involved in decision-making and social interactions); and
- the left dorsomedial thalamus (integral to cognitive functions and emotional information processing).

This differentiation highlights how emotional empathy is more about feeling, sharing emotions, and engaging emotion-related and bodily awareness regions, while cognitive empathy is more about the understanding and evaluation of mental states, involving decision-making and cognitive evaluation regions.[4]

The renowned psychologist Dr. Daniel Goleman, who brought the concept of emotional intelligence to the forefront decades ago in his 1995 book of that title, has detailed cognitive empathy as the capacity to know "how the other person feels and what they might be thinking." It doesn't absorb us in the emotional state but gives a map of that journey, allowing us to intellectualize another's emotions without feeling them firsthand.

Imagine, for a moment, you're an explorer traveling an uncharted territory. The terrain is vast and unpredictable, filled with hidden valleys and peaks of human emotion and thought. Now I want to hand you a compass—but not just any compass. This is the compass of *empathic accuracy*, a tool specifically crafted to navigate the intricate landscapes of the human psyche. Instead of pointing north, it points to the underlying emotions and motivations of the person you're engaging with.

Like an experienced explorer, you'll soon understand that the strength of this compass lies not in getting lost in the surrounding emotional turmoil, but in something else. Instead, it offers insight, allowing you to understand feelings and thoughts from a distance. You won't feel the heat of someone's anger or the cold of their indifference; still, you'll see with more clarity their origin, current situation, *and* ultimate destination, allowing you to adjust your sails and tailor your responses accordingly. It's a different way to maneuver through interpersonal relationships. Instead of getting wet from the rain of another's sadness or warmed by the sun of their joy, you remain observant and understanding. The knowledge you gain from this vantage point is invaluable. You can predict where the path will lead next, anticipate challenges, and prepare for them.

In the complex web of human interactions, cognitive empathy has evolved as a sophisticated intellectual tool. Our ability to perceive minute facial cues, interpret subtle shifts in voice tone, intuit the meaning of body language, and interpret language has been honed over millennia, enabling us to decipher what someone else might be feeling or thinking. While these processes might seem intuitive or automatic, they're underpinned by complex neural mechanisms, with regions like the medial prefrontal cortex playing a pivotal role in perspective-taking.

Consider its applications in pragmatic scenarios such as everyday negotiations with difficult people. With cognitive empathy as an ally, negotiators can perceive their counterpart's emotional and mental state, predict potential counter-moves, and adjust their tactics to align with the situation. Thinking back to Joel and his challenging work in Middle East peacebuilding: his ability to empathize isn't about emotional alignment but a precise insight into the other party's position, motivations, and likely responses. Imagine Joel entering a room with what he would say is the most emotive, high-stakes negotiation in the world right now. He reads the room, gauging facial expressions, tones, and nonverbal cues. Armed with cognitive empathy, he's equipped to interpret these signs, anticipate the emotions and thoughts driving every party, and thereby strategize effectively. It's worth reiterating that emotional involvement is not only unnecessary here but perhaps even self-defeating; instead, the power lies in the clarity of understanding and the strategic advantage it offers. Without that, Joel's already difficult task becomes futile because of the very nature of *his* work as distinct from that of others. Cognitive empathy is the ability to understand without getting entangled.

With so many differences between emotional and cognitive empathy, including the areas of the brain they each activate, you may wonder why we call them both "empathy." In other words, what do cognitive and emotional empathy have in common that makes them both "empathy" rather than, say, "sympathy" or "compassion"?

Emotional empathy and cognitive empathy are both categorized under the umbrella term *empathy* because they share a fundamental aspect: the ability to relate to and understand the experiences of others. Despite their different processes and brain activations, they converge on this key element. They both are intellectual processes involving understanding others, connection and relatability, and a response to others' experiences. Their primary distinction lies in how we process and react to the information about someone else's situation or emotions. The reason they're distinct from sympathy or compassion lies in their focus and depth. Recall that sympathy generally involves feeling concern for someone but from a more detached perspective, and compassion involves a desire to help or alleviate suffering. Empathy, in both its forms, implies a deeper, more personal sharing of emotional states, whether that awareness is emotional or cognitive.

Empathy Collapse and Using Cognitive Empathy to Prevent It

As we've now explored, empathy, the bedrock of human connection, allows us to resonate with the experiences of others, fostering understanding and support. However, the ability to empathize is not inexhaustible. Empathy collapse (typically accompanied by general compassion fatigue and apathy) is a state where the capacity to empathize diminishes or ceases temporarily. This decline is often triggered by repeated exposure to distressing situations, overwhelming emotions, emotional exhaustion, or a fear of the vulnerability that comes with emotional ties. While commonly observed in high-empathy-demand professions such as healthcare, social work, and counseling, this phenomenon is not confined to these fields. Consider, for example, continuous exposure to distressing news and images of war or poverty on social media resulting in people feeling desensitized. A caregiver for a chronically ill parent may become emotionally numb, community activists in high-crime or impoverished areas might suffer empathy collapse, or those in customer service roles who daily encounter complaints and negativity may become disengaged with customers' frustrations.

Empathy may collapse in scenarios we perceive as harmful, particularly where there are power imbalances—such as negotiations where the weaker party may see empathy for the stronger as a liability, leading to what we might call "strategic empathy collapse." The deliberate withdrawal from empathetic engagement here is not driven by emotional exhaustion but by a calculated response to threats to personal interests or justice. For example, empathizing with an employer's financial constraints during salary negotiations may result in someone settling for less, while empathizing with a ruthless counterpart can be seen as terrifying, risking emotional attachments that might lead to compromising one's stance. This concern is rooted in the fear that empathy equals agreement or concession, potentially weakening one's position across various contexts, from professional to intimate relationships.

The symptoms of empathy collapse are varied and complex, encompassing feelings of detachment, numbness, cynicism, or irritability when confronted with the distress of another person or group of people. If you've experienced this, you may have found yourself becoming less responsive or indifferent to situations that once elicited strong empathetic responses from you, as if your emotional reservoir has run dry. Or perhaps you've observed similar effects on others, shocked by how little feeling they're showing in a situation that's obviously emotion-provoking.

The impact of empathy collapse extends beyond an individual person to affect those around them. In professional healthcare settings, it can lead to a decline in the quality of care and support for clients or patients. In a political setting, it can numb an entire population to the pain of those different from them. In personal relationships, it can weaken bonds, leading to isolation and a sense of detachment. People experiencing empathy collapse may also struggle with feelings of guilt, frustration, or inadequacy due to their changed emotional responses. Some even seek professional help, fearing that there's something fundamentally "wrong" with them.

As a result, it serves us to learn more about what empathy collapse is and how we can avoid it by revealing empathy for what it *can* be in those high-stress situations: a strategic understanding rather than an emotional surrender—the unique utility of "cognitive" empathy. The challenge, then, is not to allow empathy to collapse in these situations but to redefine and reframe how we use empathy.

Empathy *can* in fact involve comprehending the other party's perspective and constraints while we still advocate firmly for our own needs and rights. This balanced approach can lead to more effective negotiations where both parties feel heard and respected, more consistent healthcare where doctors and nurses aren't traumatized to the point of ineffectiveness, long-term care for a chronically ill relative without numbness, and a mutual appreciation of both corporations' needs for long-term growth during a merger without leaving a lot on the table. It's also very useful when emotional resonance is challenging due to cultural, societal, or personal barriers. In these situations, cognitive empathy serves as a bridge, enhancing our circle of compassion by helping us understand a broader range of experiences and viewpoints.

It's worth repeating that compassion and empathy, *even cognitive empathy*, can coexist harmoniously, allowing us to *care* about the outcomes of the other without being emotionally connected to them. Focused listening (to understand others' perspectives), active reflection (considering others' emotions and motivations), and setting boundaries (to manage personal limits) are key components of cognitive empathy. Engaging in constructive conversations, rooted in understanding rather than immediate feeling, keeps empathy at play without leading to emotional exhaustion or an unfair negotiation in power-imbalance situations. This process naturally turns us away from the misconception that empathy is synonymous with weakness, concession, or even emotional connection and toward a view of empathy as a calculated tool for insight, impact, and influence. This understanding can transform the way we approach negotiations, power, and responsibility toward others, allowing empathy into the situation even when we are emotionally drained or afraid of vulnerability—turning empathy from a perceived threat into a valuable resource for achieving fair and satisfactory outcomes. Cognitive empathy, akin to using a compass to recognize direction without walking the path, allows us to acknowledge another's emotional landscape without experiencing it personally.

In the realm of many interpersonal and power dynamics, the interplay of cognitive and emotional empathy becomes particularly interesting. The decision to use emotional versus cognitive empathy in negotiations shouldn't be automatic but an intentional choice that evaluates multiple factors. There is, in fact, a significant difference in how we should approach negotiations with a beloved spouse on the one hand and parleys to avoid a hostile business takeover on the other hand.

Back to my friend Joel, the peacekeeper: When it comes to conflicts of the sort he deals with, most of us put our hearts and minds into solidarity with a particular side, starting with the phrase (whether on social media or on a flag) "I stand with." During these times, understanding the other side can be more than uncomfortable—it can feel downright wrong. But most of us aren't peace workers.

"If you want to work in peacebuilding," Joel says, "there needs to be a recognition that this work is supposed to make you uncomfortable and get you in a space where you're trying to get people to nonviolently lose, because that's ultimately what peacebuilding is. You need to truly understand where each part of society is coming from to be able to develop a strategy to satisfy, build peace across worldviews, or find ways that peace doesn't shatter someone's worldview, without judgment."

I use Joel's example not to convince anyone to take a neutral position with respect to any conflict or issue; I, myself, have rather strong opinions and advocate with profound emotion for a variety of matters. Rather, Joel's example demonstrates that strategically using empathy that leads to understanding the *other* in a time of strife, negotiation, conflict, or urgency, in order to help us or others, is sometimes necessary. And as we learn in this book, it *is* possible in nearly all aspects of our lives. Consider, for example, the following dynamics:

- *Parenting:* Emotional empathy is crucial when soothing a child who is upset, as it allows the parent to genuinely feel and share the child's emotions, providing comfort and validation. However, cognitive empathy becomes more important when guiding the child toward a solution or helping them see the situation from a mature perspective, where realizing their emotions and thoughts is key without necessarily sharing in those emotions.
- *Workplace Leadership:* For leaders, emotional empathy can be vital when an employee is facing personal challenges, as it fosters a supportive environment by genuinely sharing in the employee's feelings. In contrast, cognitive empathy is more appropriate when making team or organizational decisions, where understanding diverse perspectives and needs is essential without becoming emotionally entangled, or amid an urgent crisis or high-risk business scenario.

- *Healthcare:* Doctors, nurses, and therapists might be at particular risk for empathy collapse, but they need to remain connected with their patients on a human level to better offer solutions to their healthcare problems. Cognitive empathy can therefore be critical for maintaining clinical detachment and objective decision-making, ensuring that providers understand patient needs without becoming emotionally overburdened.
- *Conflict Resolution:* At times of conflict, cognitive empathy is essential for recognizing each party's viewpoint and the root causes of the conflict objectively. Emotional empathy is *not necessary* to note and validate the emotions involved (tools that facilitate a more compassionate and effective resolution). If, however, the particular conflict is in the backdrop of a meaningful and long-term relationship, such as with a spouse, child, parent, or dear friend, complete emotional detachment would eradicate vulnerability and could harm the relationship in the short and long term.
- *Teaching:* Educators often employ cognitive empathy to understand students' challenges and perspectives, which aids in tailoring teaching methods effectively. Without emotional empathy, however, we might not feel the genuine joy we experience when a struggling student learns to succeed, making the challenges of an emotional tie worthwhile. The balance is ours to draw in different situations.
- *Client Relations:* In customer service, cognitive empathy is key for understanding client needs and perspectives, leading to effective problem-solving. Even if a seller's number goal (a higher sales volume) seems in contrast with their moral values, they can utilize compassion through cognitive empathy so they never lose themselves in the negotiation.

- *Community Service:* Social workers often use cognitive empathy to understand the complex issues facing people from diverse backgrounds from a professional standpoint. Emotional empathy can be exhausting for these overworked and underpaid public-service professionals, and its usage is going to be up to each person through a determination of their capacity for bearing the emotional toll of secondary trauma.
- *Labor Union Negotiations:* In these union negotiations, cognitive empathy is critical for insight into the employer's constraints and objectives, aiding in formulating realistic demands. Emotional empathy plays an important role as well in creating genuine bonds with union members, understanding their struggles and concerns, ensuring their needs are adequately represented, and ultimately feeling fulfilled from the feeling of comradery that comes along with successful collective bargaining.
- *International Diplomacy:* Diplomats use cognitive empathy to understand other countries' complex social, cultural, and political frameworks so they can make informed decisions. In these situations of complex, weeks-long, multiparty negotiations, emotional control is necessary for the long-term stamina needed to succeed.
- *Business Mergers and Acquisitions:* During major business negotiations, cognitive empathy helps negotiators understand the other company's strategic goals and concerns, vital for structuring beneficial deals. They use it to gauge the emotional tone of the negotiation and understand stakeholder concerns, facilitating smoother negotiations and overcoming apprehension. Emotional empathy can also be useful, particularly during postmerger integration, to build two teams into one cohesive unit. Generally speaking, emotional empathy is more likely to have a role in a voluntary M&A that

parties who mutually respect each other entered into versus a hostile takeover by a much larger entity seeking to take advantage of the weaker one.

Significantly, empathy can and typically does include a mix of both cognitive and emotional components—it's hardly ever an entirely binary choice. In any scenario, the choice of how much cognitive versus emotional empathy is appropriate depends on the specific needs of the situation—whether it requires a deeper emotional connection or a more objective understanding. But, as you can see, strategic use of empathy is *not* the same thing as emotionally manipulating your counterpart but rather a necessary tool to gain power and influence when you're in a place of powerlessness, preserve relationships while succeeding in negotiations, and maintain compassion when collapse might have been a likely outcome.

Strategic Empathy

Strategic empathy represents an artful and deliberate fusion of cognitive and emotional empathy, carefully adapted to each unique situation. This approach involves a conscious dance between understanding another's emotional and mental states (cognitive empathy) and participating in their emotional journey (emotional empathy). More than just aligning emotionally or understanding intellectually, strategic empathy is a sophisticated strategy for harnessing empathy's full power. It allows us to influence outcomes, forge deeper attachments, and skillfully navigate complex social dynamics. By masterfully deploying strategic empathy, we deepen our comprehension of others and bolster our capability to respond, negotiate, and lead across various contexts. Essentially, it transforms our entire empathetic capacity into a dynamic instrument for empowerment, connection, and positive change.

Also known as *tactical* or *intellectual* empathy, strategic empathy extends beyond traditional empathic boundaries by infusing strategic intent. It transcends mere perception or sympathy for the other party's position, utilizing that insight as a tactical advantage. This method requires a delicate equilibrium: enough empathy to earn trust and insight, yet sufficient detachment to maintain objectivity and goal-oriented focus. The central aim is to employ empathy—predominantly cognitive empathy—to unearth the other party's deepest emotional drives and thought patterns, positioning oneself as a mind reader in the room. This entails active listening, astute questioning, and sharp observation to genuinely comprehend the counterpart's viewpoint. However, the ultimate goal is leveraging this deep understanding to guide the conversation or negotiation favorably.

The crux of strategic empathy lies in its intentional use as an interaction tool. It involves modulating between cognitive and emotional empathy, not just for empathy's sake but to unearth crucial information that one can use strategically in various contexts. This method requires focusing on the counterpart, setting aside personal biases to truly grasp their perspective and emotions. Strategic empathy's essence is in its calculated nature—making the counterpart feel genuinely heard and understood without necessarily agreeing with them. It's about delving into the reasons behind their views, revealing both their underlying emotions and thoughts. This process fosters an atmosphere of trust, which is pivotal in swaying the interaction toward desired outcomes.

As we move our discussion to this realm, let's pause to consider *what* and *who* we're trying to affect through this strategy. Take a moment to complete the exercise below. Remember that strategic empathy is the deliberate combination of cognitive and emotional empathy, carefully tailored to each situation. It involves understanding another's mental and emotional states and using this insight to influence outcomes and build deeper rapport. To determine the right balance of cognitive versus emotional empathy and deliberately decide how much emotional versus intellectual connection is wise, it's crucial to be mindful of who you're negotiating with and what you're negotiating about. If you are negotiating with someone in a personal relationship, you might need to use more emotional empathy, compared to a professional setting where cognitive empathy might be more appropriate. The Who/What Exercise is designed to help you identify the people you negotiate with regularly, allowing you to consider the consequences of using more or less emotional connection in each context. Note that in this exercise we look specifically at the negotiation setting because it's perhaps the most contentious and conflict-prone form of interaction. It's highly illuminating to examine the impact of empathy in such a challenging situation.

THE WHO/WHAT EXERCISE

Who do you generally negotiate with on a regular basis; and What do you generally negotiate over?

First, list the "small matters" (minor issues), breaking them up into professional and personal. Remember to list the who and the what.

- Minor Professional Negotiations. Examples:
  - With co-workers over client-management issues or leadership roles
  - With clients over product delivery times or invoicing matters

- Minor Personal Negotiations. Examples:
  - With family over your working late hours
  - With friends over how to spend free time

Then, reflect on the "big matters" (major concerns). Again, remember to break it up into professional and personal.

- Major Professional Negotiations. Examples:
  - With co-workers over your partnership percentage or with associates over salaries
  - With client during a bidding-for-business process or with opposing counsel over major deal points

- Major Personal Negotiations. Examples:
  - With a spouse over whether to move for one of your careers
  - With a parent or ex-partner over which religion to raise your kids in

Exercise Reflection Chart		
	Minor	Major
Personal		
Professional		

Negotiations most frequently occur within the circle of those we are closest to—our family, friends, and colleagues. Proximity paradoxically breeds conflict: The more intimately connected we are to someone, the more likely we are to encounter disagreements. It seems counterintuitive at first. Why would our closest relationships endure the most discord? The answer lies in the comfort and familiarity inherent in these bonds. This ease can lead us to lower our guard, making our interactions less cautious and, paradoxically, more prone to misunderstandings and conflicts. The frequency and depth of our interactions with these people amplifies such a scenario, as their decisions, actions, and emotions tend to have a more significant impact on our lives than those of acquaintances we see infrequently.

This exercise will help you reflect on your negotiation experiences, enhance your awareness and empathy in both professional and personal contexts, gain clarity on your negotiation behaviors, and make informed decisions about the type and degree of empathy to employ in your negotiations. For more detailed instructions and the printable reflection page, please visit my website, www.sherminkruse.com.

In the evolving dynamics of parent-child relationships, for instance, the choices children make as they grow and develop their own identities—like selecting a career path or a college—become more than milestones; they're potential negotiation grounds within the family. As comfort solidifies in these bonds, parents may find themselves engaging more freely, sometimes at the risk of overlooking the nuanced nature of these discussions. Here, the challenge for parents is to consciously balance their own hopes and fears with an empathetic realization of their child's aspirations and anxieties. This requires a fine balance between cognitive empathy, to understand the child's reasoning and perspective, and emotional empathy, to connect with their hopes and concerns. It's crucial in these deeply personal dialogues that familiarity doesn't lead to careless communication.

The same principle applies to long-standing friendships, which, over the years or decades, develop a layer of comfort that can occasionally result in less guarded interactions. When a friend decides to relocate for a job or undergoes a significant lifestyle change, these seemingly minor decisions can evoke strong emotions and necessitate adjustments in the friendship's dynamics. The ease of long-term friendships often leads to more open exchanges of thoughts and feelings. Yet, in these situations, it's essential to maintain a balanced empathy. Understanding the friend's motivations (cognitive empathy) can be as crucial as connecting with the emotional aspects of their change, like feelings of loss or joy (emotional empathy). This balanced approach is often key to navigating transitions of this sort, preserving the strength and depth of the friendship and ensuring that the comfort of the relationship doesn't inadvertently lead to misunderstandings or conflicts.

Let's consider scenarios where a predominance of cognitive empathy might be more effective. Suppose you find yourself in a situation where the relationship with your negotiating counterpart is not long-term or deeply personal. In such instances, maintaining an emphasis on cognitive empathy allows you to remain analytically detached, focusing on understanding their viewpoint without getting emotionally entangled. This approach is particularly beneficial when dealing with a counterpart who may not share your interests or may even be openly hostile. Here, an excess of emotional empathy could cloud your judgment or weaken your negotiating position. Similarly, in situations where you possess less power or leverage, relying more on cognitive empathy enables you to preserve your objectivity and strategic focus, crucial for navigating power dynamics effectively.

Conversely, there are circumstances where tilting the balance toward emotional empathy yields better results. This is often the case in long-term relationships, whether professional or personal, where a deeper emotional connection exists. In such scenarios, engaging more with emotional empathy can strengthen relational bonds and foster a cooperative atmosphere, making negotiations smoother and more amicable. This approach is especially fruitful when the counterpart is cooperative, as it builds on mutual trust and understanding, paving the way for more collaborative and mutually beneficial outcomes. Additionally, when you find yourself in a position of equal or greater power, leaning in to emotional empathy can help create a more equitable and respectful negotiating environment, which not only benefits the immediate interaction but also lays the groundwork for a stronger ongoing relationship.

Internalizing these dynamics is crucial in mastering strategic empathy. By evaluating the nature of your relationship with the counterpart, their stance toward your interests, and the power balance in the negotiation, you can more effectively decide the blend of cognitive and emotional empathy to apply. This tailored approach not only enhances your negotiation skills, but also contributes to building more meaningful and productive collaborations, whether they're fleeting or long-standing.*

As the next few chapters will detail, however, strategic empathy isn't just about oscillating between cognitive and emotional empathy. In the intricate realm of interpersonal communication, tactical empathy stands out as a formidable skill set, requiring you to discern the subtle cues and underlying motivations of your counterpart. In other words, you need to *use* the empathy you've cultivated, which can be cognitive, emotional, or both (though it tends to be much more cognitive heavy to gain the information necessary to connect with the counterpart on a human level). You then use analytical

* If you're someone who struggles with the emotional control required by cognitive empathy, you'll love the second half of this book, because stoicism is the foundation of emotional regulation and control. If you are someone who struggles with emotional empathy, you can start from a place of cognitive understanding and go from there to develop vulnerability and openness. Stoic teachings are essential here as well, because they'll help you overcome whatever past events or future concerns are holding you back.

skills to strategically process the information you've gathered. The key is to create a sense of trust and safety, which encourages the other side to open up and share more freely, thereby providing valuable insights you can use tactically, being careful to stay at the right level of emotional attachment.

Strategic empathy unfolds in a series of interconnected stages, beginning with the pursuit of understanding. This initial stage involves a deep dive into the thoughts and emotions of others, engaging with a blend of attentiveness and sensitivity. The goal is to grasp the complex layers of their perspectives, recognizing that true insight is both an intellectual and emotional tie. As this understanding solidifies, it naturally progresses to trust. Trust is the invisible thread that weaves through the fabric of human relationships, a fundamental element that transforms simple interactions into opportunities for meaningful bonds. It's within this framework of trust that communication finds fertile ground to grow. Defensive posturing relaxes. Dialogues become richer, marked by openness and the free exchange of ideas and feelings.

An environment of open communication is pivotal for the discovery of crucial information. It's through candid conversations that key insights come to light, not as a result of aggressive probing but through the voluntary sharing that occurs in a climate of mutual respect and trust. With the unveiling of information comes the opportunity to exercise influence thoughtfully. Here, influence is not a manifestation of control but a subtle guiding of the interaction toward positive outcomes. It's about using insights to inform decisions and actions in a way that's considerate of all parties involved.

In essence, strategic empathy is a transformative process that begins with a profound understanding and moves through trust and communication to responsibly inform our ability to positively shape the interaction. It's an approach that recognizes the significance of emotional connection in all forms of human exchange.

Thus, the leverage and power we gain through strategic empathy are the direct result of:

- *Understanding:* Engaging deeply to truly know the other person's viewpoint. Example: A manager takes the time to listen to an employee's concerns about work-life balance, genuinely understanding the stress they're under.
- *Trust:* Building a reliable and safe space for open exchange. Example: A therapist consistently respects confidentiality, allowing the client to feel secure enough to share personal struggles.
- *Communication:* Facilitating a two-way dialogue that's both open and effective. Example: Two business partners regularly schedule meetings to transparently discuss the progress and setbacks of their joint venture.
- *Discovery:* Uncovering key insights that are shared in the spirit of trust and openness. Example: A doctor asks thoughtful questions and discovers a patient's symptoms are linked to an issue they hadn't considered, leading to a correct diagnosis.

Through strategic empathy we send a powerful message to those around us: "I see you. I hear you. Your perspective matters." This is where others lower their guards, communicate more genuinely, and reveal information that shifts even the most futile situations toward a positive outcome. By transforming empathy from a simple tool to a comprehensive communication philosophy we call "strategic empathy," we can astutely maneuver between cognitive and emotional empathy.

More than just stepping into another's shoes, strategic empathy is:

- intentionally entrenching ourselves in others' viewpoints;

- discerning which empathy type best fits the unfolding situation;
- utilizing empathy tools to uncover the information; and
- still remaining compassionate or sympathetic.

Our relationships weather disputes without sacrificing mutual respect; we revolutionize interactions, create deep bonds, and achieve desired outcomes.

"There are definitely people I stand with," Joel says. "My work has been around endowing those who are trying to do good with as much legitimate resource as possible. You have to be human and let it affect you sometimes, of course, but you also have to understand *your* role in the conflict and where you can have the most impact."

As we turn the page from becoming familiar with the nuanced dance between cognitive and emotional empathy, we learn that empathy isn't just a state of mind but also a suite of actionable skills. This chapter has laid the foundation, illustrating how a deep, strategic understanding of empathy can navigate the complex interplay of human emotions and thoughts, particularly in high-stakes situations. We learned that empathy, in its purest form, is about balance—a delicate equilibrium between awareness and feeling, between engaging the mind and involving the heart.

Now, in Chapter 3, we pivot from theory to practice, from contemplation to action. We take the theoretical framework of empathy and transform it into concrete tools that can be wielded with precision and purpose. "Three Concrete Tools of Strategic Empathy" introduces us to the practical applications of empathy in real-world situations. Here, we will explore how to harness empathy as a strategic resource—how to deploy it to defuse conflicts, foster understanding, and build bridges of communication even with the most challenging people and in the most daunting scenarios.

Chapter 2 Takeaways

In this chapter, we've outlined the following critical ideas:

- Detangling the concept of empathy sets the foundation for its practical application through strategic empathy.
- Distinguishing empathy from related concepts like sympathy and compassion helps clarify its unique role.
- Elaborating on the two primary types of empathy, Cognitive and Emotional, provides a deeper understanding of its nuances.

CHAPTER 3

THREE CONCRETE TOOLS OF STRATEGIC EMPATHY

You never really understand a person until you consider things from his point of view . . . until you climb into his skin and walk around in it.

— HARPER LEE, *TO KILL A MOCKINGBIRD*

When I was nine years old, I had to start covering my hair everywhere in public. Seven years had passed since the Islamic Revolution. There was an arms embargo against Iran, which the Reagan administration violated by selling arms to Iran and Iraq simultaneously (in a scheme later called the "Iran-Contra Affair"). Those two neighboring nations used the weapons in bids to conquer each other. The war, in turn, caused the Islamic regime to tighten its grip on its own people. Although the mandatory hijab for all women (regardless of their religion) wasn't the most violent demonstration of the regime's grip—not by far. They also rounded up and forced 14-year-old boys to detonate landmines by running through them (clearing the way for troops to advance) and held public executions for seemingly minor violations such as drinking alcohol. But requiring headscarves was, and still is, the daily physical and symbolic constant reminder of it all. For my defiant little nine-year-old mind, navigating up to six missile raids a day, bread lines around the corner, cold baths, and electricity shortages was hard enough without having to daily battle the dark practices of the morality police. The hijab is required to attend school (even for kindergarteners), but you could leave school and immediately rip off your headscarf—until the age of nine. Nine was when the requirement began for all public places. It's also the legal age of marriage (at the request of a parent).

I turned nine on May 12, 1986. It wasn't more than a week or two afterward that I first saw the power of tactical empathy on display. My mom masterfully modeled it for me. We were in Tajrish Bazaar, a food marketplace in northern Tehran. I don't remember why I wasn't in school, what we were shopping for, or why I didn't have my headscarf on, but I do remember as a freshly-turned-nine-year-old that sometimes Mom would let me go out without my headscarf, and she herself would let a bunch of hair fall out of the sides of her scarf. Until that day, we'd gotten away with it. I was a scrawny little thing, looked seven or eight years old at most. If a guard asked, I could lie about my age. It's not like I had to carry ID. And if someone yelled at my mom for not being properly covered up, she'd typically tuck the hair in and that'd be the end of it. We relished the slight act of defiance. It made us feel slightly more free. But that day, we came to regret the decision not to cover up.

She was massive—the female morality police coming our way. Or seemed that way, anyway, maybe because of my small-statured self. Or maybe it was the big, Russian-style assault rifle hanging across her chest that made her so enormous to my eyes. Her steps heavy, like the stomps of a giant. The grip on her rifle was so unrelentingly tight that I felt if she sneezed, the trigger would go off by accident. Her words were miserly and loud—something about my mom's headscarf being too loose, about me not having one at all. She asked me how old I was, and for some odd reason, I told her the truth! I'd just turned nine! As morality police, her job was enforcing compliance with religious laws like keeping your headscarf on. The armed, fist-pounding, enormous human screaming at my mom and me, she was just doing her job.

I was frozen with terror. She had the power to arrest us on the spot and we'd be powerless to do anything about it, unless my mom somehow negotiated our way out of it. If she did, maybe we'd get off with a warning. If she didn't—arrest, detention, maybe even a lashing for my mom, large fines . . . they might even search our house and find our illegal records and homemade alcohol, and then we'd be in *real* trouble.

My mom locked her kind eyes with the guard's and said, "You seem very frustrated."

"Yes, I'm frustrated!" the guard responded.

My mom was silent for a beat.

The guard continued, "Do you know how frustrating it can be to give the same warning and threat, day after day?"

"Day after day," my mom said warmly.

"Some days are really hot, you know? I've gotta cover up too while I walk up to them to repeat the same warning, to person after person."

"Yes, you have to cover up too—in this heat."

"Why can't people just comply?"

"Your work sounds really hard. For us, you know, my daughter *just* turned nine. They grow up so fast. How can we convince you to let it slide this time?"

The guard hesitated for a few seconds, then released her hand from the grip of her weapon and just turned and walked away.

Without knowing what "strategic empathy" was, my mom used its core tactics to negotiate with a well-armed and government-empowered morality police guard. We didn't get arrested that day. Living out those days in Iran, when thousands of people were being detained or even killed, my family managed to stay safe.

Strategic empathy is the act of expanding your understanding of the other side both gaining and using empathy, then using that knowledge to create leverage. In this chapter, we're going to learn which tools to use to engage in this process, and how to use them. Our strategic empathy tools cause the other side to feel "heard," thus creating a feeling of trust and breaking down the barriers to effective communication, leading to the discovery of critical information necessary for successful influence. It's true, the old adage: "Knowledge is power." When you have less power than others—whether it's because of your political position, economic status, race or ethnicity, gender or gender identity, sexual orientation, or immigration status—tactical empathy is a highly effective method of rising up.

After years of practice and research, I've organized various empathic methods into **five tools**, three of which are basic tactics that we'll discuss in this chapter: **Affect Labeling** (simply naming someone's emotions), **Silence** (a dynamic break in talking), and **Active Listening** (more than just hearing). The final two tools are more advanced: **Mirroring and Repeating** (words, but also body language), and **Probing Questions** (asking "how" and "what" questions). We'll cover those in Chapter 4.

Using empathy strategically by moderating the cognitive-emotional spectrum and utilizing the tools in this book is converting empathy into a superpower. Empathy used in this way gives us incredible influence in many contexts, from personal relationships to professional negotiations. By understanding and responding to the underlying emotions and motivations of others, we can guide conversations and outcomes in our favor. This transformative approach allows us to connect deeply with others, build trust, and foster cooperation, ultimately leading to more successful and meaningful interactions. Embracing strategic empathy enables us to navigate complex social dynamics with skill and compassion, making it an invaluable asset in any interaction.*

Affect Labeling: The Powerful Effect of Identifying Emotions

The first thing my mom said to the morality guard yelling at us while clutching her weapon that day, in a very calm voice that ended with warm, downward inflection, was, "You seem very frustrated." She literally just labeled the guard's primary feeling; gave it a name: *frustrated*. This is the first tactical empathy tool she used, which we call *Affect Labeling* (or *Emotion Labeling*). This tool works differently depending on whether the emotion being labeled is negative or positive.

---

* While the three basic strategic empathy techniques in this chapter and the two advanced techniques in the next chapter are primarily ***cognitive*** empathy tools, intended to understand the other side and thus gain leverage in a power dynamic, using them doesn't foreclose emotional empathy. When the situation calls for it, emotional empathy can and should be used. The difficult questions of how to act with more cognitive empathy by regulating our own emotions are reserved for the second part of the book, on stoicism.

To better appreciate how this tool of Affect Labeling becomes powerful during confrontations, especially when the other person is engulfed in negative emotions, it's crucial that we delve into the science behind emotional regulation. This brings us to the amygdala, the part of our brain that's pivotal in managing our emotions. Understanding the amygdala's role provides insight into why labeling emotions is so effective in situations where someone, like the guard, is overwhelmed by hostile feelings.

When you're feeling stressed, angry, afraid, or threatened—the classic *negative* emotions—your amygdala is activated, triggering a fight, flight, or freeze response. Meanwhile, your frontal lobe, the part of your brain responsible for rational, logical thinking, suffers as a result. You go into what neuroscientists disparagingly call "lizard brain," and your higher cognitive functional capabilities decrease.[1] As Jill Bolte Taylor, renowned neuroscientist and author who gave a viral TED talk about diagnosing and studying her own stroke, says, "Just like children, emotions heal when they are heard and validated."[2]

This means that in most instances, you're literally less smart when you're stressed out. There is such a thing as a positive stress-related impact on your brain, but this is typically not the response when you're facing real danger. Positive stress responses usually happen when you're responding well to a rigorous but beneficial challenge, like getting a raise at work, taking your new baby home from the hospital, or saying, "I do," at the altar.[3] This type of stress can increase your alertness and productivity. If we stick with my nine-year-old self back at the Tajrish Bazaar in Tehran during the morality guard's verbal assault, I was feeling good, old-fashioned negative stress, which is what any of us feel in a high-intensity situation where we're feeling powerless and stand to lose something that's important to us. My eyes were glued on the veins of the guard's hand flexing as it gripped the rifle. This is the kind of stress that makes you less smart—explaining why my lizard brain was too full of anger to make sense of anything. More importantly, and this is something my mom understood very well, this explains why the morality guard was so agitated. Her entire professional life consisted of roaming the streets in search of rule breakers—hunting them down, intimidating them, and arresting them for their transgressions. It's not just the people she encountered who were in lizard-brain mode, either terrified of her (a flight response) or yelling at her (a fight response), but like in many soldiers, her amygdala was also triggered. Probably over and over again.

So that's what happens to the brain when it's triggered by negative emotions. This was what the *guard's* brain was going through when she was confronting my mom. Remember that what my mom did in response was put words on the guard's feelings: "You seem very frustrated."

It shouldn't be surprising that putting feelings into words (affect labeling) helps manage negative emotional experiences; just ask anyone who's ever had talk therapy. But most people aren't really sure *why* this is happening or exactly *what* mechanism is doing this in the brain.

Then, in 2007, along came Dr. Matthew Lieberman, Harvard-trained and running a social and cognitive lab at UCLA, to study how it is that affect labeling soothes our brain.[4] Lieberman, along with a group of neuroscientists and social psychologists, conducted a study that looked specifically at functional magnetic resonance imaging (fMRI) scans of the brain and compared three groups:

1. Subjects who looked at images of faces expressing negative emotions;
2. Subjects who matched images of faces together, based on the emotions expressed on the faces (for example, match the two sad faces, or match the two angry faces);
3. Subjects who matched images of faces with words labeling the emotions those faces were expressing; and
4. Subjects matching images of faces with words describing the genders of the faces pictured (for example, match the face of the woman with the label "Helen" instead of the label "Samuel" based on presumed gender).

This study shows that when we put our feelings into words, it decreases activity in the amygdala (the part of the brain that processes emotions) more than when we match faces with emotions or just look at negative images. This means that naming our feelings helps reduce emotional responses. Interestingly, think about the fourth bullet point above, which summarizes a pretty incredible finding in the context of comparing emotion labeling to gender labeling (naming the gender of a face): labeling emotions specifically reduces activity in the amygdala and other emotional parts of the brain, but other forms of labeling do not have that same effect. Thus, it is the labeling of the *emotion* that reduces the amygdala activity (and therefore helps to control the negative emotion), not just the act of labeling.

Not long after this, Dr. Katharina Kircanski, a UCLA- and Stanford-trained scientist working at the National Institute of Mental Health, teamed up with Dr. Lieberman and others to take a closer look at this phenomenon, but with the stimuli ramped up. Instead of just examining patients whose amygdala activity increased because they saw an image of an angry face and lessened when they labeled it "angry," they studied patients who were *experiencing* the negative emotions more directly and profoundly than that. Specifically, they decided to take arachnophobia by the horns (or the legs?). They took spider-phobes and showed them actual spiders. Not images of scared people. Not even images of spiders. *Actual* spiders. Then they had the subjects describe their feelings about the spiders *to* the spiders, and they looked at any changes in the subjects' physiological fear response (for example, variation in the electrical characteristics of their skin).[5]

It turns out, even if you're crushingly terrified of spiders, if you tell the spiders you're afraid of them, you'll be less afraid. In fact, the more "fear words" participants verbally used while talking to the spider, the less anxious they became. What's even more incredible is that this effect was not just in the moment; the subjects were less afraid of spiders for up to a week afterward.

Similar studies in addition to this one in a variety of settings and contexts cumulatively tell us that the mere act of **labeling a negative emotion** reduces the amygdala's activity, allowing your frontal lobe to function better. And, as you can see, the impact of affect labeling on negative emotions isn't limited to just the "talk therapy" setting. This is why you feel better about your breakup after talking to your friends about it, why you may have been able to tame someone's negative emotions in the middle of a high-conflict situation at work by acknowledging those feelings, or why journaling your emotions helps you regain calm. Simply naming your negative feelings decreases them, helping you think rationally again.

Now, what happens when you label a *positive* emotion? Surprisingly, the opposite. In a series of four studies in 2021, scientists asked subjects to view images of positive emotions, then compared the participants' emotional reports based on whether or not they labeled their emotions.[6] It turns out that putting words on positive feelings reinforces them. Several studies have duplicated these findings using a variety of measurement criteria, such as fMRI machines measuring activations in inhibitory networks in the prefrontal cortex and reduced activations in the amygdala (which, as we've seen, is an area involved in emotional responses). A team of Stanford and Harvard researchers further validated and applied these studies in the workplace setting in 2021 through six separate experiments and a compilation summary of dozens of prior experiments.[7]

This tells us why giving a pep talk to yourself in front of the mirror before a big meeting actually makes you more confident, or why your spouse complimenting you on your outfit as you dress for an important event can make you feel more attractive.

We'll explore these experiments more in the second part of this book in the context of emotional control. For now, the takeaway is that labeling negative emotions reduces their intensity, while labeling positive emotions reinforces those feelings.[8] This is the case whether or not you're trying to create that effect. It just happens, implicitly.

All of this made intuitive sense to my mom that day in the bazaar. She's not a neuroscientist, and these experiments hadn't been conducted back in 1986. But she innately understood the tactical empathy concept. She affect-labeled when she said to the morality guard, "You seem very frustrated." The guard's response was, "Yes, I'm frustrated!" But right after she said that, because my eyes were frozen on her hand gripping the rifle, I could see the tension in her hand relaxing just because her emotional state had been labeled. The guard would now be more capable of cognitive function and less likely to be erratic.

The affect-labeling technique requires you to grasp the other person's mental and emotional states and then label them to decrease negativity, reduce hostility, reinforce positive feelings, and expand rational capabilities. Note that your labeling isn't limited to just the most basic feelings of *happy*, *sad*, and *angry*. There are myriad ways that you can describe your counterpart's emotional state. Consider the following possibilities:

Affect-Labeling Language		
It seems like you feel	It sounds like you are	It looks like you feel
You seem	You sound	You look

Potential Emotion Labels				
Sad	Happy	Hurt	Panicked	Angry
Depressed	Amused	Isolated	Anxious	Annoyed
Crushed	Glad	Shocked	Troubled	Agitated
Upset	Pleased	Let Down	Uncomfortable	Furious
Frustrated	Optimistic	Wounded	Unsure	Irritated
Dismayed	Enthusiastic	Rejected	Stuck	Disgusted
Heavy	Delighted	Hurt	Mixed Up	Outraged
Sorrowful	Eager	Betrayed	Desperate	Fed Up

So, for example, your labeling might look something like "It sounds like you're annoyed with the service you received," or "It looks like you're feeling uneasy about the proposal."

When you've labeled their affect, your counterpart is more amenable to what you want. Thus, the affect-labeling tool gets to the heart of tactical empathy: using your understanding of the other side to gain leverage. The exploration of Affect Labeling in our interactions, and all of the potential labels in the graphic above, highlights its potency in tactical empathy, yet it also underscores a challenge: accurately identifying emotions to label them.

This brings us seamlessly to our next tool: Dynamic Silence. While Affect Labeling requires us to pinpoint and verbalize emotions, Dynamic Silence offers us a powerful method to gather the emotional information we need.

Active Listening: Full Attention before Response Articulation

Complete this brief exercise before you continue reading:

> Read this paragraph. After you've finished that, put this book down, close your eyes, and try to focus only on the external noise around you for about a minute. (Unless you're in a soundproof studio, there's always some noise—birds chirping, sirens, a vacuum cleaner, the laughter of children, cars driving by, dogs barking, and so on.) Then pick up the book again and read on.

Ready? Go!

* * *

What did you hear during that minute after I asked you to focus your listening that you were not hearing before? Chances are, you noticed sounds previously overlooked in the background noise of your environment, whether it was the distant hum of traffic or the intermittent beeping of a pedestrian crossing, the rustling of leaves in the wind, or the gentle hum of a refrigerator. But how is this possible? After all, your body's biological process of hearing did not change. During both time frames (pre-listening instruction and post-listening instruction), sound waves entered your outer ear, your eardrum vibrated and sent signals to your middle ear, which then sent the vibrations to the cochlea in your inner ear, causing the fluids inside to ripple. Hair cells rode the waves of the ripple and moved up and down, causing your stereocilia (microscopic, hairlike projections) to bend, leading chemicals to rush into the cells and creating an electrical signal to your brain that let you recognize and understand the sound. Long medical jargon short, literally nothing about the way your hearing *works* changed between those two time frames. All that changed was that you *decided* to mentally process the sounds and thus listened more consciously.

What's more interesting is that it's possible your listening began even before the paragraph ended—when you read the first sentence asking you to pay attention to external noise, even if you were not supposed to begin that work until after you finished reading the paragraph. In fact, even if you didn't actually follow my instructions, didn't put the book down at all, and kept reading, chances are that upon reading my words prompting you to tune in to outside noises, you *did* just that on some level, hearing things you weren't hearing before. So even aside from you actively choosing to listen, my mere prompting you to listen subconsciously affected your listening, giving you access to information you didn't have a moment ago.

This exercise in tuning in to ambient sounds serves as a microcosm of the broader skill of active listening, especially crucial in conflict situations. Just as you chose to focus on and process previously unnoticed environmental sounds, active listening in a conversation, particularly during conflict, involves a similar conscious decision. It requires you to attentively absorb not just the words, but also the underlying emotions, tones, and perspectives of the other person. This deliberate focus in both scenarios—whether on the hum of your surroundings or the nuances of a heated dialogue—demonstrates how active listening shifts our perception and understanding. In conflict, such focused attention tends to defuse tension, foster empathy, and pave the way for resolution, just as it brought awareness to the rich tapestry of sounds in your environment.

There are two lessons in the above active-listening exercise. The first lesson emphasizes the vast reservoir of information available to us, accessible through the simple yet profound act of actively listening. This information encompasses not just the spoken words but also the underlying emotions and thoughts of those we interact with. Active listening enables us to tune in to these subtle cues, granting us a deeper understanding of others' perspectives and feelings. The second, equally crucial lesson from active listening is its power to build trust. When we actively listen, we demonstrate to the other person that we value their thoughts and feelings.

This validation is a fundamental human need and fosters a sense of safety and respect. In a world where people often feel unheard or misunderstood, being an active listener sets you apart as someone who genuinely cares and pays attention. It creates a bond of trust, crucial for any meaningful relationship or interaction. Our world is full of distractions. Active listening is the ability to focus entirely on a speaker, understand their message, and comprehend the information. In this way, you aren't just gaining information about the counterpart's thoughts and feelings but also empowering your counterpart. There are few aspects of human existence more powerful than our desire to be heard. The affirmation in that makes us feel connected to the person listening to us, have more trust in that person, and let our guard down.

Trust gained through active listening is foundational for influence. People are more likely to be open and receptive to those they trust. They feel more comfortable sharing their genuine thoughts and emotions, which are essential for empathetically responding to them. This openness not only helps in personal attachments but is also critical in professional settings, where trust facilitates teamwork, more effective leadership, and successful negotiations. Moreover, trust isn't just about getting others to agree with you; it's about creating an environment where mutual understanding and respect contributes to more collaborative and constructive outcomes. In essence, active listening doesn't just open a door to the world of others' inner experiences; it lays the groundwork for a relationship characterized by mutual respect and understanding, where influence is a byproduct of genuine connection and empathy.

But listening successfully is surprisingly challenging. Before I practiced active listening (and still now from time to time), even when my mind wasn't wandering off to my to-do list or the notifications popping up on my cell phone, even while in an interesting conversation or professional discussion with a colleague or friend, I hardly ever waited for the other person to stop speaking before mentally formulating my response. My brain would work on the right example with which to agree, or appropriate language to disagree, while the other person was still talking. I'd wait until they were finished before I spoke (most of the time!), but not before thinking of what I was going to say. This was the case whether I was at a cocktail party, talking with a friend about her boyfriend problems at the office, negotiating a raise with my boss, or having a dialogue with a judge in a courtroom. When talking to a junior associate about their performance review, they'd be justifying their constantly late submissions *while* I was preparing my "but" response, even though I'd wait until they finished their sentence before speaking. Having a couple of drinks at happy hour with a good friend, I'd be formulating my anthropology-based response on the uselessness of reality television even while she was still going on about the season finale of *Love Is Blind*. Most conversations consisted of me just waiting to talk. In the courtroom context, there are some advantages to this form of mental process and being quicker with a logical reply. But even in that rare context, there were drawbacks to my jumping the responsive gun too quickly—I'd miss all the information and mental connections, because my brain was too busy moving on to the response.

I wasn't unique. Research shows only about 10 percent of us listen effectively. Even if we think we *are* listening, we're usually trying to figure out how to jump in with our own story, making mental judgments, considering advice to offer, distracted by who just walked into the room, or altogether zoned out. It's inherent in the human condition and central to the way our brains function to begin composing our response to an event (including a verbal statement) as it's occurring, rather than wait for it to conclude. Whether you agree with what the other person is saying or not, your brain begins to formulate a response. Listening for a response isn't true active listening. Neither is giving advice people didn't ask for or solving their problems for them. Even agreeing isn't listening. In fact, any kind of reply is different altogether from the act of *listening*.

This pattern tracks on social media too. Social media hasn't just revolutionized the way we talk to one another person-to-person, but also how corporations engage with their employees and customers. This "social listening" is our interpersonal dialogue with others through the domain of social media. Dialogue and multilogue have found a new normal in the social-listening online space, often taking the place of telephone or in-person conversations. As a result, social-media platforms are becoming increasingly popular tools for customer relationship management.[9]

How many of us can really say, when in a heated social-media dialogue, that we're actually reading to *understand* what the other person is trying to communicate, rather than to judge or to formulate a response? That's certainly not what I did when I Facebook-debated people on the merits of vaccinations during Covid or against the so-called "Muslim ban" during the Trump administration. I wasn't engaged to listen and understand what my counterpart was trying to say. Instead, I was looking for loopholes in their argument to exploit. The ability to do this well served me sometimes as a litigator, and critical-thinking skills are key to success in a multitude of settings. But sometimes you've got to know when to listen. As corporate leaders trying to better understand our consumer base, listening allows us to anticipate customer needs while turning complaints into solutions on a professional level. It helps innovate products and strengthen customer loyalty.

When in doubt of the applications of active listening in a business setting, think of Lee Iacocca, who led Ford, developed the Mustang, and then revived Chrysler from near corporate death. He said, "I only wish I could find an institute that teaches people how to listen. Businesspeople need to listen at least as much as they need to talk. Too many people fail to realize that real communication goes in both directions." Other corporate geniuses who value listening above nearly all other traits include Indra Nooyi (PepsiCo and Amazon), David Abney (UPS), Angela Ahrendts (Apple), and Sir Richard Branson (Virgin Group), among countless many others.[10]

As leaders in companies, learning to actively listen can revolutionize our business. As humans generally, when we do it right, social listening helps us reconnect to old friends, keep track of our teens, and maybe even build bridges across political divides.

When my mom was confronting the morality police that day in Iran, her focus on the guard's emotional state amid the chaos of the bustling bazaar and the possibility of her own detention made the guard feel a rapport between them. In a tense and dangerous situation such as the one we faced, where the power dynamics were so one-sided—the morality officer had significantly more political and physical strength than my mom—my mom's active listening placed the two women a bit more parallel to each other. It evened things out a little—not because of force, but because of the empathic tool of active listening.

At the end of the day, listening is the deceptively difficult task of releasing your own ego. In doing so, you can build trust and connection, and discover the hidden emotions and agenda of the people around you, which helps you gain influence.

Balancing one's ego with the need for active listening in conversations is crucial for effective communication, empathy, and collaboration. Consider, for example:

- *Debating a Topic:* Your ego wants to win an argument and prove your point, but active listening demands that you genuinely understand the other person's perspective, even if it contradicts your own.
- *Receiving Feedback:* Your ego may want to defend yourself or justify your actions, but active listening requires you to consider the feedback openly and understand the giver's perspective.
- *Managing Conflict:* In a conflict, your ego might push you to focus on your grievances and what you want to say next, while active listening requires you to focus on understanding the other person's feelings and viewpoints.

- *Negotiating:* Your ego may strive for the best possible outcome for yourself, but active listening necessitates understanding the needs and constraints of the other party to find a mutually beneficial solution.
- *In a Team Meeting:* Your ego might urge you to dominate the conversation or highlight your contributions, but active listening means valuing others' ideas and fostering a collaborative environment.
- *Learning Something New:* Your ego might resist admitting ignorance or vulnerability, but active listening involves being open to new information and admitting when you don't understand something.
- *In a Relationship:* Your ego may want to prioritize your needs and viewpoints, but active listening is crucial for insight into your partner's needs and fostering a healthy, balanced relationship.
- *During a Performance Review:* Your ego might focus on highlighting your achievements and minimizing your weaknesses, but active listening allows you to understand your areas for improvement and how you can grow professionally.
- *Mentoring or Coaching:* Your ego might lead you to focus more on imparting your wisdom, but active listening is essential to truly understand a mentee's challenges, goals, and needs.
- *Resolving Customer Complaints:* Your ego may make you defensive when faced with criticism, but active listening is key to grasping the customer's experience, resolving their issue effectively, and improving your service.

In each of these examples, managing your ego and prioritizing active listening can lead to more productive, empathetic, and understanding interactions.

Limit your mental interruptions and pay close attention to what's being said for its total meaning, context, and subtext, rather than what you want to say or what you want to hear. Sometimes, it's being okay with silence, the next tactical empathy tool on our list.

Silence: A Dynamic Beat

Strategic empathy is thoughtful but uncomplicated. The goal is simply to make the other side feel heard, which induces trust and breaks down the barriers to critical information. While I've been fascinated by *why* the techniques work, studying and perfecting their use for years, my mom didn't have to know why and how they work to be intuitively great at them. That day in the marketplace, after affect labeling ("You seem frustrated") and active listening (being focused on the guard's words and body language), my mom did the oddest thing—and that was to do nothing. She used the third strategic empathy tool I just mentioned: She was silent. Not for a long time, but for a dynamic beat.

The thing about silence is that people like to fill it.

In the space that my mom's silence created, the guard started talking about how *frustrating* it was to give the same warning, the same threat, the same reason for arrest, to person after person after person, every day. How *frustrating* it was for her to walk those streets, day in and day out, yelling at women for running or having their hair slip out of their scarves. Why couldn't folks just comply? Her face squinted at the hot sun peeking through the Alborz Mountains; the Tajrish Bazaar is at the foothills of those peaks. Through my mom's silence, the guard was talking to and looking at her as if she was the person with the answers the guard needed for her life to make sense. As Leonardo da Vinci said, "Nothing strengthens authority so much as silence."

This is exactly the "verbal reveal" we're looking to get in a power-imbalance situation. My mom's affect labeling followed by her listening and silence made the guard, the massive human with the rifle who only encountered others in an adversarial context and whom everyone hated, feel like someone was invested in her feelings. It's unlikely that anyone else she encountered in the streets made her feel this way. Were they afraid of her? Sure. Interested in her perspective? No way. This was her chance to be seen. The rifle was still hanging on her, but she had been emotionally disarmed. Even better, the guard was talking about her feelings and experiences, giving my mom tons of information about her motivations and frustrations.

The guard didn't bring up religion or morality. Even if she felt that women's hair should be covered and that the Islamic Republic was right to enforce it (and maybe she did), if you really listened to her words, that's not what she was saying. She wasn't justifying the hijab requirements or saying anything about why women *should* cover their hair. Instead, she seemed unhappy with her job. She talked about it like she was Sisyphus, the mythical Greek founder and king of Ephyra whom Hades punished for cheating death by forcing him to roll the same rock up and down a mountain for all eternity.

Of course, morally speaking, the guard should have just quit a job where she not only accomplished nothing useful but in fact assisted in the oppression of her own people. Instead, she had for some reason accepted her role in all of it. Nevertheless, she didn't see herself as the villain. Most people don't. Most people see themselves as good. Even if they don't like their actions, they justify them somehow for whatever ends they've told themselves they're accomplishing. Think of your own conflicts. How often, amid an argument, do you see *yourself* as the bad guy? You fight for your side because you believe it's the right side and justify any questionable conduct on the basis that the result will be just. Maybe you reconsider your actions later, upon reflection, but in the moment, you're much more likely to be "right" while the other guy is "wrong." Rather than attributing her discontent to the moral deficiencies of her actions enforcing corrupt laws, the morality guard on the streets that day complained about the frustrations of her job. However wrong her conduct, the guard had justified it. But just now maybe she wasn't so sure.

At that moment, standing in the streets and watching her heavy breathing and rattled voice, I could see these justifications softening, causing fractures in her authority. In that space of silence, there was trust and vulnerability. The massive morality officer with the rifle across her chest suddenly didn't seem as powerful as before. My mom had gotten her to reveal her resentment with the same system that could see us arrested, detained, tortured, or even killed, maybe even by the guard's own hand. My mom was doing what hostage negotiators do, but without the power of the government backing her up—she was building rapport with someone trained to be an adversary, someone far more powerful than she. And she was doing it simply by labeling emotions, listening, and being silent.

An awkward moment of well-timed and dynamic silence creates space not only for the other person to reflect about their position and open up about their motives, but also for the silent person to center themselves emotionally. My mom must have been as afraid as I was, but you couldn't tell by looking at her.

Silence here doesn't mean being quiet for an extended period of time. Rather, it's for a beat—a dynamic moment timed appropriately to allow the other person to feel heard, respected, but also a little awkward; uncomfortable enough to fill the silence. Using silence too much, or at the wrong moment, can be detrimental in several ways. First, it may create unnecessary tension or discomfort, leading to a breakdown in communication rather than fostering an open dialogue. If the other person perceives the silence as uninterest or disengagement, it can erode trust and make them feel undervalued or ignored. In a sensitive or emotionally charged situation, this might escalate the conflict instead of resolving it. Additionally, excessive silence might be misinterpreted as indecision or lack of confidence, potentially weakening your position in a negotiation. Proper timing is crucial: You should use silence strategically to encourage reflection and expression, not to intimidate or disconcert. So, it's important to balance silence with active engagement to ensure it serves as a tool for empathic understanding rather than a barrier to effective communication.

Dynamic silence has many applications beyond my marketplace experience. Indeed, Charles De Gaulle, the person who led France to a free republic against Nazi Germany and whom a military court sentenced to die but then played a significant role in restoring French democracy, said that "Silence is the ultimate weapon of power." Let's turn to an example in the world of corporate negotiations and the particular case of Steli Efti. In addition to being unofficially known as Silicon Valley's most prominent sales hustler and a big fan of using silence during negotiations, Efti is the CEO of Close.io, a seven-figure company providing communication software platforms for sales companies. Here, he tells *TechCrunch* magazine the story of negotiating outstanding licensing fees due to a third-party software company whose tech Close.io didn't need to use anymore. Here is Efti recalling the negotiation—pay particular note to how he used silence not only to shift the dynamics of a conversation but also to save hundreds of thousands of dollars.[11]

> The next day my phone rings: "Hey, Steli, this is John [not his real name]. Is this a good time to chat for you?" Me: "Yes, sure, let's chat."
>
> John: "I really want to help you. You guys are a struggling startup and I have a huge soft spot for entrepreneurs. I put up a huge fight with the finance department and got you an amazing deal. I think you'll love it. You'll be super thrilled to hear that instead of $250,000 you just need to pay us $100,000 to get out of the contract."
>
> I just had $150,000 taken off my shoulders. I felt like doing a happy dance. This was the moment to use the simplest and most powerful negotiation tactic ever. Silence.
>
> After a couple of moments of awkward silence, he continues to say, "Well, Steli, you know, it's really important to us that our relationship stays healthy and I want you to know that [insert a huge pile of bullshit here]. This is really the best I can do for you, I already took a lot of heat from finance for this. I hope you'll understand."
>
> 23 . . . 22 . . . 21 . . . 20 . . . 19 . . .
>
> He continues: "You know, one thing we might be able to do, if you postpone canceling the contract till January next year is probably give you a much better deal, maybe something between $25,000 and $50,000 instead of $100,000."
>
> This was November. Waiting for two more months was no problem.
>
> "January. Twenty-five thousand. Sounds good to me."

> John: "Ehhm . . . great, I'm really glad that we can part on good terms. I will send you all the information later today."
>
> . . . That phone call saved us $225,000. I couldn't have negotiated that kind of deal if I had said something.

Thus, silence, when used thoughtfully and dynamically, is not merely the absence of sound but a powerful tool for fostering communication, understanding, and achieving strategic objectives.

A Parenting Case Study: Active Listening, Silence, Affect Labeling

Combining silence with empathy tools can lead to remarkably successful negotiations, even in everyday situations—for example, negotiating tech time with children. Recently, when I was sitting at the kitchen table, absorbed in writing this very book, my son, Pierce, approached me. He had this hopeful look in his eyes, the kind that told me he wanted something.

> "What can I do for you, Pierce?" I asked, not looking up from my screen.
>
> He hesitated for a moment and then said, "Mom, I think I should get an hour of extra tech time because of all the extra reading I did."
>
> I glanced up briefly, acknowledging his point. "I know you've been reading more. And I'm proud of you for that." Then I paused my typing and remained silent, not immediately responding further, allowing the silence to hang in the air and continuously surprised by how that beat can open up a space for more.
>
> Pierce shifted uncomfortably. "Yeah . . . and, um, remember I took those recycling boxes out last night. I know, taking out recycling is already my chore." He was trying to fill the silence. I gave him a slight nod while still looking at my screen, encouraging him to go on.
>
> He continued, "But I also helped put Cole to bed like so many nights last week. I've been doing more, you know? So,

maybe an hour extra tech time?" he asked, his voice laced with hope and uncertainty.

I finally looked up from my laptop, still silent but now giving him my full attention. As soon as I began actively listening, I heard something different than just a kid asking for more frivolous tech time.

After a moment, Pierce sighed and said, "Actually, I also want the extra time because . . . well, there's this new game my friends are playing, and I just . . . I don't want to be left out."

This reveal is what I had been looking for: information that gets behind the why, information that I didn't have before. Now when I speak further with Pierce about this issue, I can offer other things besides additional screen time that address his underlying concern. I can try to put him in the same basketball class as some of his friends, or overall increase the number of get-togethers, or allow him to play video games when his friends are over (something I don't usually allow). I'm learning more about his needs as he gets older and slides deeper into the teenage years. I'm sure he also just wants to play shoot-'em-up video games because he's at that age and they're fun. But balancing my concern about the impact of those games on a young mind and mindful now of his need for social connection, I respond more thoughtfully, combining my earlier silence with affect labeling, gaining influence with my son, remaining mindful of his struggles, and strengthening our relationship all at the same time.

I softly responded, "It sounds like you're feeling a bit left out with your friends. That can be really tough."

He nodded, looking relieved to be understood. "Yeah, it's tough. I just want to play with them."

I nodded knowingly. "I appreciate you sharing that with me, Pierce. Let's talk about how we can balance your tech time and make sure you feel included with your friends."

Reflecting on this conversation, I realized how the blend of silence and active listening, coupled with affect labeling, not only provided me with more insight into Pierce's needs but also helped him feel heard and understood. Sometimes, the most powerful tool in communication isn't the words we say but the silence we allow and the empathy we show.

Significantly, the example of Pierce's technology use reflects more of an ongoing negotiation situation than a short-term bargain that concludes with a definitive long-term result (conversations balancing technology access with all my kids continue to this day). Neither silence nor any other strategic empathy tool can singlehandedly win every negotiation, particularly tough ongoing ones. In many cases, this is appropriate because in ongoing negotiation situations the facts evolve. For example, with my kids' tech use, the equation changes as they grow older. This dynamic nature of negotiations is key, especially when dealing with loved ones. The tools we're discussing aren't about manipulating loved ones into doing what we want. Rather, strategic empathy is about gaining the information and empathic understanding necessary to wisely reach our goals through influence. In the case of my discussion with my son, the goal of using silence, active listening, and affect labeling wasn't to change his desires so he didn't want the tech, but to gain more insight into why he *did* want it and what pressures *he* was facing, so that I could meet both my goals of protecting his brain and fostering his social connections.

Whether on the streets of Iran, in a heated negotiation worth hundreds of thousands of dollars, or in a screen-time conversation with your child, a dynamic beat of silence allows the issue to sink in, for you and for the others involved in the discussion. Affect labeling, active listening, and silence can make your counterpart feel respected, give them an opportunity to reveal more information, defuse anger, or create a slight awkwardness that usually goes to your advantage. In my mom's case with the morality guard, she did not utilize emotional empathy at all. She never felt the guard's pain, but rather understood it and used that information to get the *guard* to feel emotionally connected to *her* and give her what she needed. In the case of my discussion with Pierce, on the other hand, I felt some of Pierce's pain, particularly given my own childhood experiences of feeling excluded. I found a way to relate with him and to find solutions together that addressed my concerns about his adolescent brain's exposure to too much gaming, screens, and violence, but while balancing his interests and needs to connect to his peers with fun activities. Meanwhile, the business cases offer examples of various in-between cognitive- and emotional-empathy states, reminding us to apply tools of strategic empathy with flexibility and intention. Affect labeling, active listening, and silence also magnify the impact of the other, more advanced tactical empathy tools we will discuss in the next chapter: "mirroring and repeating" and "probing questions."

Like the superpower it is, strategic empathy gives us incredible influence in various contexts, from personal relationships to professional negotiations. By understanding and responding to the underlying emotions and motivations of others, we can guide conversations and outcomes in our favor. This powerful approach allows us to connect deeply with others, build trust, and foster cooperation, ultimately leading to more successful and meaningful interactions. Embracing strategic empathy enables us to navigate complex social dynamics with skill and compassion, making it an invaluable asset in any interaction. In the next chapter, we'll delve deeper into this remarkable capability by studying the advanced tools of mirroring and repeating, as well as probing questions, further enhancing our ability to influence and connect with others effectively.

Chapter 3 Takeaways

In this chapter, we've set out the three most concrete tools of strategic empathy to foster a genuine connection, trust, and leverage:

- Understanding the impact of Affect Labeling highlights the importance of recognizing and expressing the emotions of others.
- Utilizing Silence as a powerful strategic tool aids in introspection, deepens comprehension, and shifts the appearance of control.
- Engaging in Active Listening fully involves understanding the speaker's narrative, emotions, and intentions.

CHAPTER 4

ADVANCED STRATEGIC EMPATHY TOOLS: MIRRORING/ REPEATING AND PROBING QUESTIONS

The great gift of human beings is that we have the power of empathy, we can all sense a mysterious connection to each other.

— Meryl Streep

At least once a semester, I test out mirroring body language with my students as the test subjects. It's typically the second class, so I've already introduced myself to the students and made them aware of my relative power position as their professor. I enter the classroom and confidently walk to the front, taking up a dominant stance with my arms crossed over my chest. "Good morning, everyone. I'm glad you could all make it today. As you know, we have a lot to discuss, so let's get started." Then I pause and watch. I look to see how many students mirror my body language by crossing their arms over their chests. Without fail, a good portion of them changes posture to mirror mine. This is when I unfold my arms and gesture toward the presentation materials. "As you can see, today's class compares and contrasts various types of leadership styles . . ." But what I'm really doing is watching to see who uncrosses their arms.

In this chapter, we delve into two advanced techniques that will elevate your understanding and practice of empathy: "Mirroring and Repeating" and "Probing Questions." These strategies are designed not just to enhance your interactions but to transform them, providing you with tools to engage more deeply and effectively with others.

The Mirroring and Repeating technique we'll explore in the first part of this chapter isn't just about copying the words or body language of your counterpart; it's about tapping into the power of the brain's mirror neurons. By mirroring the language and gestures of others, we activate a profound neurological process that fosters connection and trust. You'll also learn about the intriguing Gauchais reaction and its effect on the brain's mirror neurons, providing a scientific basis for this technique. We'll also look at real-world applications of this method, including insights from Travis Bradberry, the chief people scientist at LEADx, to illustrate the practical impact of mirroring in professional and personal interactions.

The other skill, Probing Questions, is trickiest of all. Moving beyond the typical *why* questions that often put people on the defensive, we will focus on the power of *how* and *what* questions. These types of inquiries are less confrontational and more effective in peeling back the layers of a discussion. We'll explore examples from the realm of luxury-goods negotiations, showcasing how probing questions can lead to deeper understanding and more successful outcomes.

As we progress through this chapter, remember that these advanced techniques are tools to enhance your empathetic engagement with others. They're not just strategies for negotiation, but pathways to building stronger, more meaningful bonds and exerting greater influence over your own life and interactions. Let's embark on this next phase of your Stoic Empathy journey, equipping you with the skills to interact with greater understanding, compassion, and effectiveness.

Mirroring and Repeating: Adopting Words, Gestures, and Tones to Build Connection

Researchers have known at least for decades that our emotions mirror those around us, creating empathic connections. Mirror neurons are likely the reason that mimicking someone, which neuroscientists call the Gauchais reaction, is associated with a greater liking for the mimickers and a greater feeling of affiliation, often leading to more positive social behavior toward the mirroring person. Related to this physical mimicking is the concept of mirror neurons and the mirror neuron system's involvement in empathy, which we discussed in Chapter 2.

The Gauchais reaction's effect on mirror neurons is why waitresses who emulate the body language, vocal patterns, or tones of their customers get larger tips.[1] Why the department store sales clerk leans on the same hip you do; you'll probably like him more and buy more merchandise if he physically mirrors you.[2] Why we're more likely to be romantically interested in a potential partner at a speed-dating event if they verbally resemble us than if they don't.[3] The Gauchais reaction is also why your tone, speech speed, and even your dialect is more likely to simulate those in your social circle or your friend group than that of someone you don't like. In 2010, a group of researchers found that when someone mirrors your behavior, the areas of your brain that activate are the same ones that process rewards and make you feel good.[4] Mirroring someone's body language or words activates their mirror neurons, which creates empathy in the person mirrored. With empathy comes rapport and a deeper level of communication.

As Travis Bradberry of LEADx put it, "The next time you need to win someone over to your way of thinking, try nodding your head as you speak. People unconsciously mirror the body language of those around them to better understand what other people are feeling."[5] Travis should know. LEADx runs an app that combines AI and microlearning to teach leadership-competency skills. The world's leading corporate body-language consultants agree with him. One such expert, Susan Young, said, "Mirroring and matching works at the sub-conscious level and serves to make the other person feel more 'comfortable' and connected to you. These subliminal actions can create a subconscious feeling of unison and connection that demonstrate how much you have in common."[6] Perhaps she was a fly on the proverbial wall when my mom clashed that day with the morality guard.

Remember the morality guard's verbal reveal in response to my mom's silence, active listening, and affect labeling on the streets of Tehran? This was when my mom mirrored. Verbally, she'd just summarize the guard's sentence or repeat a few of the key words.

> "Do you know how frustrating it can be to give the same warning and threat, day after day?"
>
> "Day after day," my mom would say warmly.
>
> "Some days are really hot, you know? I've gotta cover up too while I walk up to them to repeat the same warning, to person after person."
>
> "You have to cover up too—in this heat."

And there it is. The guard just revealed how frustrated she was, not only with the people against whom she was enforcing the oppressive hijab laws, but with the law itself! The reveal was amazing. It never would have been said were it not for how my mom handled the situation. At that point, my mom physically mirrored the guard. As the guard's posture relaxed, so did my mom's tension. Re-creating my mom's postures in my mind, I see her shoulders lower along with the guard's hand on the rifle.

Having understood the profound impact of mirroring and repeating on our neural pathways and social interactions, let's pivot our attention to the practical application of these techniques. How do we mirror and repeat effectively, especially in contexts where words carry significant weight, such as in professional negotiations?

Let's consider a common, real-life example of these techniques in action during a tense negotiation:

> You're in the midst of a high-stakes salary negotiation with your boss. The office air is thick with tension, making every word crucial. Your boss, showing signs of stress, leans forward and confesses, "I'm at my limit with the budget." This is a critical juncture.

As an adept negotiator understanding the power of mirroring, you echo their posture and words, leaning in and reflecting back, "You're at your limit with the budget." This mirroring does more than show you're listening; it prompts your boss to open up further.

Feeling heard, your boss explains, "There's no room for adjustment."

You mirror this sentiment as well: "So, there's no room for adjustment." Your repetition, followed by a thoughtful pause, acts as a silent encouragement for them to elaborate.

This strategy leads to a breakthrough. Your boss, now less on guard and feeling understood, divulges, "We can't adjust the budget, because our department's funding was cut." This insight, this reason behind the budget constraint, is precisely what you aimed to discover. It shifts the discussion from a dead end to exploring solutions, such as reallocating existing resources or discussing nonmonetary benefits that could compensate for the salary limitation. Maybe something like this:

You say: "Thanks for being up front about the budget issues. I get where we're at, so how about we think about other ways to balance things out? Maybe we could look at flexible work options or some extra time off?"

"What kind of work flexibility were you thinking about?"

"Well, maybe working from home a few days a week could work. It'd save me on travel and I think I'd actually get more done."

"Okay, but what about the extra vacation time?"

"An extra week off could really help with keeping a good work-life balance, don't you think? It'd be a great way to make up for not moving up in salary."

"I see what you mean. Let me chat with HR and see what we can do. I'm open to these ideas and will get back to you after some discussions on our end."

This example illustrates the power of mirroring and repeating in a negotiation context. By carefully echoing the counterpart's words, you create a space where they feel heard and are thus more inclined to open up, providing you with invaluable insights into their constraints and perspectives. This approach isn't about manipulation; it's about fostering understanding and empathy, which are the cornerstones of effective communication and negotiation.

The versatility of the mirroring technique extends beyond the mere repetition of words. It encompasses the nuanced realm of body language. Consider the scenario of a negotiation meeting:

- *Context:* You're in a crucial negotiation meeting with a potential business partner. The stakes are high, and establishing a connection is key to influencing the outcome favorably.
- *Action:* As the meeting begins, you observe your counterpart's body language closely. They lean slightly forward, hands clasped together on the table, indicating a mix of eagerness and caution. Recognizing this, you subtly mirror their posture, leaning forward as well, showing engagement and openness.
- *Empathetic Response by Mirroring Body Language:* As the conversation progresses, your counterpart mentions the challenges their company is facing. You nod in understanding, maintaining your mirrored posture. Your body language reflects a genuine interest in their concerns, not just a passive acknowledgment.
- *Strategic Use of Empathy:* Utilizing this empathetic link, you then offer insights or solutions that align with their challenges. Your body language remains congruent with your words, signaling sincerity. This alignment of verbal and nonverbal communication enhances your credibility and persuasiveness.
- *Result:* Your counterpart, feeling understood and valued, becomes more receptive to your proposals. The mirrored body language, combined with empathetic listening and relevant responses, builds trust and rapport, increasing your influence in the negotiation.

- *Further Application:* As the meeting progresses, you notice a change in their body language—a relaxation of shoulders, a more open stance. You adapt accordingly, easing your posture, signaling that the conversation has entered a more comfortable and cooperative phase. This continued mirroring reinforces the growing rapport, making the negotiation process smoother and more productive.

In this scenario, you use body-language mirroring strategically to create an empathetic connection that you then leverage to influence the negotiation positively. The key is the seamless integration of empathetic listening and relevant, sincere responses, all while maintaining congruence between verbal and nonverbal cues.

Mirroring and repeating proves its efficacy even in scenarios where physical presence is absent, such as during a Zoom call, where you have more limited cues. You can still mimic the motions of the person's eyes, such as gaze direction and blink speed. If they're drinking from a mug, go grab your own mug and take a sip a few seconds after they do. If they tap their pen in their teeth, go for it. Just be subtle and wait 5 to 30 seconds before you mirror. You can even mirror on phone calls. If the person is obviously smiling, you can hear it. Smile in turn—and they'll perceive your smile as well. Match their voice tone and volume, as well as speed.

Besides mimicking words and body language, you can practice mirroring someone's vocal cadence. Vocal cadence is the way your voice flows. It's the pauses between your words and how the rhythm sounds. It might help if you think of each person's voice like a song with its own unique lyrics and melody. Since research shows that we prefer voices that sound like our own, try also mimicking the pauses and flows of a person's voice.*

* Mirroring happens unconsciously too, and in romantic settings. For example, if your breathing pace is aligned with your partner's, you're more likely to have stronger feelings for one another—or so says a 2002 article in *Bride* magazine quoting Tonya Reiman, a well-known body-language expert. Significantly, *Science Daily* agrees, citing a 2017 study by Goldstein, Weissman-Fogel, and Shamay-Tsoory published in the journal *Scientific Reports* in support of the proposition that "when lovers touch, their breathing, heartbeat syncs, pain wanes" (See Lisa Marshall, "When Lovers Touch, Their Breathing, Heartbeat Syncs, Pain Wanes, Study Shows," *Science Daily*, June 21, 2017, https://www.sciencedaily.com/releases/2017/06/170621125313.htm.)

Imagine, for example, you're on a crucial conference call with a key stakeholder. Even though you can't see each other, the principles of mirroring remain just as potent. As the conversation progresses, you notice the tone and pace of the stakeholder's speech—perhaps a hint of anxiety in their voice or a rapid tempo indicating urgency. Subtly, you begin to adapt your own vocal qualities to match theirs—not mimicking, but mirroring the essence of their speech patterns. If they're speaking quickly, you slightly increase your pace while ensuring clarity and understanding. If their tone carries a sense of concern, you mirror that sentiment in your voice, maybe with a softer tone, signaling empathy and comprehension. This vocal mirroring, though seemingly minor, can create a subliminal bond and a sense of alignment, even without visual cues.

Mirroring, an integral technique in empathetic communication, can be challenging to master effectively. The biggest mirroring mistake is mirroring people's unique traits, mistakes, or imperfections. Never mirror a person's dialect, specific speech impediments, or any unique expressions. To ensure it's applied successfully and respectfully, it's important to understand both what to mirror and what to avoid. Here are some key principles for effective mirroring:

- *Respect for Individuality:* Always be mindful of a person's unique traits and characteristics. Avoid mirroring aspects deeply tied to someone's identity, such as dialects, specific speech patterns, or unique expressions. Respecting distinct identities is crucial, as these traits are often connected to a person's cultural background and personal identity.
- *Avoid Mockery and Insensitivity:* Be cautious not to mirror speech impediments or any characteristic that might be perceived as a personal imperfection. Mirroring these aspects can come across as insincere or even mocking, which may damage trust and the empathetic connection you're trying to build.
- *Focus on General Nonverbals:* Effective mirroring should concentrate on broad aspects of communication.

This includes body posture, gestures, vocal tone, and speaking tempo. These general nonverbals can be mirrored to show empathy and understanding without the risk of mocking or offending.

- *Cultural Sensitivity:* In our globalized environment, cultural sensitivity is paramount. Mirroring someone's unique cultural traits or dialect is subject to misinterpretation as a lack of respect or understanding of their culture.
- *Building Authentic Connections:* The ultimate goal of mirroring is to foster genuine connections. This is best achieved through subtle, respectful mirroring of common behaviors and avoiding overmirroring or mimicking unique traits that might render interactions artificial.

In addition, when you mirror, make sure that you're prioritizing positive nonverbal cues that promote engagement and empathy, not negative actions, because those won't advance your empathic link.

- *Mirror Positive Gestures:* Engage in mirroring gestures that convey openness and interest, such as nodding in agreement, leaning forward slightly, maintaining eye contact, and reflecting affirmative hand gestures.
- *Avoid Negative Body Language:* Be cautious not to mirror negative nonverbals like turning away, folding arms in a blocking manner, closing eyes, or looking away. These actions can signal uninterest or disagreement, hindering the empathetic connection.

By focusing on mirroring positive nonverbals and avoiding negative ones, you'll significantly reduce misunderstandings and facilitate a more empathetic, connected communication environment. By focusing on general, positive aspects of communication and respecting individual uniqueness, mirroring effectively builds rapport and enhances empathetic attachments without causing discomfort or offense.

Probing Questions: Avoiding Shutdowns and Receiving Deeper Responses

Remember, strategic empathy is the capability that provides access to information and creates the trust necessary to achieve your goals, even when you start from a position of relative weakness in a negotiation. At its core, strategic empathy involves oscillating between emotional and cognitive empathy skills to understand others' thoughts and feelings. This helps them lower their guard and reveal information, strengthening your connection with them. You can then use this knowledge to determine your path and increase your power, whether you're leading a team, negotiating a higher bonus, hitting a sales target, or managing a classroom of preteens.

We've discussed several empathy tools for revealing the information needed to build trust, influence, and leverage: affect labeling (identifying emotions), active listening (versus passive hearing), silence (a dynamic pause), and mirroring (mimicking body language or words). A somewhat obvious but often overlooked technique to gain information is simply asking questions. But what kinds of questions are most likely to yield usable information in daily interactions, and how should you ask them?

As a litigator, I learned how to cross-examine a witness, and to do it well. I've made witnesses break down their barriers, confess what I wanted them to, even outright cry on the stand and a deposition seat. Sometimes it's as easy as knowing what a witness is going to lie or be inconsistent about, then being prepared to expose the lie in front of the judge and jury. For example, at trial, I'd ask a question I knew they'd answer with yes while knowing they'd answered it with no during their deposition. I would let them give the yes and then play the recording of them saying no. Even if it related to a small, tangential subissue, once I'd exposed their lie in public, the witness was in the palm of my hands. Tears were likely. They were humiliated. This is when I'd start peppering them with fast, interrogation-style questions, mostly yes-or-no questions I could ask quickly. The witness wouldn't have enough time to think before answering, getting them to a final answer to a final question that'd help me win the case or completely discredit that witness.

Yes, I can cross-examine with the best of them. But what works well in a court of law doesn't necessarily work well in the rest of life. For example, I *could* also beat my husband or a co-worker in virtually any argument, but making colleagues or family members cry by catching them in a logical "gotcha" moment is *not* the goal in the real world. I'd lose my relationships, maybe even lose my marriage and my job. Winning arguments in exchange for a lonely and miserable life isn't winning.

Outside the courtroom, the vast majority of our power struggles and negotiations are split into two types, neither of which have much use for confrontational, cross-examination–type questions. **First** are contexts wherein we're in long-standing relationships with our counterpart, such as with our boss, employees, vendors, customers, spouse, friends, parent, children, neighbor, or fellow school parent. For these situations, the entire concept of a cross-examination can be severely self-defeating. Maybe we'll win that argument, get that raise, sign the new contract, convince our spouse we should spend the holidays with our family, but are we really winning? How will that "win" affect our overall relationship with the people with whom we're spending the majority of our life? How will the next day or year look for us at work or at home? Consider that cross-examining the people closest to you in life, those with whom you hope to have positive and enduring relationships, can:

- *Erode Trust:* Cross-examination is inherently confrontational and is often perceived as aggressive or accusatory. In personal and professional dynamics that rely on trust and mutual respect, such an approach erodes the foundation of trust that's been built over time.
- *Create Defensiveness:* This method puts the other person on the defensive, leading to closed communication rather than open dialogue. It may cause them to withhold information, be less honest, or become more adversarial, which is counterproductive in a relationship based on collaboration and mutual support.

- *Damage Long-Term Bonds:* Relationships in your personal and professional life are ongoing, unlike a courtroom setting which is situation-specific and transient. Aggressive questioning can damage these relationships, leading to long-term repercussions that affect your work environment, home life, and social interactions.
- *Neglect Emotional Intelligence:* Cross-examination lacks the nuances of emotional intelligence required in lasting relationships. It doesn't consider the feelings, perspectives, or emotional states of the other party, which are crucial for healthy, long-term interactions.
- *Miss Opportunities for Constructive Dialogue:* This approach often misses the chance to engage in constructive, empathetic dialogue where both parties feel heard and understood. In ongoing relationships, it might be more important to find common ground and mutually beneficial solutions rather than to win an argument.
- *Impact Personal Reputation:* Consistently using cross-examination tactics can lead others to view you as combative or uncooperative. This perception can impact your personal and professional reputation, affecting current and future collaborations.
- *Create Psychological Harm:* Repeatedly being subjected to such questioning causes stress, anxiety, and discomfort for the other person, leading to a deterioration of the relationship quality.

If we were to look at this from a game-theory lens, we could classify our daily negotiations and power struggles into two categories: finite games and infinite games, each demanding distinct strategies to optimize long-term outcomes. Finite games, such as court battles, have clear endpoints, rules, and winners, emphasizing immediate victories and resolutions. In contrast, infinite games, much like our interactions with colleagues, friends, and family, have no defined endpoint; the goal is not to win but to perpetuate the game. Success in infinite games is measured by the ability to maintain and enhance relationships over time, requiring strategies that prioritize mutual understanding, trust, and collaboration. Adopting an infinite-game mindset in our personal and professional lives encourages us to look beyond the immediate win, focusing instead on continuously improving relationships and creating environments where all participants can thrive. This approach recognizes that, in the long run, prioritizing the quality and sustainability of our relationships is crucial. These relationships not only shape the outcomes of individual encounters but also drive the overall harmony and productivity of our shared endeavors.

The **second** category of situations where cross-examining your counterpart or reducing them to tears with a confession is misplaced is where a controlled cross-examination simply won't work—it won't be effective—particularly if you're the powerless one. A lawyer conducting a cross-examination in court has authority and power over the witness. Unless the judge sustains an objection, the witness is obligated to respond or face being in contempt of court—they can't suddenly decide to stand up and leave if they don't like the question. Unlike the morality guard that day on the streets of Tehran, the witness in a court of law can't arrest, detain, torture, or murder the lawyer who's questioning them. But the cross-examination paradigm just doesn't extend well outside a legal case in front of a judge or jury.

Cross-examination is simply not of much use outside a courtroom. Some questions get the other side to say what you want them to say but damage your relationships and harm you more than help you. Other questions and situations make people shut down even more, get the wall that your earlier work lowered right back up again, decrease trust, and reduce information outflow. The wrong question can also just end the conversation; the person can simply walk away from you.

What *is* useful in these circumstances is *probing* questions—a powerful tool in communication, particularly when the goal is to gather in-depth information and build trust without jeopardizing the overall relationship. The essence of these questions lies in their ability to delve deep into a subject, seeking to understand the underlying reasons, opinions, or feelings. This approach facilitates a more comprehensive understanding of the situation or the person involved. Let's take a closer look at both cross-examination–type questions and probing questions:

- *Cross-Examining Questions: Why* and *but* questions can help your case by attacking a witness's credibility or even encourage a confession in a controlled, courtroom-type setting, but in other situations, these types of questions are often perceived as challenging or accusatory, leading to a defensive response. For example, asking someone "Why did you choose that method?" can imply doubt or criticism of their decision-making process. Similarly, *but* questions can undermine someone's statement, creating a sense of contradiction or opposition, which might close off communication channels. For example, "You claim that this timeline is nonnegotiable, but haven't similar projects been completed faster in the past?"
- *Probing Questions:* The focus on *how* and *what* questions tends to foster a more open and constructive dialogue. *How* questions are particularly useful for encouraging a detailed narrative or explanation. They invite respondents to describe processes, thoughts, or feelings in depth, providing a platform for comprehensive understanding. For instance, asking, "How did you approach this challenge?" allows the person to explain their methodology and reasoning, revealing a wealth of information about their decision-making process, skills, and attitudes. Similarly, *what* questions are invaluable for gathering precise and specific information. These questions help you drill down to the facts and details of a situation. They're straightforward and direct, yet devoid of the confrontational tone that *why* questions might carry and focus the conversation on specific actions, leading to clear and focused responses. For example, you may ask:

"What steps did you take to resolve the issue?"
"How can we solve this?"
"What are we trying to accomplish?"
"What brought us to this situation?"
"How can I earn your confidence that I can lead the team?"

Thus, by emphasizing *how* and *what* questions—the probing type—the conversation becomes more about exploration and understanding rather than judgment or contention. This approach not only yields richer and more useful information, but also contributes to a more positive and collaborative communication environment. The key lies in crafting these questions in a way that is nondirective, encouraging the respondent to share openly and at length, which leads to insights that might not emerge through a more confrontational questioning style.

The way these questions are posed is crucial in building trust and strengthening relationships. When probing questions are asked with respect and empathy, they make the other person feel heard and understood. This not only helps us acquire valuable information but also fosters a sense of mutual respect and trust.

The effectiveness of probing questions is significantly influenced by the context in which we ask them and the flexibility with which we use them. Understanding and adapting to the specific circumstances of each conversation is crucial for several reasons. First, every situation is unique and requires a tailored approach. For instance, the type of questions that would be appropriate in a casual conversation with a colleague might differ vastly from those you would use in a formal performance review. In a casual setting, a more relaxed and open question might encourage sharing, while a structured and specific question could be more effective in a formal evaluation. Second, the emotional state and relationship with the respondent play a significant role. If someone is feeling defensive or stressed, even well-intentioned probing questions might be met with resistance. In such cases, it might be more effective to use softer, more empathetic questioning techniques, perhaps starting with more general questions before gradually moving to more specific ones.

When strategizing your questioning approach, align it with the conversation's objective. For gathering factual information, direct questions may be most effective. These are typically closed-ended, eliciting precise, concrete answers. For instance:

- Question: "What time did the meeting start?"

  Potential Response: "The meeting started at 9 A.M."

- Question: "What steps did you follow in this procedure?"

  Potential Response: "First, I logged into the system, then I uploaded the files, and finally, I sent an e-mail confirmation."

These questions aim to obtain specific information and usually lead to straightforward answers. Conversely, if your objective is to use empathy strategically to understand thoughts or feelings, frame your *what* questions to be more open-ended and reflective. This invites the respondent to share detailed and nuanced responses. For example:

- Question: "What were your thoughts when you were met with this challenge?"

  Potential Response: "I felt initially overwhelmed. But then, I started to break down the problem into smaller parts, which made it more manageable."

- Question: "What were you feeling when this was happening?"

  Potential Response: "During the experience, I felt a mix of excitement and nervousness. It was uncharted territory for me. Then again, I was pretty eager to learn and adapt."

In these instances, *what* questions delve into the respondent's internal experiences or perceptions, inviting broader answers that reveal more about their perspectives or emotional states. Remember, cultural nuances influence how questions are perceived. In some cultures, direct questions might be seen as intrusive, while in others, they're valued for their clarity. The key is to be flexible and actively listen, ready to adjust your line of questioning based on the responses. This might mean exploring an unforeseen yet significant topic or refraining from a line of inquiry that causes discomfort.

Being adaptable and sensitive to the unique context of each conversation is key to using probing questions effectively. A flexible approach attuned to the specifics of the situation, the emotional state of the respondent, the relationship dynamic, cultural norms, and the conversation's goals will ensure that your questions are not only appropriate but also more likely to yield insightful and meaningful responses.

I remember a particularly heated negotiation at the peak of my legal career. Most of my work was for high-end luxury-goods companies, but in this case, I was representing a fashion start-up company whose owner I'd met at a local fashion show. Her company didn't in any way compete with my bigger clients, and she was, in many ways, a struggling artist. Let's call her company Fancy Bags. She needed me to negotiate a supply agreement for her start-up with a clasp manufacturer—let's call it Clasp Makers—whose products would be used in making Fancy Bags collections. Fancy Bags made very exclusive items sold at high prices, but it was new in the local marketplace and had no market power compared with much more established international brands. As a fashion company, brand integrity was a pivotal component of its business model, so Fancy Bags didn't want its clasps to look like those on any other handbag. As a result, it insisted on an exclusivity agreement wherein its supplier would not provide any other handbag company with accessories of any kind that could be used on bags. The negotiation, summarized here, took place mostly over e-mail, using affect labeling and probing questions.

Clasp Makers: "This is a no-go. We can't agree to an exclusivity agreement. We'd lose seventy-three percent of our business."

Fancy Bags: "You seem concerned about profitability if you agree to contract only with us."

CM: "Yeah! I mean, most of our business is making metal accessories for handbags. You guys are still small potatoes. We'd go out of business!"

FB: "I understand. My client is concerned that their handbags will look like everyone else's that you provide clasp components to. As you know, their trademark and brand integrity is really important to them, and people buy their bags because of their distinctiveness. What do you suggest we do to ease their concerns?"

CM: "They don't have anything to worry about, because we don't make clasps like these for anyone else! The metal accessories we make for other brands, they don't look anything like these clasps!"

FB: "How can my clients be sure of that, or sure that won't change?"

CM: "Well, we can give them a report on what else we produce."

FB: "Can we agree to make it a regular report?"

CM: "Yeah, maybe that could work. We can define the parameters to exclude the other metalwork we do."

FB: "Sure. We can even identify the other metalwork as specifically allowed in the contract. And you let us know on a regular basis if you're making changes so we can update the contract to allow more metalwork that doesn't look anything at all like our clasps—as long as we put a guarantee in the contract that you won't make anything like these clasps."

CM: "Yeah, we can talk about how that might work."

Remember that while engaged in strategic empathy, your efforts are focused on discovering information about your opponent—information you can use to your advantage. The goal is to keep the conversation going and coax the other side into speaking more.

Using a *how* question helped Fancy Bags to understand the Clasp Makers' concerns and find creative ways of resolving them, whereas a *why* or *but* question would've felt more like a cross-examination. Here are some examples of how those types of questions might have been framed.

Why Questions:

- "Why can't you agree to an exclusivity agreement?"
- "Why are you so concerned about losing other business if our products are distinct?"
- "Why haven't you considered the unique value that Fancy Bags brings to your business?"

These questions might put Clasp Makers on the defensive by coming across as challenging their business decisions and priorities.

But Questions:

- "But isn't it true that our exclusivity would differentiate your product offering?"
- "But don't you see the potential for long-term gains with our brand?"
- "But isn't it better to have a unique product rather than catering to many common ones?"

But questions could be perceived as undermining or disputing the concerns that Clasp Makers raises, potentially leading to a more contentious negotiation dynamic. The supplier could've just hung up on me and walked away from my client's relatively small order, and my client would be out of luck.

In contrast, the use of *how* and *what* questions in the actual negotiation led to a more collaborative and solution-focused dialogue, because they encouraged Clasp Makers to think about possible solutions and express their concerns more openly. The *how* question got the supplier thinking about how *they* could solve *my* client's concerns—triggering empathy for my client. That's the power of probing questions: They elicit empathy for you by a counterpart, changing the framework of the discussion for your benefit.

These types of questions are thoughtfully designed to make your counterpart feel like they're the ones in control of where the discussion is going, even though you're the real driver. When you're at an impasse with a loved one, asking *them* how to solve the problem will flip their mental switch from a defensive mode to one that gets their cognitive juices flowing toward finding a common solution. It triggers empathy for your situation, at a minimum, demonstrating the adverse impacts that their proposed solutions will have on you.

Getting back to my mom and the morality guard: She used this tool expertly. What she did was get the *guard* to have empathy. Mom said, "Your work sounds really hard. For us, you know, my daughter *just* turned nine—they grow up so fast. How can we convince you to let this go? What can I do right now?" There are many zealots among the morality police who are morally committed to their jobs. This didn't seem to be this particular person's story. She seemed sick of her job and ready for a break. When my mom asked her what she could do for the guard to let us go, she flipped the switch and put the onus on the guard to think of a solution that would free us versus cognitively focus on the many tasks that come with an arrest.

I remember this part as clear as day, because this is when the guard released the hand that was gripping her weapon and just turned and walked away. And we got the heck out of there as quickly as we could.

Without knowing what these tools are called, my mom used affect labeling, active listening, silence, mirroring and repeating, and probing questions that day, all strategic empathy skills, to raise her weak bargaining position. She never felt the guard's pain, but she understood it, and she used that information to get the *guard* to feel emotionally connected to *her* and give us what we wanted. As is often attributed to Einstein, "If I had an hour to solve a problem and my life depended on it, I would use the first fifty-five minutes determining the proper question to ask, for once I know the proper question, I could solve the problem in less than five minutes."

Power comes from the ability to control and influence. The greater our influence in the room, the more favorable the outcome. When you're the less powerful one in the interaction, not just politically but also racially, economically, or genderwise, no one thing will guarantee you the win. But, just like my mom, you can strategically implement the five strategic empathy tools above to increase your odds in *every* context, whether you're hoping to increase your salary or just trying to keep your family safe.

Chapter 4 Takeaways

This chapter illuminated advanced strategic empathy tools that enhance our ability to connect and understand others on a deeper level:

- Mirroring and Repeating involves reflecting the speaker's language and body language to create rapport by showing attentiveness and understanding.
- Using Probing Questions delves deeper into the *how* and *what* of the speaker's thoughts and feelings, encouraging them to open up and providing a pathway to deeper insights and comprehension.

* * *

As we conclude our exploration of strategic empathy, we've delved deeply into the art of understanding and influencing others. We've learned how to wield empathy strategically, shifting between emotional and cognitive empathy as the situation calls for it, and utilizing empathy as an active means of creating connection and fostering trust. The techniques we've covered—affect labeling, active listening, silence, mirroring, and probing questions—have equipped us with powerful methods to enhance our empathic skills and strategically navigate our interpersonal interactions.

These tools allow us to enter the minds and hearts of others, uncovering their thoughts and emotions to build stronger bonds and gain valuable insights. With strategic empathy, we've discovered how to gently lower the defenses of others, encouraging them to reveal information that can strengthen our rapport and increase our influence. Whether leading a team, negotiating in the workplace, or simply managing daily interactions, these techniques empower us to engage with others on a profound level.

The next part of our journey shifts inward. To truly wield influence with integrity and resilience, to even be able to exercise cognitive empathy in lieu of emotional empathy when the circumstances require it, we must also master the art of self-control. This is where the ancient wisdom of Stoicism comes into play.

Stoicism teaches us to cultivate inner strength and maintain emotional equilibrium, regardless of external circumstances. Where empathy helps us navigate the complexities of others' emotions, stoicism provides the foundation for managing our own. By embracing Stoic principles, we learn to control our reactions, harness our emotions, and act with ethical clarity. In the following chapters, we'll explore the core tenets of stoicism and how they can be applied in the modern world. We will delve into the Dichotomy of Control, Discomfort Embracing, Habituation, Memento Mori, and Moral Courage—five methods of stoic self-regulation that complement the empathic tools we've already covered.

Through these stoic practices, we will gain the resilience to face life's challenges with grace, the discipline to regulate our emotions without repressing them, and the ethical compass to guide our actions. Together, these principles will not only enhance our personal growth but also empower us to engage with the world in a balanced and impactful manner.

As we transition from strategic empathy to stoicism, remember that true power lies in the harmonious balance of understanding others and mastering oneself. By integrating these timeless philosophies, we can navigate life with both compassion and strength, influencing our surroundings while staying grounded in our core values.

Join me as we embark on this next phase, where we turn inward to discover the profound power of stoic self-mastery. Through this journey, we will uncover how to fortify our Inner Citadel, harness our resilience, and ultimately, lead lives of greater purpose and influence.

CHAPTER 5

STOIC EMOTIONAL REGULATION AND MINDFULNESS

To feel these feelings at the right time, on the right occasion, toward the right people, for the right purpose and in the right manner . . . is of course the mark of virtue.

— ARISTOTLE

Even if you aren't a big enough *Star Trek* fan to sport a Bajoran earring to a convention like I would, you've heard of Mr. Spock, the half-Vulcan, half-human first officer of the starship *Enterprise*, a character who appeared in six different television series and nine different feature films, played by different actors. Juxtaposed against the cowboyesque Captain Kirk, Spock came across quite stoic. Like the Stoics, Spock would often place logic and reason above emotion. When faced with the unpredictable nature of the cosmos, Spock, much like a Stoic, would accept things as they came, relying on his logic and training, and always holding virtue in high regard. While their similarities are striking and Vulcanism aligns in many ways with Stoicism, there are significant differences. Whereas Stoics sought to recognize, understand, and transform emotions, Vulcans, including Spock, are taught from a young age to deny them entirely. Stoicism also carried with it a sense of universal belonging, an idea that every being was a citizen of the world. While the adventures of the USS

Enterprise touched upon this sentiment, it wasn't a central pillar of Spock's personal belief. This is why our chapter will not begin with Mr. Spock as our Stoic ideal. Instead, that title goes to Captain Picard, always played by the unshakable Sir Patrick Stewart.

In the boundless sea of stars, the updated *Enterprise* cut through space, led by Captain Jean-Luc Picard. Unlike many who traversed the cosmos, Picard wasn't just a man of action; he was a man of deep thought and principle. He wasn't born of a race like the Vulcans, who naturally suppressed emotion. Instead, he hailed from Earth, a world teeming with passion and chaos, making his measured demeanor all the more striking. On quiet nights, when the vastness of space pressed on the ship's hull, Picard would retreat to his quarters. Surrounded by ancient Earth literature and relics, he sought solace in the wisdom of the ages. So, he was likely to have pondered the teachings of the Stoics, an ancient Earth philosophy. Their teachings about reason, moral virtue, and acceptance would have resonated deeply with him. During the day, the bridge was alive with activity, but Picard's guiding presence was a beacon of stability. When faced with dilemmas, he would call upon reason and rely on diplomacy, much like a Stoic sage. Not merely content to react, he deliberated, aiming to align his decisions with the highest principles of justice and integrity.

The universe was unpredictable. Picard knew this all too well, having faced adversaries and undergone trials that would have broken lesser beings. Yet, in Stoic fashion, he accepted these challenges, aware of what was and wasn't within his control. His endurance in the face of adversity, always holding on to his principles, became legendary. But it wasn't just about individual trials; Picard's vision extended to a grander scale. He saw a universe where all sentient beings, regardless of origin, could coexist and learn from one another, reflecting Stoicism's universal perspective—all while regulating, rather than suppressing, the human condition of emotionalism.

Stoicism, originating in ancient Greece in the 3rd century B.C.E., promotes the pursuit of virtue and wisdom as the foundation of genuine happiness. At its heart lies the dichotomy of control: a guiding principle that distinguishes between elements of life we can influence—our reactions, judgments, and behaviors—and those we cannot, such as external events and outcomes. By internalizing this distinction, Stoics learn to navigate life's challenges with equanimity, focusing energy on meaningful personal growth while accepting the natural course of events beyond their control.

This philosophy also underscores that the true measure of good in life is virtue, with external events being neutral in the pursuit of moral excellence. By curtailing our desires, practicing indifference to life's vicissitudes, and centering our values on personal character and integrity, Stoicism provides a blueprint for a contented, purposeful existence rooted in discerning and accepting the limits of our control.

Consider a compelling episode from *Star Trek: The Next Generation*: There's a moment when Captain Picard stands on the bridge of his ship when the *Enterprise* comes across a mysterious alien probe. As he interacts with the enigmatic device, he is immediately and inexplicably transported into a world completely unknown to him or to us as *Star Trek* audience members. In an instant, Picard becomes a village man named Kamin, living on the planet Kataan, a preindustrialized humanoid society with its own unique set of challenges far removed from the starship's comforts.

The discomfort of the unknown is overwhelming at first. Picard longs for the life he'd known, the starship, and the familiar faces of his crew. But as the years pass, something within him shifts. Like a true Stoic, he lives in accordance with the dichotomy of control—the idea that there are aspects of life we can control and those we cannot. As Kamin, Picard makes a choice. He chooses to embrace this alternate life, even falling in love and having children, always continuing to search for knowledge in the stars while trying to save Kataan. You see, this world was suffering through a protracted drought due to increased solar radiation, which threatened all life on the planet.

In the end of the episode, after living an entire life as Kamin and dying of old age, Picard wakes up on the bridge of the *Enterprise*. He realizes that his entire existence as Kamin was a generated virtual-reality program. The decades of life he lived, the people he loved, every experience he'd had, was in fact a simulation in his brain that had lasted about 20 minutes in real time. Kataan is revealed to have been destroyed by its sun going nova over 1,000 years ago. The probe the *Enterprise* had encountered, the one Picard touched in the beginning of the episode that placed him in the life of Kamin, was an interactive time capsule designed to convey the history of the extinct civilization to one person through a lifetime of lived and shared experience. Before the simulation ends, the people of Kataan ask Picard to tell others about the story of their world. Because he had embraced discomfort, accepted change, and adapted to the unknown in his journey as Kamin, Picard was in the perfect position to tell the universe about Kataan: not just facts about its people's existence, but the very spirit and essence of their lives.

Picard's transformative journey made him wiser and more resilient. His stoicism provided personal growth and a richer, fulfilling emotional life, showing us that anyone could choose at any time to embrace discomfort and confront the unknown with courage, leading to personal growth and a deeper understanding of the self. What is, after all, the goal of exploring strange new worlds and seeking out new life and civilizations, if not to take our own civilization, including ourselves, to the next step of our evolutionary trajectory?

Contrary to popular belief, emotional control doesn't limit our emotional depth. But emotional control is about how we feel *and* how we manifest our feeling experience. It is not the refusal to feel emotions. It's Picard's logical approach while accepting what he cannot control and enriching his positive emotional experiences, not Spock's stubborn blocking of his human side. Stoics don't sacrifice emotional richness. To the contrary, a life of stoicism enhances our positive emotional experiences, increasing patience, resilience, grit, and kindness, allowing us to live to the fullest even in circumstances beyond our control.

Greco-Roman Stoicism: Zeno, Seneca, Epictetus, and Emotional Regulation

Stoicism is the finest example of a philosophical path that values emotional regulation: the idea that our well-being is contingent on mastering our own emotions, reactions, and perceptions. It's a Hellenistic philosophy that Zeno of Citium founded in Athens in the early 3rd century B.C.E. As Zeno once expressed, "Man conquers the world by conquering himself." In first defining Stoicism, Zeno laid its groundwork by teaching that logic, physics, and ethics were the core disciplines in leading a virtuous life. He emphasized that events themselves hold no intrinsic value; as he notably remarked, "It's not what happens to you, but how you react to it that matters." Therefore, by regulating and refining our judgments, we achieve emotional equilibrium.

While rooted in Greek beginnings and the teachings of Zeno and other Greek philosophers, Stoicism was notably refined and expanded on by Roman thinkers such as Seneca and Epictetus, making it a truly Greco-Roman school of thought. Seneca observed, "We suffer more in imagination than in reality." For him, emotional regulation was about understanding the nature of fortune and accepting the impermanence of life. By doing so, we attain a state of tranquility and inner peace untouched by external adversities.

Epictetus offers a fascinating narrative in this context. Born a slave in Rome, he served under Epaphroditos, a secretary to Emperor Nero. Despite the confines of his enslaved status, Epictetus used his circumstances as a backdrop to understand Stoic philosophy deeply. It was during Nero's reign that he somehow convinced his owners to emancipate him. Liberated from his bonds, he migrated to Nicopolis in Greece, where he established a celebrated Stoic school. As Epictetus insightfully stated, "It's not things themselves that upset us, but our judgments about these things." His teachings, recorded by his student Arrian, revolved around the dichotomy of control: discerning what's within our control from what isn't. For Epictetus, true freedom—both from his literal chains and from emotional turmoil—emerges from recognizing this dichotomy and mastering our emotional responses.

At its core, Stoicism provides a road map for emotional resilience. From Zeno's foundational teachings to the Roman adaptations by Seneca and Epictetus, the underlying message is clear: Emotional well-being isn't about denying the existence of our feelings but understanding and navigating them. By recognizing the impermanent nature of life, the unpredictability of fate, and the boundaries of control, Stoics develop an enduring contentment irrespective of external circumstances, converging on the principle that our perceptions and judgments hold the key to our emotional well-being.

While Stoicism, as a philosophy, places a significant emphasis on emotional control and how our judgments shape our emotional landscape, it's crucial to approach this within the broader Stoic framework on the nature of reality. There are thousands of texts throughout history—academic research, translations, and modern takes—on Stoicism, including articles, essays, dissertations, and other shorter pieces alongside books. Stoicism, at its core, champions the pursuit of virtue as the highest form of happiness, emphasizing that human flourishing is achieved not through the acquisition of external goods but through inner excellence. The philosophy advocates for living in harmony with the universe's rational order and coming to know the distinction between what lies within our control and what doesn't. Beyond its guidance on emotional regulation, Stoicism provides insights into societal roles, personal duties, the interconnectedness of all beings, and the transient nature of life. Through practices of reflection, discipline, and ethical commitment, Stoics seek a life that is both meaningful and in accordance with nature's design. Stoicism's ideals, however, are not without flaws.

A clear dissonance exists between Stoic philosophical principles and certain societal realities of its time. Notably, several of its key proponents, especially those from the Roman era, including Seneca and Marcus Aurelius, were either beneficiaries of or directly involved in systems of slavery. It should be self-evident that enslaving another is not merely a physical constraint but an assault on the very essence of humanity, undermining the core tenets of equality, justice, and the inviolable sanctity of the human spirit. Slavery was so deeply woven into the fabric of Greco-Roman economies and daily lives that it's jarring to reconcile their profound philosophical insights with their personal and societal complicity in this gross injustice. For instance, Seneca, who penned numerous works on the nature of humanity, virtue, and the soul, was, paradoxically, a member of the Roman elite that benefited directly from the institution of slavery. These ethical dilemmas demand our attention.

How can Stoic principles, which extol the virtues of justice, wisdom, and the inherent value of all human lives, coexist with a system that commodified human beings, treating them as mere property to be bought, sold, and discarded at will? Moreover, the long shadow of slavery's atrocities persists to this day. Generations have been shaped and, in many cases, scarred by its legacy—from systemic racism and economic disparities to deeply ingrained societal prejudices. By examining Stoicism in light of these glaring historical realities, it becomes essential to interrogate and critique the philosophy, ensuring that its contemporary adaptations don't inadvertently perpetuate or gloss over the grave injustices of the past.

Likewise, Stoicism's emphasis on emotional restraint can be perceived as promoting a lack of empathy or detachment from the realities of suffering, whether our own pain or that of others. By prioritizing personal tranquility and acceptance, there's a risk that we might become complacent or indifferent to broader societal injustices or systemic issues that demand active intervention and transformation. Thus, some of Stoicism's teachings are deeply flawed outside a modern context that respects all life and promotes ideals of equality and universal human rights—or, as this book does, highlights the essentiality of empathy.

While no single resource can encapsulate the breadth of Stoic teachings nor fully explore the potential criticism of those teachings, our goal here is not to study Stoicism. Rather, we distill impactful Stoic principles for our own use, then unveil the benefits of its interplay with strategic empathy. Thus, our approach to Stoicism is with a discerning perspective, adapting its strengths while recognizing its limitations. We engage with Stoicism actively, acknowledging its strengths, addressing its limitations, and ensuring its relevance in contemporary society. Indeed, Stoic Empathy isn't just a synthesis; it's an evolution. It merges introspection and self-improvement typical of Stoicism with the compassionate understanding that cognitive and emotional empathy bring. It may even help us in our quest to avoid empathy collapse in response to dire circumstances and tragic events. The result is a richer, more nuanced interaction with both the Stoic tradition and the complexities of our contemporary world.

At its core, this approach ensures we don't ignore history's contradictions but learn from them. We harness the insights of Stoicism, supplementing them with the virtue of empathy, and in doing so, create a framework that resonates with the ethical aspirations and challenges of today.

Throughout history, many influential figures, despite their monumental contributions, carried personal or societal blemishes. Philosophies and time periods, just like people, are complex. Often, wisdom and evil can coexist. Weaving empathy—a deeply human quality—into Stoicism elevates the Stoic principle of understanding and regulating our emotions. Engaging with Stoicism through an empathetic lens urges us to internalize its timeless lessons critically. Empathy not only allows us to appreciate Stoicism's intrinsic wisdom but also equips us to critique, challenge, and refine these teachings for modern sensibilities.

Thus in this work, we aren't urging a complete submission to ancient Stoic ideals. Rather, our goal is specific: to introduce and employ Stoic Empathy as a strategic tool, especially when navigating scenarios of perceived power imbalances. We lean heavily on the Stoic doctrines related to emotion regulation and judgment, recognizing that this is just one facet of a broader philosophical tradition alongside the values of human rights and equality that empathy fosters.

The Benefits of Emotional Regulation Versus Denial

Specifically, the capacity to manage emotions indicates differences in how people tailor their emotional reactions to fit specific situational needs. With this skill, people can effectively choose the emotions they experience, their timing, and the way they feel and convey them. This capability stands out as a vital component of our emotional tool kit.

The ancients would be astounded by the ways modern science has managed to objectively gauge the effectiveness of emotion regulation strategies. For instance, researchers can now quantify the extent to which we can alter our emotional expression based on specific instructions.[1] In these controlled lab settings, participants are directed on how they should regulate their emotions, such as diminishing the intensity of their expressive reactions, when exposed to emotional triggers like sudden loud sounds or poignant film clips. These modern methodologies in the field of affective science offer precise tools to evaluate our competency in applying emotion regulation techniques.

Studies on emotional intelligence (often referred to as EQ) have shown numerous benefits for those who can recognize, comprehend, and manage their own emotions, as well as recognize, comprehend, and influence the emotions of others. High EQ is associated with better mental health, greater job performance, leadership skills, and interpersonal relationships. For instance, a study by a group found that managers with high emotional intelligence were more likely to share strategic information with their subordinates, fostering trust and collaboration. Captain Picard's leadership style, marked by insight and effective emotional communication, reflects the benefits of high EQ in leadership roles.[2]

Studies on emotional denial or the act of inhibiting emotional expressions, on the other hand, show that while it can be adaptive in certain situations (e.g., keeping calm in a crisis), consistent suppression can have far-reaching negative consequences. Habitually avoiding emotions not only decreases an individual's experience of positive emotions but also is associated with lower well-being, less satisfactory connections, and poorer overall mental health. Suppressed emotions can lead to poorer decision-making, resurface in unpredictable ways, and potentially lead to internal stress.[3]

The ultimate goal of Stoic teachings of integrating emotion with reason, along with the error of Mr. Spock's emotion suppressing, are therefore consistent with modern neurological and psychological research.

Stoicism and Mindfulness

Given that Stoic practices aren't as widely recognized today as Buddhist mindfulness techniques, drawing parallels between the two can help those familiar with Buddhism to better grasp and relate to Stoic concepts. While Stoicism carves its unique path in the annals of philosophical traditions, it shares kindred spirits with Buddhism. Putting aside their more complex life-after-death concepts and focusing instead on their lessons of how to live while we're alive, both of these ancient wisdoms recognize the intrinsic value of moral integrity and the pursuit of a life led by virtue. And both arose as responses to the human condition, offering pathways to navigate life's challenges and attain inner tranquility. Buddhism, with its Four Noble Truths, teaches the acceptance of suffering and the impermanence of worldly desires. These Four Truths of Buddhism are *dukkha* (that negative experiences are an inherent part of existence); *samudāya* (that the primary cause of suffering is desire and ignorance); *nirodha* (that by letting go of desire and eliminating ignorance, we can achieve a state free from suffering and the cycle of rebirth); and finally, *magga* (a set of practices and principles divided into three categories: ethical conduct, mental discipline, and wisdom).

The Stoic doctrine echoes Buddhism's First Noble Truth, which asserts the ubiquity of suffering (*dukkha*). While the Stoics don't delineate suffering in the same structured manner as do the Four Noble Truths, their recognition of life's inherent challenges is evident. Seneca's assertion that "All life is a servitude" resonates with the Buddhist understanding of the inescapable nature of suffering, or what the ancient Samurai of Japan called *shikata ga nai* (wisdom in acceptance of what cannot be controlled). Similarly, at the heart of Stoicism is the dichotomy of control—the idea that some things are within our control and others are not, which we will discuss further in Chapter 7. Epictetus famously proclaimed, "Men are disturbed not by things, but by the views which they take of them." This mirrors the Buddhist Second Noble Truth, which identifies attachment or craving (*tanha*) as the root cause of suffering. For both Stoics and Buddhists, the external world is not inherently problematic; instead, it's our perceptions and attachments that lead to suffering.

Both Stoicism and Buddhism are not merely diagnostic but also prescriptive. They offer concrete paths to overcome life's challenges. The Stoics advocate living in accordance with reason, emphasizing virtues like wisdom, courage, justice, and temperance, and releasing ignorance and desire, concepts very similar to Buddhism's Third Noble Truth, *nirodha* (freedom from suffering by letting go of desire and eliminating ignorance). In both philosophies, aligning ourselves with the rational order of the cosmos and focusing on what's within our control, we attain tranquility.

Stoicism finds even greater parallels with Buddhism's Eightfold Path and its tenets of mental discipline and transformative wisdom, both offering profound blueprints for personal transformation, ethical living, and mental clarity. Their intersections lie in their shared emphasis on grasping the nature of reality, cultivating a virtuous character, and honing mental discipline to skillfully navigate life's challenges. At the heart of Stoic practice is the cultivation of an equanimous mindset toward things we can't control, focusing instead on judgments, decisions, and actions, which are the only things we *can* control. Beyond ethical conduct and mental discipline, both Stoicism and Buddhism underscore the transformative power of wisdom.

This isn't to say the two belief systems are identical. For example, while Stoics prioritize virtue as the highest good, Buddhists emphasize the cultivation of compassion and loving-kindness. Highlighting the similarities between the two, however, helps find a framework for many who may not know much about Stoicism but are more familiar with mindfulness teachings of Buddhism. For Stoics, mindfulness is about being present, conscious of our own judgments, and aligned with rationality. Similarly, in Buddhism, Right Mindfulness is a critical aspect of the Eightfold Path, encouraging practitioners to maintain awareness of their bodies, feelings, and minds. And the Stoic practice of viewing others as fellow members of the larger cosmos mirrors the Buddhist teachings on interconnectedness and compassion for all sentient beings. Thus, putting aside their differences and focusing on their many profound similarities, from their understanding of suffering to their prescribed paths to liberation, allows us to more easily transcend the challenges posed by the human condition and maintain control over our emotional state.

It's noteworthy to mention that Buddhism isn't the sole philosophical or spiritual system sharing remarkable similarities with Stoicism. The tenets of Abrahamic religions, for instance—namely Judaism, Christianity, and Islam—often converge with Stoic ideals. These religions are anchored in ancient scriptures that uphold virtues of compassion, justice, and humility. They emphasize that our value is determined more by our actions and character than by external factors or titles, highlight the importance of not being overly attached to materialistic pursuits, and value introspection.

For example, 13th-century theologian Thomas Aquinas drew deeply from Stoic philosophy. He integrated the Stoic cardinal virtues—practical wisdom, courage, justice, and temperance—with the quintessentially Christian virtues later defined by Paul the Apostle as faith, hope, and charity (1 Corinthians 13:13). Fast-forward to the late Renaissance, and we see the Flemish philosopher Justus Lipsius attempting a fusion of Christianity and Stoicism. Guided by the writings of Seneca, Lipsius posited that humans should direct their allegiance not to volatile emotions but to God. He proposed that true human freedom is realized in yielding to God's will, echoing the Stoic belief that freedom is achieved by embracing the universe's whims. While Lipsius's melding of Stoicism and Christianity was short-lived, facing significant opposition from the church, it nonetheless left an indelible mark on thinkers like Sir Francis Bacon (the father of empiricism and the scientific method), Montesquieu (whose articulation of the theory of the separation of powers in government heavily influenced the framers of the U.S. Constitution), and Montaigne (his Stoic influence helped him develop *philosophical skepticism*, making him a significant figure in the Renaissance humanist movement).

When exploring the treatment of emotions across these ideologies, an important distinction emerges. Stoicism, just like Buddhism and the Abrahamic faiths, doesn't advocate for outright emotional denial. Rather, the emphasis is on discerning emotional management and awareness. We are the most patient leaders, parents, partners, and friends if we're able to modulate and regulate our emotional reaction to external stimuli. And we *do* have this ability. Modern science confirms ancient traditional teachings that emotions aren't merely passive experiences thrust upon us. As we'll explore further in the next chapter through a deep dive into the nature of emotions according to modern science, we, all of us, including you, possess the agency to navigate and, when necessary, modulate emotional experience, intensity, and expression.

As you read, remember that the goal is to be more like Picard than Spock. Captain Jean-Luc Picard, while being a paragon of Starfleet's principles, also had a deeply human core. When navigating the vast expanse of space, his decisions weren't merely derived from Starfleet protocol. They arose from a well of emotional intelligence where feelings were acknowledged, weighed, and then directed through a lens of experience and wisdom. He often retreated to his ready room or the ship's lounge, indulging in classical music or Shakespearean drama. These moments of reflection weren't just pastimes. They were his way of introspecting, processing emotions, and drawing parallels between human nature and the myriad challenges of space. With each new mission, Picard's emotional prowess seemed to strengthen. His continual engagement with his feelings, whether in the face of a Borg cube or a diplomatic entanglement, showcased his enduring emotional evolution. Most significantly for purposes of this book, Captain Picard's decisions were informed by both reason and empathy, forging bonds that went beyond mere duty.

Spock, on the other hand, would frequently immerse himself in logical tasks and calculations, hoping that the emotional riddles would resolve themselves in the backdrop of his logical pursuits. Even when he meditated, the goal was not to accept and release, but rather to deny emotional experiences altogether. While his logic-first approach often provided clear, unbiased solutions, there were instances, especially during personal crises, where the suppressed human emotions would demand attention, leading to rare moments of vulnerability. Spock's emotional-denial practices, while often effective and providing stability, sometimes acted as mere Band-Aids over the bubbling cauldron of his dual heritage. Spock's journey served as a poignant reminder of the complexities of identity and the perils of ignoring our feelings. While his Vulcan logic was a powerful asset, the moments when he embraced his human emotions were often the most transformative, highlighting the richness of a holistic self.

As you were reading through the preceding sections, an inevitable and pressing question might have formed in your thoughts: Is it truly *possible* to exert mastery over our myriad emotions—especially when we need them the most, such as in critical bargaining scenarios? Indeed, gaining control over our emotions is complex and not easily achieved. It requires sustained effort, determination, and resilience. But it *is* achievable, and countless people throughout history have successfully harnessed their emotions, deepening their emotional acuity in the process. Throughout this book, I provide strategies and insights on *how* to harness and navigate your emotions, building on the lessons of yesterday and today. The intricacy of this "how-to" question necessitates that before we delve into methods and strategies for emotional control—with the ultimate goal of enhancing our bargaining positions—we must first establish a solid foundation of emotional understanding. To do so, we're going to explore how emotions work, looking at what recent scientific studies and discoveries tell us about them. Perceiving these details is crucial for us to begin managing our emotional reactions effectively. Just as Captain Picard confronted and adapted to unforeseen emotional landscapes in his experience as Kamin on Kataan, we'll develop deeper connections with our own emotional universes, preparing ourselves to navigate them with wisdom and grace, especially when the stakes are high.

Chapter 5 Takeaways

We've accomplished the following pivotal goals in this chapter:

- Introducing Greco-Roman Stoicism.
- Distinguishing emotional regulation from emotional denial (controlling, not repressing, our emotions).
- Comparing Stoicism with mindfulness and other Buddhist philosophies.
- Integrating stoic control with our nuanced understanding of empathy.

CHAPTER 6

ASPECTS OF EMOTIONS AND YOUR POWER OVER YOU

I don't want to be at the mercy of my emotions. I want to use them, to enjoy them, and to dominate them.

— OSCAR WILDE, *THE PICTURE OF DORIAN GRAY*

As we journey toward mastering our emotions and perceptions through the principles of Stoicism, it is important to remember the empathic applications that are central to this book. The power we gain from understanding others while controlling ourselves lies at the heart of our exploration. In the Stoic worldview, emotion unfolds in two phases. First, there's the initial automatic reaction. Ever stood before a crowd and felt a sudden rush of nervousness? Or participated in a sports match, with adrenaline making your heart race? Have sudden feelings of guilt, anger, or fear ever taken hold of you? These are spontaneous bodily reactions. They signal potential risks, whether they're physical, mental, or social. The Stoics of old didn't judge these responses, which they titled *propatheiai*; they saw them as neither good nor bad but rather as neutral and innate responses to potential harm rooted in our humanity. There's no reason for shame or resistance to these.

How many times, however, in those exact same situations where you encountered that automatic reaction or *propatheia*, have you taken a moment to accept the emotion, examined its source, then channeled your adrenaline into your performance; or used a breathing technique to calm your nerves; or used visualization to see yourself succeeding? These reevaluations, said the Stoics, were the second phase of the emotional experience, which they called *pathe*. Pathe, therefore, are more developed emotions that arise when we provide our assent to and evaluate the initial impressions through a cognitive process.

Modern neuropsychologists would agree with the ancients, expanding from the propatheiai and pathe into a more comprehensive, five-pronged view of human emotional experience wherein lies more control. Here are the prongs:

- *Neurophysiological Response:* Increased heart rate, hormone release, muscle tension, or changes in skin temperature
- *Behavioral Expression:* Smiling when happy, body language, tone of voice, or even specific actions like slamming a door when angry
- *Motivational Tendency:* Fear might motivate someone to escape a situation, while love might motivate someone to care for another person
- *Subjective Feeling:* The internal, personal experience of the emotion, the warmth of happiness, the burn of anger, or the weight of grief
- *Cognitive Process:* Thoughts, appraisals, or evaluations; i.e., "I'm being treated unfairly."

Nearly every aspect of the emotional experience, both in modern neuroscience and ancient Greek terms, can be somewhat in our control. The sophisticated interplay between self-regulation and empathic engagement allows us to navigate complex interpersonal dynamics with greater finesse and ethical consideration. In practical terms, strategic empathy enables us to approach negotiations, conflict resolution, and even everyday conversations with a deeper sense of awareness and control. By combining our emotional regulation skills with a strategic-empathic approach, we position ourselves to maximize our influence in a just and ethical manner. This means not only achieving our objectives but doing so in a way that promotes mutual respect, understanding, and, where possible, beneficial outcomes for all parties involved. Moreover, the consistent application of strategic empathy reinforces our Inner Citadel, strengthening our mental fortitude against external pressures while enhancing our ability to remain calm and logical. As you integrate these practices into your daily stoic living, you'll not only transform your personal and professional relationships, improve your daily life, and elevate your power dynamics, but you'll also contribute to a more empathetic and compassionate world.

Let's delve deep into the interplay of mind and body to understand the nuanced choreography that crafts our emotional experiences. We'll begin with the relationship between emotions and our very *neurophysiological functioning*, which echoes in our brain's circuits, hormonal cascades, and even our posture, turning abstract signals into tangible bodily responses. Next, we'll examine how our sometimes eloquent, sometimes clumsy *behavioral expressions* speak the language of our hearts through silent dialogues etched in smiles, frowns, or the softening of our gaze. Then, we'll evaluate our *motivational tendencies*, revealing our emotions' primal origins: the evolutionary impulses that drive us toward love or push us away in disgust, compelling us to seek joy or escape threats, each hinting at our shared ancestry yet manifesting uniquely in every human. After this, we'll probe into the very core of emotion: its *subjective nature* and those deeply personal concerts of feelings, from the profound depths of sorrow to the soaring heights of joy. Mastery of emotions, an endeavor both challenging and rewarding, requires as much consistent reflection, purposeful strategy, and unrelenting effort as navigating a ship through a long oceanic journey. Last but not least (perhaps better described as "first" if we consider the early impact of philosophical thought thousands of years old), *cognitive processes* serve as the mind's tapestry—woven of attention, memory, perception, beliefs, and expectations—acting as a compass guiding our emotional journeys.

Through this dissection, we set a firm foundation for our mastery over ourselves and prepare for our journey through a life of Stoic Empathy. While we neither can nor would want to fully dictate our emotions, as philosophers have stated for millennia, we're not passive recipients of our emotional state either. As Confucius said, "He who conquers himself is the mightiest warrior." This Buddhist sentiment, also echoed by Taoism (in the writings of Lao Tzu) as well as ancient Japanese Zen and Samurai teachings of *Jisei* (self-mastery), captures the consistency of these Asian philosophies with the Greco-Roman Stoicism's emphasis of our inner strength and self-control.

Once we're able to better understand *what* we can regulate and have explored tools on *how* we can regulate it, in Chapters 7 and 8, we'll delve deeper into stoic living and developing our Inner Citadel. We'll begin to cultivate a robust and harmonious way of life, balancing emotional regulation with wisdom, courage, and justice, much of which is integrated into or completed by the strategic empathy concepts we've learned thus far, to gain power.

Neurophysiological Responses

When we experience emotions, our bodies respond in various ways, such as with changes in brain activity, heart rate, hormone levels, and muscle tension. When we feel joy, there's a noticeable positive reaction in our brain's reward centers. In contrast, feelings of fear activate our amygdala, a region in the brain associated with threat responses. These emotional experiences trigger a cascade of hormonal reactions: The weight of stress can lead to increased cortisol levels, while cherished moments of closeness can elevate oxytocin. Our heart rate, too, sets its rhythm in concert with our emotions, increasing during times of excitement or stress and slowing during more peaceful moments. Muscles respond, tensing up in reaction to anxiety or stress and relaxing when we're at peace or contented. Overseeing all these reactions is our endocrine system, regulating hormones like adrenaline, which spikes during fearful situations, and serotonin, which rises during moments of happiness.

For instance:

- *Brain Activity:* Neuroimaging shows an exaggerated response in your amygdala when you remember a tragic incident, like a car crash, even if you weren't hurt during the accident. The amygdala is associated with processing emotions, particularly the emotion of fear, and plays a crucial role in storing emotion-laden memories.[1]
- *Heart Rate and Emotion:* Imagine entering a boardroom for an intense negotiation, or meeting someone you have a crush on. In both scenarios, your heart races. This increased heart rate is a sign of heightened emotional arousal, whether stemming from excitement or anxiety.[2]
- *Hormonal Responses:* Whether you're pushing through the last mile of a marathon, pulling a challenging all-nighter at work, or staying up with a crying baby, your body can release a surge of adrenaline empowering you to conquer the challenge. Such hormonal responses, especially adrenaline and cortisol, prepare our body for demanding scenarios by increasing alertness and energy.[3]
- *Muscle Tension:* Whether at a tough job interview for your dream position or at the movies watching a stressful and action-filled scene, sometimes you can literally feel a stiffening in your shoulders and neck. This muscle tension is a body's typical response to stress, signaling the need to be alert.[4]
- *Sweating:* How many times have your palms moistened amid a tense situation? This sweating isn't from the room's temperature but is your body's automatic response to the situation's perceived stress.[5]

These physiological reactions offer a window into our emotive framework by explaining *both* the instantaneous and seemingly involuntary response to strong emotional stimuli (or Stoic propatheia), opening the door to exploring our secondary control over them (or Stoic pathe).

EXERCISES

Let's discuss just a handful of neurophysiological control mechanisms—such as meditation (mindfulness), exercise (adrenaline burn-off), muscle relaxation, and grounding touch—then explore the contemporary science supporting their effectiveness, and review exercises to help practice them:

Exercise: Brain Awareness/Mindfulness Meditation

Mindfulness meditation has attracted significant modern scholarly and public attention. As a comprehensive two-decades-long analysis published in *Nature Reviews Neuroscience* in 2015 reported, there's a growing body of evidence supporting the practice's myriad benefits. Some studies, for example, show that meditation can increase attention (by impacting the anterior cingulate cortex) and reduce stress (through altering the brain's fronto-limbic networks).[6]

If you're new to meditation, try what I call the simple yet effective 3 × 3 Mindfulness technique. Dedicate just three minutes, three times a day, to fully engage with the present moment through meditation. This practice involves immersing yourself in your current activity with your utmost attention. Whether you're pouring cereal, noticing the delicate dance of flakes cascading into the bowl and the milk weaving its way through the gaps, or taking a shower, tuning in to the symphony of water droplets and the sensations they evoke on your skin. Even the daily drive home transforms into a journey of discovery as you observe every turn and the dynamic life at street corners as if seeing them for the first time. This method is designed to fit seamlessly into your routine, making mindfulness an accessible and practical part of your day.

Exercise: Adrenaline Burn-Off

Adrenaline is a crucial component of the body's stress-response system. Produced in the adrenal glands, it's released into the bloodstream in times of acute stress, preparing the body for immediate action. This so-called fight-or-flight response is an evolutionary mechanism that was designed to help our ancestors react quickly to threats, like predators we should run away from or physical defeat. When this hormone floods our system, we might experience rapid heart rate, increased alertness, and a surge of energy.

In today's world, most stressors don't need a physical response. For instance, when faced with a tight work deadline or a confrontational e-mail, actually running or getting into a fistfight are obviously not the appropriate actions. Nevertheless, our body still reacts by releasing adrenaline, leaving us in a heightened state of arousal without a clear outlet for that energy.

Exercise offers a valuable means of utilizing this excess adrenaline. Physical activities metabolize it, restore emotional balance, and diminish feelings of stress or unease. By doing so, they help metabolize and clear out the extra adrenaline from our system. But it's not just about burning off this hormone; the act of physical exertion also stimulates the release of endorphins and neurotransmitters that act as natural painkillers and mood elevators. Endorphins can counteract the effects of stress, leading to feelings of relaxation and euphoria post exercise, often referred to as the "runner's high."[7]

Regular physical activity also encourages neuroplasticity, the brain's ability to adapt and change. It can promote the growth of new neurons, especially in the hippocampus, an area vital for learning and memory. Given that chronic stress can hamper hippocampal function and contribute to mood disorders, exercise offers a dual benefit: immediate relief from current stress and long-term resilience against future stress.

On a day-to-day basis, even if you don't have time, energy, or the financial capability for a full workout, try the Hourly Energy Shift trick. Combat the effects of stress and reinvigorate your body by breaking up every hour of desk work with a short burst of physical activity. It's simple:

- Commit to 10 jumping jacks, infusing your body with a quick energy boost and utilizing excess adrenaline.
- Dance in the shower, turning a routine activity into a joyful movement session that not only cleanses your body but also your stress levels.
- Opt for jumping, rather than walking, from room to room at home, making each transition an opportunity for a mini workout.

This playful approach not only helps in metabolizing excess adrenaline but also injects fun into your day. While it might raise some eyebrows in the office, it's a surefire way to keep energy levels high and stress at bay. By integrating these brief, invigorating exercises into your daily schedule, you're not just burning off adrenaline; you're fostering a resilient, joyful state of mind that enhances both physical and mental well-being.

Exercise: Muscle Relaxation

Your muscles ache because of the day you've had, or the day you're about to have. You wish you had time and money for a massage, but alas, no such luck. You can, physiologically, alter your muscle tension through a 5-to-10-minute exercise while sitting at your desk.

In the early 20th century, Dr. Edmund Jacobson introduced muscle-relaxation therapy, commonly known as progressive muscle relaxation (PMR). This therapeutic technique was designed to help people identify and release tension in their bodies by making them more aware of their physical sensations. The PMR process typically begins with deep-breathing exercises to establish a calm baseline. A practitioner then systematically tenses specific muscle groups for a few seconds and then releases the tension, moving progressively through various regions of the body. This sequence, when practiced regularly, not only alleviates physical stress but also promotes mental relaxation and awareness of the body's tension points.

Thus, systematically tensing and then relaxing each muscle group will physically alter your muscles' tension and can significantly alleviate stress.[8]

The exercise I suggest for this is the one I find most people need: Sleep-Ready Muscle Release. This simple practice is designed to alleviate insomnia and signal to your body that it's time to rest. In just a few minutes, you can ease muscle tension and prepare your mind and body for a restful night.

- ***Prepare for Sleep:*** As you lie in bed, ready to sleep, take a few deep breaths to center yourself and create a calm state of mind.
- ***Tense Your Muscles:*** Gently tense all the muscles in your body as much as possible without causing discomfort. Hold this tension for a full four seconds. This act of tensing is crucial—it heightens your awareness of bodily sensations and prepares you for the next step.
- ***Release and Relax:*** After four seconds, release all the tension in your muscles simultaneously. Feel the wave of relaxation sweep through your body, from your head down to your toes. Notice the contrast between tension and relaxation and allow this sensation to guide you deeper into a state of relaxation.

This exercise, when practiced nightly, serves as a powerful signal to your body that it's time to sleep. By consciously transitioning from tension to relaxation, you're not only releasing physical stress but also inviting mental tranquility, making it easier to drift off into a deep, restorative sleep.

Exercise: Grounding Touch

Why do you immediately bring your hand to the spot on your shin that you've just hit against a table, or hug your child tight when they're distressed? Why is touch even a social aspect of our well-being? These aren't meaningless habits that we've accidentally associated with comfort over time. Rather, there's a direct relationship between human touch and changes in our neurophysiological state. For example, a romantic partner's touch lowers arousal levels by reducing heart rate, because a welcomed social touch reduces the activity of brain areas involved in alarm processing, promotes recovery following a stressful event, and diminishes pain perception.[9]

But even aside from a pleasant social human touch, we can alter our neurophysiology and thus our emotional states quickly by touching inanimate objects. "Holding your breath and putting cold water on your face, or just an ice pack, will trigger the diving reflex, which dramatically decreases your heart rate," says Dr. John Campbell, professor of biology at the University of Virginia. "Essentially all mammals have this reflex, from mice to humans to blue whales, which likely helps us stay underwater longer."[10] You can try something similar to this practice through what I call the Cooling Clarity Technique, ideal for leveraging the body's natural reflexes to create calm in moments of high stress or before stepping into the spotlight:

- *Find a Source of Cold Water:* At the first sign of anxiety or just before a performance or speech, locate a tap or a container of cold water.
- *Submerge Your Wrists:* Run cold water over your wrists for a few seconds to a minute. The cold sensation is not just refreshing but triggers a physiological response that can help lower your heart rate.
- *Focus on the Sensation:* As you do this, take deep, slow breaths and focus on the feeling of the cold water against your skin. This mindful attention helps in further reducing anxiety levels and centers your mind.

- *Embrace the Calm:* After you've run the cold water on your wrists, gently dry them, and take a moment to feel the calmness enveloping your body. Notice any decrease in your heart rate and a sense of heightened awareness and clarity.

This technique, based on the diving reflex, is a quick and effective way to signal to your body that it's time to calm down, thereby reducing anxiety and improving performance. It's a practical tool that you can use anytime, anywhere, to regain control over your emotional state and sharpen your focus.

The question arises, then: If we can alter these physiological responses, can we in turn affect our disposition? Does changing our heartbeat or adrenaline levels help us regulate our feelings? This would be the very transition to pathe emotions that the Greeks discussed: feelings arising when we provide our assent to and evaluate the initial impressions. The answer, according to psychology and neuroscience, is "sometimes." Remember that neurophysiological response is just one of the aspects of our five-pronged emotion experience, and just changing it is typically not enough to control the entire emotional experience. But in some cases, you *can* alter your heart rate, muscle tension, and other neurophysiological aspects of your emotional experience and thus change the emotion. Returning to Dr. Campell's diving reflex and its impact on anxiety, as Dr. Campbell himself says, "Interestingly, recent research has shown that heart rate alone can affect anxiety . . . and ongoing research in my lab suggests the opposite may also be true—that decreasing heart rate can decrease anxiety. So, triggering your diving reflex will decrease your heart rate, which may make you feel less anxious."

Whether you understand the connection between your neurophysiological responses and your emotions in depth enough to let you control your emotions, the knowledge alone empowers you and provides tools to proactively navigate your myriad emotional experiences. Armed with this awareness and these strategies, achieving a more profound equilibrium and mastery over your feelings is more attainable, placing true emotional well-being firmly within your grasp. Let's now move on to prong two of the human emotion experience: Behavioral Expressions.

Behavioral Expressions

It should come as no surprise that behavioral expressions reflect our emotional condition. The more difficult and interesting question is: Will turning that frown upside down make you happier? In other words, does manipulating our behavioral expressions allow us to better control our emotions? Christie Brinkley was confident in this advice when interviewed about her *Sports Illustrated Swimsuit* cover shots and CoverGirl spreads in the 1970s and '80s: "A smile is like an instant facelift and an instant mood lift." Scientists refer to this idea as "facial feedback hypothesis," and it dates back to at least the 1800s, when Charles Darwin himself first discussed it. While researchers used to believe the answer to that question was a resounding yes, recent research reveals the issue is far more complicated than initially believed.

In 2022, a research team engaged in a meta-analysis that conducted and reviewed hundreds of studies across the globe to find out not only whether smiling makes us happier, but also the extent to which our behavioral expressions impact other emotions in a positive or negative way (Does frowning make you sad? Does scowling make you angry?). They published their work in the journal *Nature Human Behaviour*, showing that in each case, if there was an impact, it was context dependent (whether the expression was a smirk or a beaming smile) and very small.[11] While the idea is controversial that manipulating our facial expressions can have a significant effect on our emotional state due to facial feedback, another one has gained massive neurological support: emotions are contagious. So, a genuine smile might not make you happy, but it'll lift the moods of those around you, and then their smiles can uplift you.

Recall our discussion in Chapter 4 of the Gauchais reaction and mirror neurons—brain cells that fire both when a person acts (smiling because they themselves are happy) and when they observe another perform the same action (the other person smiling with happiness). This was a component of the scientific backing behind our Mirroring and Repeating tool. The mirror neurons can do so much more than just lower our opponent's guard through mirroring and repeating strategic-empathy techniques. Since the neuron "mirrors" the behavior of the other, as though the observer (the person seeing the emotion-based behavior) was experiencing it themselves, we can literally influence the emotions of others through our own emotional expressions. Here's the science behind how it works:

Our brains are naturally inclined to mimic the emotional states of those around us, so we are, each of us, in effect, an "emotional contagion." In fact, it's believed that both the affective (how we feel) and motoric (how our body reacts with movements) information are activated by mirror neurons.[12] Consider the scenario where a friend bursts into laughter in a social gathering; it's almost inevitable that the rest of the group will follow suit and succumb to laughter themselves, even if the reason for the amusement remains unknown to them. This involuntary chain reaction is because the mirror neurons facilitate a shared emotional experience, fostering a sense of unity and empathy among the group. The act of yawning operates under the same principle; how many times have you heard someone say, "Yawning is contagious"? Well, it kind of is! Witnessing someone yawn often triggers an automatic response in others to yawn as well, a testament to the interconnectedness of our emotional states and the instinctual mirroring of those around us.

Remarkably, this is even the case when the feeling states we're encountering are digital. For example, a study published in the *Proceedings of the National Academy of Sciences of the United States of America* found that emotions expressed online influence our own emotions, constituting experimental evidence for massive-scale emotional contagion via social networks and explaining anxious teenagers everywhere.[13] Here's an example highlighting this phenomenon:

> Fifteen-year-old Olivia is scrolling through her social media feed and encountering multiple posts, stories, or videos from friends or influencers expressing sadness, frustration, or disappointment because of personal issues, global events, or societal problems. Even without direct physical interaction, she begins to feel a sense of sadness, empathy, or anxiety. The constant exposure to such emotions, especially if the content is emotionally charged or relates to an issue Olivia finds personally significant, leads to a heightened state of emotional contagion. Over time, this exposure can contribute to a general sense of unease, sadness, or anxiety, reflecting the emotional states encountered online. This mechanism is partly why there's growing concern about the impact of social media on mental health, particularly among teens. The digital platform amplifies emotional contagion because it exposes users to a wide range of emotional expressions from a vast network of contacts, often without the mitigating factors present in face-to-face interactions, such as physical comfort or immediate clarifying conversations.

Since our emotions can arise internally ("self-initiated") or as mirrors of others ("externally generated"), learning to *distinguish* between the two equips us to better navigate our emotive reactions and decision-making processes. This understanding can also enhance empathy training, making it more targeted.[14] Recognizing that our emotions can influence those around us also helps guide our behavior, promoting more harmonious interactions. For instance, consciously projecting positive emotions in a group setting can foster a collective positive atmosphere, anticipating the likelihood that others will mirror these emotions. We become more deliberate in our expressions, understand and connect with others better, and improve our emotional communication. Likewise, if we're consistently observing negative or anxious emotions from others, it might indicate that we're experiencing these same emotions, whether we're aware of it or not. Identifying this is an important step toward self-modulation. Here are some helpful exercises to enhance your ability to distinguish between self-generated emotions and mirrored emotions, increase your empathic and stoic abilities, and help you decide whether you want to engage in regulation or simply to feel:

- *Charades:* Not just a fun party game, charades is also an exercise in understanding and conveying emotion without the crutch of verbal language. The challenge for participants is to portray a range of emotions using only their body language and facial expressions. This practice serves a dual purpose: it fine-tunes your ability to pick up on subtle emotional cues in others, and it also reinforces your capacity to communicate complex emotions nonverbally.
- *Keep a Diary:* Here's a reflective exercise that encourages you to pay closer attention to your surroundings. By dedicating a week to recording observed behavioral expressions and the emotions you infer from them, you begin to cultivate a heightened sense of awareness that can help you identify consistent patterns in emotional displays. Over time, as these patterns become more evident, your intuitive ability to interpret nonverbal cues from others will become sharper, allowing for more accurate emotional readings.
- *Empathy Training:* Watching a movie scene without audio turns a passive activity into an interactive exercise in empathy. With the dialogues muted, you're compelled to interpret the story and the emotions of the characters based solely on their visible expressions and actions. This sharpens your ability to understand emotions without relying on spoken cues. Discussing your interpretations with peers afterward allows for exposure to a diverse range of perspectives, further refining your empathetic skills.

- *Mindful Meditation on Emotions:* Particularly when you center it around emotions, mindful meditation fosters a deepened sense of self-awareness. By remembering past emotional experiences and reflecting on your behavior and body language during those moments, you're not only building a richer emotional vocabulary but also understanding your personal emotional triggers and reactions. Over time, regular sessions of this kind of introspection can lead to enhanced emotional regulation and a better grasp on your emotional state.

In essence, simply manipulating our physical expressions of emotions might not significantly affect our mood, but Christie Brinkley's "smile for a mood lift" advice wasn't wrong. Grasping the role of mirror neurons in our interactions provides an enriched perspective on emotional self-awareness, regulation, and interpersonal efficacy. Having explored neurophysiological responses and behavioral expressions, let's turn to prong three: Motivational Tendencies.

Motivational Tendencies

Consider a data analyst whose entire role consists of generating routine reports by extracting data from databases and creating charts, a fast-food cook diligently preparing standardized menu items day in and day out, or a shelf stocker at the produce aisle constantly arranging and rearranging the garlic and apples. Try to imagine their daily dialogue, likely centering around the details of their tasks—shortcuts and efficiency tips, perhaps. You'd expect tired eyes, vacant expressions, and disingenuous smiles. They do it for the paycheck—to put food on the table, get braces for their kid, pay their tuition, or some other form of external motivation. After all, who would do such jobs for the intrinsic joy of it? Marcus Aurelius said, "It is not death that a man should fear, but he should fear never beginning to live."

Nevertheless, occasionally you meet someone who genuinely seems to get fulfillment from the repetitive task itself rather than just the paycheck. Perhaps the analyst views datasets as representations of people's lives and not just abstract numbers, glimpsing the myriad possibilities behind their numerical evaluations. Maybe the short-order cook appreciates feeding people good and affordable food a lot more because he fasts every Friday night and so knows what it's like to go hungry. And sometimes the grocery clerk's meticulous arrangement of apples, with stems positioned just so, can become a work of art.

Why do we engage in the activities we do? What motivates us? What drives *you* personally to go to work every day? Is it inherent joy in the work (intrinsic motivation) or the pay (extrinsic achievement)? And how can changing our motivations alter our emotional state?

What motivates us helps explain why we make certain choices and how we get along with others. Basic human urges like fear, curiosity, and love are primal and come from our early history as humans; they helped our ancestors survive and form strong connections. But what drives us today has evolved beyond these basic instincts. Our motivations in today's world are shaped by our personal experiences, what our society values, and our own goals to succeed in our careers or increase financial security so we can pay for that vacation in Mexico or our teen's braces. But we can also enjoy learning and the unique pleasure that comes with the acquisition of knowledge, find a spiritual place (whether through meditation, prayer, or any other means), experience the joy of creating everything from a work of art to spaghetti for our family dinner, and appreciate rare moments of solitude (at least they're rare for me—did I mention I have four kids?).

Historically, scholars like Dr. Abraham Maslow illuminated the multifaceted structure of human motivations. Maslow introduced his now-renowned hierarchy of needs in 1943, setting out the progression of human motivation from satisfying basic physiological needs to achieving self-actualization. Building on this work, the study of motivation has expanded considerably in the last 80 years, with the last quarter of a century of research and philosophy revolving around Deci and Ryan's self-determination theory.[15]

According to self-determination theory (the modern version of the hierarchy of needs), fundamental to human functioning and growth are **three** core needs:

- autonomy (the need to feel in control of our own actions and decisions);
- competence (the need to feel capable and effective in our actions); and
- relatedness (the need for social connection, belonging, and positive relationships with others).

This theory, now supported by more than two decades of neurological and psychological research, states that when the basic psychological needs of autonomy, competence, and relatedness are met, we're more likely to be *intrinsically* motivated. So, if an activity makes us feel somewhat in control, competent, and in healthy relationships, we tend to engage in it for the sheer enjoyment, interest, or satisfaction it provides. Stacking apples and garlic isn't a pointless menial task but an opportunity to create art (control) that's unique and unexpected (competent), and the co-worker we have lunch with every day admires it, as do our regular customers (relatedness). But when our three core needs aren't met, our motivations are left up to extrinsic motivations, such as rewards, recognition, or avoiding punishment. So, for example, if the floor manager in the produce aisle is a real jerk about how much time we spend pointing those apple stems a particular direction, maybe we won't meet our control or relatedness needs, but "Hey, it's a paycheck."

This world is not black and white, of course; instead, we live in a motivation continuity, a lot of which is formed by our own perspectives. We could, after all, focus more on the co-worker we like, covertly twist apple stems as part of a private joke, and feel good about the ability to keep food on the shelves particularly during times of shortage.[16] In general, when we act within the framework of feeling empowered, competent, and connected to others, we act with more intrinsic motivations (personal growth or passions) and, generally, experience greater life satisfaction and lower stress and anxiety. On the other hand, if we feel controlled, disabled, and isolated, extrinsic motives drive our actions (money or status); we are more likely to be depressed or discontented. We can, however, still find immense happiness and elevate our quality of life through externally motivated action *if* our actions align with our overall values. For example, you're not stacking groceries at the upscale grocery store that you can't afford to shop from, but at the neighborhood food pantry that feeds your community. Even the jerky boss dictating how you spend your time might not dampen your day—not with all those hungry bellies you're helping to feed.

Put more succinctly, we can control our emotional state by reorientating our motivations.[17] This ability to reorient thus runs deep and significantly advances our emotional-regulation journey. Some motive-redirection techniques include redefining our goals and mapping our motivations:

- *Redefining Goals:* A core component of emotional regulation is the understanding that our emotions are, in part, driven by our motivations and goals. As we grow and evolve, our motivations may change, leading to a need to redefine our ambition. For instance, if right after grade school your goal was to earn a certain amount of money, but you later realized you value work-life balance more, adjusting your vision could bring more contentment. Setting goals that resonate deeply with our core values or true passions ensures that the emotions we experience during their pursuit are more fulfilling and uplifting.
- *Motivation Mapping:* Mapping your motivation is akin to creating a blueprint of your ambitions. Start by listing out both your personal and professional objectives and then introspectively analyzing the motivations behind each, creating a road map of your desires. This not only brings clarity on what drives you but also aids in aligning your actions with those drives. A clear motivation map serves as a guide when you're faced with crossroads, so that you make decisions in harmony with your true desires.

Example 1:

Objective: Achieve a managerial position in my current field.

Motivation: Desire for leadership and to influence the direction of projects.

Actions: Pursue leadership training, seek mentorship, take on more responsibility in current role.

Example 2:

Objective: Run a half-marathon within the next year.

Motivation: Improve physical health and challenge personal limits.

Actions: Create a training schedule, join a running group, research nutrition plans.

Harnessing and directing our motivations is just as pivotal in navigating our emotional world as managing our neurophysiological reactions and behavioral expressions.

Fourth in our five-prong evaluation of emotions is Subjective Feelings.

Subjective Feelings

Many traumatic events darkened my daily life in postrevolutionary, midwar Iran, yet I rarely felt sad or afraid. A substantial component of my overall positive emotional framework was due to my parents. Maman and Baba always made me feel somehow protected and positively connected to my world. This can't, however, fully explain my affective state. After all, during that time there were many moments of sheer terror no child should have to face, not to mention the difficulties and inconveniences that war brings: food shortages, electricity blackouts, and no such thing as a hot shower. Lots of kids around me were panicked and afraid. Adults, too. Why wasn't I?

In contrast, my recollection of the profound loneliness following my family's first few years in Canada post immigration is strangely grim. I was safe from war and an oppressive regime, surrounded by lavishly large grocery stores full of food, all the hot showers I wanted, and a wide-open field of possible futures. There were, to be sure, reasons to be melancholy. We were displaced. We hadn't just left behind our soil; we were no longer the same people. Gone was any status we might have had as a family who owned their own home, the hugs and kisses of aunties, our language, the giggles of cousins, and our way of understanding the world. In more childish terms, I "understood" kid politics in Iran. But the kid politics in Canada were nothing like that, and given the language barrier, our economic position, and our total and complete fish-out-of-water syndrome, I couldn't even begin to understand this new world. I wore the wrong things. When I managed to speak a bit of English, I said the wrong things. I ate lunch alone at school—every single school day—for over a year. I was severely bullied for my Kmart clothes and hairy legs and face. If it hadn't been for my sisters, I don't know that I would've had any friendships at all.

Of course, the brain's interpretations and interactions with trauma are relative. Now, as a middle-aged parent living in America, I'd be devastated if my children were bullied and isolated at school and would be certainly concerned with the potential emotional impacts of that. This, however, doesn't really answer the question of the truth of my own subjective feelings in my childhood. Comparing *me* at, say, 11 to *me* at 12ish—was I really "fine" amid Iran's war and darkness but suffering much sorrow in Canada because we were renters and kids at school were mean to me? Were the perils of oppression, rockets, and sirens really *better* for my emotional stance than the mundane problems of everyday, first-world citizens? Again, we're asking the question as it relates to *me* as I experienced them *both* within approximately the same time period.

Thinking back, I wonder if I really *knew* what I was feeling when I was a child in Iran at the time I was feeling it, back when I thought I was "fine." Because at that time, it wasn't safe to feel overwhelmed.

This is the domain of Subjective Feelings: our conscious awareness of an emotion and its impact on the emotional state itself. Subjective feelings are how we perceive, recognize, and label our own emotions. For example, if you feel sad, your subjective feeling involves recognizing that you're indeed experiencing sadness: "I am sad right now." It's not just the physiological changes or behavioral expressions associated with sadness but also your awareness and interpretation of that emotion.

Think back to a moment when you were overwhelmed by the beauty of a sunset, the melody of a song, or a memory from the past. While the emotion—be it joy, nostalgia, or sorrow—might be identifiable, the depth and texture of what you felt are uniquely yours. This internal sensation, like a fingerprint of the soul, defines subjective feeling. In today's world of hustling complexity, the palette of our subjective feelings is deeper. Each interaction, whether you're scrolling through social media (your quiet melancholy while scrolling past travel pictures), engaging in virtual realities (fear of falling from a virtual roller coaster), or the myriad shades of personal connections (the feeling of warmth at a note from a long-lost friend), evokes a spectrum of feelings.

It might seem that our ability to be aware of our feelings is inherent and automatic, but emotions can sometimes be surprisingly complex and elusive. This can be especially true during times of intense duress, when our emotion-cognition bridge is paused or stunted. There are myriad reasons why we might misunderstand our own emotion condition at any given time. Perhaps the feeling isn't fully crystalized yet, or we're experiencing more than one feeling and they're oddly fused, making them difficult to decipher from one another. Maybe it's because we've never felt this way before—say, the first time we've had an anxiety or panic attack. In the case of civilians and even soldiers caught up in armed conflict, they could be disassociating from the emotion as a survival mechanism.

For purposes of our stoic training, improving our ability to identify our subjective feelings through introspection and reflection is an essential part of managing emotions. To regulate emotions, we must process them, and to process them, we should know what they are. As the Oracle of Delphi (the Pythia) said, predating the Stoics by several centuries, "Know thyself."

Here are some tools to improve our emotional detection capabilities and thus better control the Subjective Feeling aspect of our emotional experience:

- *Emotion Journaling:* Establish a dedicated space, either digitally or in a traditional journal, to chronicle your emotions daily. Take a few moments each day to record feelings tied to significant events. Writing without judgment, let your thoughts flow freely. This habit can illuminate patterns or emotional triggers over time, helping you gain a deeper understanding of your emotional landscape.
- *Mindful Meditation:* Yes, we keep coming back to this one. Engage in this ancient practice, focusing on the present moment and your current emotional and physical sensations. Allocate quiet moments in your day to close your eyes, center on your breathing, and acknowledge any arising emotions or thoughts. Label these feelings without judgment, and gently return your focus to your breath. This routine not only aids in emotional recognition but also in processing those emotions.
- *Feelings Artboard:* Channel your emotions into art, a medium that allows for a tangible expression of intangible feelings. Whether you sketch, paint, or collage, let your chosen art form mirror your inner emotional world. Using art in this manner can be therapeutic, providing an avenue to process and represent emotions that might otherwise be challenging to articulate.

This journey toward Subjective Feeling literacy, Motivational Tendency awareness and control, Behavioral Expressions awareness, and Neurophysiological Reactions understanding helps us navigate our complex emotional landscapes while also enhancing our ability to connect with and understand others. As we continue to build our foundation for a more empathetically resilient self, let's turn to the last and arguably the most traditionally "stoic" aspect of emotions: Cognitive Processes.

Cognitive Processes

"Men are disturbed not by things, but by the view which they take of them," Epictetus said. The principle that our emotional reactions aren't dictated *entirely* by external events themselves but rather are substantially *influenced* by our cognitive interpretations, judgments, and beliefs concerning these events is a central aspect of Stoicism's emotional-regulation philosophy. Stoics fervently emphasized the importance of distinguishing between those elements within our cognitive control and the unpredictable nuances of the external world. They believed that by honing our cognitive processes and making sure they align with a reasoned understanding of events, we achieve a state of emotional tranquility, largely untouched by external disturbances (an Inner Citadel).

More specifically, while the propatheiai were automatic to the Stoics, the pathe were in our hands—or, more accurately, in our minds. In other words, by utilizing reason to evaluate the world, we decide whether to "assent" to our preliminary impressions of events. By subjecting our initial perceptions to cognitive scrutiny, the Stoics thought, we can anchor that emotion in truth and prevent it from being swayed by misinterpretations. In this way, genuine emotional well-being stems from our own internal cognitive state, not fluctuating external circumstances.

This Stoic emphasis on how cognitive processes shape emotions remains a timeless insight, echoing in contemporary approaches to understanding human emotion and well-being. Modern fields of psychology, psychiatry, and neurology confirm ancient Greco-Roman wisdom: Every emotion is either impacted or framed by our cognition, a masterpiece woven thread by thread with our nuanced perceptions, discerning evaluations, and profound (and sometimes absurd) interpretations. In other words, our emotions *do* partly come from how we think about the world, while in turn influencing the very perception that gave rise to them.

Modern scientific conception of how cognitive mechanisms impact our emotions is more complex than the Greco-Roman propatheiai-pathe distinction. Today's neuroscience generally subdivides the cognitive aspects of our emotions into five parts: Attention, Memories, Beliefs, Perceptions, and Expectations.

To put these parts in context, consider that the way our focus can affect our feelings (Attention decides whether we're noticing potential dangers or appreciating life's beauty) has a *different* cognitive impact on emotions than the way we remember a traumatic past event (Memories can convert a touch from a kind gesture to an invasion of personal space). Similarly, our Beliefs (making us passionate when supported or livid if they're challenged), Perceptions (we can read a situation as either dangerous or exciting), and Expectations (the distress we feel in the gap between hopeful expectations and stark reality) are different from one another. As we learn more about these five cognitive processes, we find a treasure trove of regulation tools, each offering the promise to guide our emotional odyssey. Let's talk about how each of these cognitive categories plays a role, because this will really help us to reshape our emotional-control journey.

1. Attention

Research proves that the mind's spotlight genuinely influences how we perceive and navigate our world, so the amount of *attention* we give to particular emotions can shape them profoundly. Attention acts as a gatekeeper for sensory perception and therefore significantly affects decision-making. Dive into the world of anxiety and depression, for example, and you'll find a fascinating landscape defined by attentional biases. Ever since the groundbreaking cognitive revolution in psychology began decades ago (with legends like Aaron T. Beck and Ulric Richard Gustav Neisser), a pattern emerged. Researchers found that anxious people often direct their attention on negative or emotionally intense events, whereas those grappling with depression tend to shadow out the positive, spotlighting only the gloomy. This skewed focus isn't just harmful to our emotional state; it can also impair our cognitive abilities. Even our everyday skills, like driving, are impaired when we're in this state because we have a harder time processing crucial information.[18] Attention profoundly influences our emotional experiences, steering our focus and impacting decision-making.

2. Memory

Consider the following scenarios:

- For nearly 10 years, Jamie endured the torments of an abusive relationship. Today, even the faintest hint of aggression from a man evokes traumatic memories, igniting a profound rage in her.
- In contrast, the mere aroma of an ice-cream parlor envelops Cole in a cocoon of warmth and nostalgia. It takes him back to cherished childhood moments of going to an ice-cream shop with his mother on Sunday afternoons. This sensory memory–evoked sentimentality is precisely why movie theaters infuse the air with the smell of popcorn or why stores like Nike use the scent of rubber-soled basketball sneakers and the fresh undertones of soccer cleats in grass; these atmospheres help to anchor consumers in positive associations, subconsciously prompting them to shop.
- Mahsa, an aspiring lawyer, found a unique stress balance in her studies that works perfectly just for her. During her preparation for exams, a calibrated dose of stress, precisely timed during her memory formation, optimizes her retention. Being too relaxed or too stressed reduces her memory abilities. But *just* the right amount of stress at *just* the right time really does help her retain information. The timing of stress in relation to these stages is paramount, underscoring

the nuanced influence of stress and other emotions on memory dynamics.

- For Ali, the beach isn't a haven of relaxation. On a beach a decade ago, his then wife told him the heart-wrenching news that she was filing for divorce. This same phenomenon is the reason you can train participants in a study to be afraid of blue squares—just give them a little shock to the wrist when they see a blue square; all it takes is a few shocks.[19]

Memories and emotions are inexplicably intertwined. They share overlapping neural structures. The amygdala, for instance, plays a crucial role in both emotion and the formation of emotionally charged memories. When an event evokes a strong emotion, the amygdala enhances the consolidation of that memory, making it more likely to be remembered. Emotions can also enhance or dull memories, because an emotional charge acts as a marker, like a road sign literally signaling to our brains that "this memory is significant" or "this memory is okay to forget." This is why you tend to remember emotionally charged events, whether positive (a wedding day, assuming you still like the person you married) or negative (a tragic accident) more vividly and for longer durations than neutral events. Our emotions can also serve as context cues for memory retrieval the way hearing a particular song might transport you back to a specific time or place. In addition, research shows we have "state-dependent" memories, meaning people might better recall events when they're in the same affective state as when the memory was formed. So, you're more likely to remember a sad memory when you're feeling down about a recent breakup, or a joyful one while you're laughing with friends. Not only this, but our emotions "color" our memories; if you're in a positive mood, you might remember past events *more positively* than remembering that *same* event when you're in a negative mood. In cases of traumatic experiences, the emotion (typically fear or horror) can become so deeply intertwined with the memory that recalling the memory can evoke the emotion, and experiencing the emotion can bring back the memory.

From an evolutionary perspective, the connection between memory and emotion has adaptive value. Consider a caveman encountering a saber-toothed tiger at dusk. This experience would certainly trigger a strong emotional response—fear. The emotional intensity of the encounter helps to solidify the memory of the event in the person's mind. Because of this emotional impact, the caveman remembers the details of the encounter—the tiger's fangs, the location near a particular grove of trees, and that it was darker outside when the encounter occurred—more accurately compared to a less emotionally charged event. Now, the next time this caveman or others in their group notice similar environmental cues—the distinctive silhouette of the tiger at a distance, the peculiar tracks left by its large paws, or that dusk is close—the vivid memories resurface, prompting a cautious retreat. The strong memory of fear associated with the saber-toothed tiger helps avoid potential danger, increasing the likelihood of survival and the chance to pass on their genes, but also making humans naturally afraid of the dark.

In essence, emotions are powerful modulators of memory. They influence how we encode, store, and retrieve information.[20] Because of this relationship, we don't just remember facts but also the sensations that came with them, offering a multidimensional mosaic of our past memories. Emotions and memories are deeply interconnected, shaping how we perceive, remember, and respond to events. Whether it's Jamie's trauma, Cole's nostalgic sensory cues, Mahsa's balancing act between stress and retention, Ali's poignant associations, the early human's avoidance of saber-toothed tiger tracks, or the stories you thought of when you were reading this section, emotions play a profound role in shaping our memories, guiding our decisions, and enriching the fabric of our experiences.

3. Perception

Judging an emotion seems straightforward, doesn't it?

Take a look at the image at the top of the next page. What emotion do you perceive from the man pictured? If you were to encounter him, how would his emotional state make *you* feel?

Now shift your attention to the image below, which provides context to the same image. This drawing depicts Jim Webb, not in anger but in elation, celebrating the 2007 election victory that restored control of the U.S. Senate to the Democrats.*

* Drawings by Rachel Meyers, based on photographs published in *Trends in Cognitive Science*; see Endnotes for the full citation.

Did your initial interpretation miss the mark? You're in good company. Distinguished professor and researcher Dr. Lisa Barrett, among the top 0.1 percent most cited scientists in the world for her groundbreaking work in neuroscience and psychology, published a pivotal study with her team in 2007 that demonstrated emotional experiences are content-rich events. In that study, Dr. Barrett and her team ask us to "consider the fact that 60%–75% of the time, people see facial portrayals of fear as 'angry' when the images are paired with contextual information typically associated with anger." As Dr. Barrett's team stressed in the study, "You can imagine the consequences when, in war, a soldier enters a house and sees a civilian as angry instead of fearful (or vice versa)." This terrifying reality has daily implications in our personal professional lives too.[21]

My husband, for example, has a penchant for sarcasm. He's typically a direct person and resorts to sarcasm primarily in jest or to be playful. But at the end of a very exhausting day, I can easily misinterpret his playful sarcasm as a slight, which causes emotional discord. It's not an unreasonable perception; sarcasm often serves as a passive-aggressive critique. Still, having known my husband closely for two decades, I'm well-versed in his communication nuances and know his intentions. If I'm mindful of what I know to be true about him and his motives, not only will I not feel hurt, but I might even crack my first smile in hours. If perceptions heavily influence our emotions, then the ability to cognitively reframe them becomes crucial for emotional regulation. But a vital question remains: How can we ensure our cognitive reappraisal is accurate and not self-deceptive?

I worked for years with a colleague who consistently reframed any critique of him as either praise or a mere oversight. His unwavering self-assuredness rendered him seemingly critique proof. We've all known people like this. They just don't see it. They're a nightmare to work with and even harder to live with. Thus, while perceptual reframing is essential for emotional management, it needs also to be balanced with an attempt to understand the capital-*T* "Truth" of a situation.

4. Beliefs

Martin Luther King Jr.: This man's profound belief in nonviolent resistance and racial equality shaped his emotions of hope, resilience, and determination, driving the Civil Rights Movement in the United States.

Frida Kahlo: The famous Mexican artist had strong beliefs about her national identity; her political convictions were integrated into her art and deeply influenced her emotions.

The Spartans: Belief in the importance of military prowess and discipline shaped the emotions and mentality of every Spartan. From a very young age, Spartans were conditioned to value strength, courage, and honor above all else.

Beliefs are deeply entrenched convictions that we hold about ourselves, others, and the world around us. Derived from a combination of personal experiences, social conditioning, and neural processing, these foundational lenses shape our emotional responses. Interestingly, our beliefs about *whether* emotions are *controllable* or *uncontrollable* have significant impact on our emotive states (the more control we believe we have, the less likely we are to experience depression).[22]

It stands to reason, then, that changing our beliefs will impact our emotions. Research confirms this. Unlike moment-to-moment perceptions or transient expectations, however, beliefs are more enduring and general. They are cognitive constructs often formulated over time and can remain resistant to change, even when confronted with contradictory evidence.

5. Expectations

It's hardly an astute insight that having high expectations for something can lead to greater disappointment if expectations aren't met, but this could also lead to heightened feelings of joy, satisfaction, or accomplishment when they *are* met or exceeded. Thus, expectations can serve as an anchor. When reality diverges significantly from our expectations, the emotional impact (whether positive or negative) can be amplified. Generally, a more positive outlook can be associated with better stress coping and overall well-being, while low expectations can protect against disappointment but might also limit feelings of achievement. Meanwhile, the higher our expectations about meeting a goal, the greater our sense of responsibility toward meeting that goal, and the harder we'll work to meet it. There is also the possibility of cognitive dissonance when expectations and reality don't align: a psychological state where we hold contradictory beliefs, causing feelings of unease, tension, or confusion, prompting us to either adjust our expectations or rationalize the discrepancy.[23]

So, learning to tell the difference between unrealistic high expectations and healthy optimism and adjusting them to conform to various circumstances is essential to emotional regulation.[24]

The ancient wisdom still holds true: Our thoughts influence our emotions. By tapping into these cognitive processes, we navigate our emotions with more precision, fostering better emotional health and a more enriched life. Modern neuropsychologists and cognitive behavioral therapists echo this age-old understanding, but with the added advantage of solid scientific backing for their techniques.

Remember that we're still focused here on the fifth prong of the human emotional experience—Cognitive Processes and its five key processes: Attention, Memories, Beliefs, Perceptions, and Expectations. This exploration was a crucial step in enhancing our journey toward better emotional control. For instance, we've seen how our focus—or *attention*—shapes our emotional landscape, determining whether we perceive a situation as threatening or uplifting. Similarly, *memories* play a significant role, as they can transform our interpretation of current experiences based on past events. Our *beliefs* about the world influence our emotional reactions, either igniting passion or sparking anger. The way we *perceive* events can dramatically alter our emotional response, reading the same situation as either hazardous or exhilarating. Last, our *expectations* set the stage for potential emotional distress or satisfaction, depending on how reality aligns with them. Through understanding these five cognitive domains, we have unlocked a range of tools for regulating our emotions, each providing unique insights and strategies to navigate our complex emotional journey.

Now that we've better understood these processes, let's discuss two standout methods in emotional regulation that began with the philosophies of the ancients but continue with the backing of modern science today. These are Cognitive Reappraisal (reevaluating how we see a situation) and Cognitive Distraction (shifting our attention from negative to positive or neutral thoughts).

Cognitive Reappraisal

According to the National Institute of Mental Health, 75 percent of people say that public speaking is their biggest fear. And having to prepare a speech at the last minute with no prior warning only increases your anxiety. So, if you want to design an experiment on how to better manage fear, why not expose your subjects to an impromptu and imminent public-speaking requirement? A little sadistic, perhaps, but it's all for science. In 2009, Professor Stefan G. Hofmann did just that.[25] He recruited 202 undergraduate students from introductory psychology classes at Boston University for an unusual experiment in his lab. He instructed each of these unfortunate participants to stand in front of a camera and, without any advance notice or preparation opportunity, discuss three topics for 10 minutes. To make the situation even more stressful, the topics weren't benign, easy-to-discuss matters like "why your kids are adorable" or "a list of your favorite foods and why you like them." No. They were the Iraq war, compulsory seat belt regulation, and capital punishment. Once in the lab, the volunteers learned that specialists would assess their presentations and monitor their heart rates during the entire process. Remember, it was for science!

Participants were divided into three groups. As I'm sure you can imagine, they were all stressed and anxious before they even began to speak.

- *Suppression:* The first group was told to manage their anxiety by suppressing their feelings. They were not to let any anxiety show and to behave the same as someone who was not nervous.

- *Acceptance:* The second group was advised to simply accept their anxious feelings, because it's "quite normal that an impromptu speech creates some level of discomfort or even fear." They were asked to experience their feelings fully and "not try to control or change them in any way."
- *Reappraisal:* The third group was asked to reappraise the situation as a coping mechanism. Specifically, they were advised to recognize that the situation didn't present an actual threat, because it was just an experiment. Doing this requires recalibration of various cognitive aspects of our emotions, such as memory, beliefs, perceptions, and expectations: We use past *memories* of actual danger to determine there is no physical danger that comes with the speech; we shift our *belief* from "I can't do this" to "I can do this"; we decide to *perceive* the situation as a great opportunity to speak in a safe environment about our feelings on a controversial international war, and we work on setting low *expectations* because our speech may not convince the world of our views, and that's okay.

The question the researchers were studying was which coping mechanism (suppression, acceptance, or cognitive realignment) works best to regulate the emotion of anxiety. If Epictetus were somehow to be transported directly into Dr. Hofmann's laboratory about 2,000 years into the future and asked to predict the answer, he would immediately say, "Cognitive realignment." He would tell us that physiologically, feelings of anxiety closely resemble those of excitement. What differentiates them is our perception, influenced by the situation and our personal biases. Since our understanding of these emotions has a cognitive element, then we have some power over how we experience them. By reinterpreting the physical signs of anxiety as those of excitement, people often handle tasks more efficiently and cope with stress in a better way. Because the Stoics didn't promote emotional denial or blocking, Epictetus would say trying to just reduce anxiety from a high- to a low-arousal state isn't the answer. Nor, in this case, would he urge pure acceptance. Remember that while the Stoics urged acceptance over matters not in our control, they were steadfast that our judgments and emotions *are* controllable. So we would *accept* the fact that we have to speak publicly, but not *accept* anxiety as an inevitable consequence. Rather, he would tell us, the subjects should shift the narrative surrounding the anxiety to change their perspective on it. By changing our *response* to the anxiety, we can control the pathe—the secondary phase of the emotional experience. Cognitive realignment would likely be Epictetus's favored method of emotional regulation, as it's very closely aligned with Stoic virtues.

So, what did Professor Hofmann's study find?

The Suppression group, poor souls, experienced a significant rise in heart rate and reported more anxious feelings compared to the Acceptance and Realignment groups. The Acceptance group had some success; they were able to lower their heart rates by accepting their fate, but their anxiety was undeterred. Thus, while acceptance of their emotional state enabled physiological regulation, it only went so far without cognitive reappraisal. Reappraising was the most effective means for moderating *both* heart rates *and* the subjective feeling of anxiety than attempts to suppress or accept the feeling—in Dr. Hofmann's lab and many others—just as Epictetus told us 2,000 years ago.

Anxiety can be challenging, magnifying perceived threats and twisting our attention toward them. Cognitive reappraisal tempers these biases, enabling us to perceive the world more accurately. Although this method doesn't negate anxiety, it offers a competing emotion to help manage it. The same is true for reappraisals' ability to manage other emotions.

For example, someone afraid of flying might shift their perspective by emphasizing the safety statistics of air travel or the expertise of pilots, steering clear of the dread of worst-case scenarios and focusing on the exciting aspects of the anxiety. Similarly, in situations that provoke anger, this strategy can defuse the tension. Suppose you're angry because a colleague didn't say hello to you in the hall. Instead of taking offense, you might consider that the colleague was simply preoccupied with their own thoughts. Or you might shift your focus to gratitude for the colleagues with whom you *did* have warm interactions that day. For emotions like sadness, cognitive reappraisal can offer a fresh viewpoint. After experiencing a breakup, we might opt to focus on the potential for personal growth or the prospect of future meaningful relationships rather than dwelling solely on the sense of loss. Even when it comes to feelings of disgust, say, in reaction to a particular food, cognitive reappraisal can come to the rescue: By understanding the food's nutritional merits or its cultural relevance, we can begin to change our emotional response to it.

When we use cognitive-emotional processes such as memory, beliefs, perceptions, and expectations to convert nervous energy into a useful stress, we prime our body and mind to harness their resources efficiently. By channeling stress positively, we associate it with resilience, enhanced cardiac efficiency, improved cognitive performance, and even antiaging effects. This isn't just theoretical; studies show tangible benefits—like a nearly 9 percent boost in GRE math scores, being perceived as more persuasive and competent in public speaking, better performance in sports like golf, and even heightened accuracy in activities like karaoke, all because of "useful stress."[26] Nelson Mandela even harnessed the power of cognitive reappraisal to foster cohesion in South Africa after apartheid by using what's colloquially referred to as "rugby diplomacy." By championing the South African rugby team after his release from prison and throughout the 1995 Rugby World Cup, Mandela transformed what was once a symbol of white supremacy into a powerful catalyst for national harmony.

This is not to say that cognitive reappraisal is a panacea. If this chapter has demonstrated anything, it's the complexity of our emotional state. But cognitive reappraisal (changing emotional response by reinterpreting the triggers) is a very effective technique, among many others, for emotional regulation. When we engage in this perspective-shifting technique—for instance, from viewing criticism as a personal affront to viewing it as constructive feedback—we "slow down" the emotional rush, allowing more time to process and respond. This approach resonates with Stoic beliefs that events are neutral in themselves and it's our interpretation that assigns them emotional significance.

The positive-psychology techniques of Socratic questioning,[27] schema therapy, and gratitude journaling are common tools used on a daily basis to help people cognitively reframe their negative concerns. Socratic questioning involves asking ourselves a series of focused, open-ended questions that encourage us to reflect on our thoughts, while schema therapy addresses unhelpful frameworks we've developed through time.[28] We can also combat feelings of disappointment with expectation alignment, which involves listing the initial expectations and the reality, then identifying areas of mismatch and resetting expectations to align more closely with what's actually likely to happen. We can even challenge *core* beliefs through various exercises, such as writing down a deeply held belief, listing evidence supporting and opposing it, and over time, aiming to modify or soften extreme beliefs to create a healthier emotional landscape.

Cognitive reappraisal's efficacy underscores the potent influence of our beliefs. By believing that stress can propel us forward, we can harness its energy positively rather than letting it stymie our potential.

Cognitive Distraction

Seven-year-old Sarah had been a fighter since she was a toddler. Diagnosed with a rare blood disorder called beta thalassemia major, she required regular blood transfusions to replace her diseased blood with fresh, healthy blood. Every three weeks, Sarah and her mom made their pilgrimage to Chicago's Lurie Children's Hospital while her brother went to swim class. The transfusions were lifesaving for Sarah. They were also torture to a child: hours of waiting, multiple needle pricks, and the discomfort of being hooked up to machines. The monotony and repetition of this routine, combined with the physical discomfort, made these trips immensely daunting for little Sarah. Her radiant spirit, usually so evident in her vivacious laughter and endless energy, would dim just thinking about her upcoming hospital visits. How she wished she could be in the pool with her brother instead of the waiting room of the hospital for hours on end, only to be poked and prodded in a cold bed.

Sarah's mom noticed the mounting anxiety her daughter felt with each visit. While it's true that stress can sometimes act as a catalyst for growth and resilience, often it serves as a significant obstacle, or debilitating stress, impeding our ability to think clearly, make decisions, and maintain our physical and emotional well-being, as it did with Sarah in this case. This can be particularly harmful if the body is already weakened with an illness, because over time, unmanaged stress can weaken the immune system, elevating our risk for both physical and mental health complications. Stress physically expands blood vessels, trims neurons in our brain, and releases hormones linked to depression and heart disease. Clearly, the adverse effects of stress on our judgment and decision-making abilities underscore the urgency to address it. Lurie's is familiar with what young people like Sarah go through and how harmful stress can be for their health. So, this top-of-the-line pediatric hospital implemented a transformative approach for its young patients that is parallel to another Stoic cognitive-control tool: Cognitive Distraction.

During one of Sarah's particularly difficult procedures, the doctor handed her a pair of virtual-reality (VR) goggles, part of the hospital's innovative cognitive-distraction protocols. As Sarah placed them on, the cold, sterile room transformed into a vibrant underwater adventure. The goggles became Sarah's escape, an experience in a world where her illness didn't define her even as she was receiving treatment for that very illness. The VR experiences during her treatments didn't just impact the attention and perception aspects of her cognitive-emotional experience; they also impacted her memory. Sarah no longer remembered these visits with pure dread and even began to look forward to her virtual snowboarding adventures, sometimes alternating the ocean with space explorations or treks through dense jungles. It was in these worlds that Sarah found solace, strength, and a respite from the reality of her condition. The virtual realm effectively distracted Sarah's mind, reducing her anxiety and pain, and it made the time pass sooner too.

In this way, while cognitive reappraisal tends to slow down the feeling of time passage as we reframe our anxious feelings, cognitive distraction tends to speed up the sensation of time, helping it pass more quickly.

Since I live in Chicago and have four kids, I'm familiar with the cognitive distractions that Lurie Children's Hospital uses. By controlling the attention, perception, and memory aspects of our cognitive-emotional experience, the hospital benefits thousands of children struggling with pain, fear, and anxiety. The tools Lurie uses extend beyond VR to include vibrant murals, playrooms, aquariums, and even occasional visits from therapy animals. For a moment, a child can forget they're in a hospital as they paint a picture, play with toys, or cuddle an adorable dog. If plagued by a distressing thought, instead of dwelling on it, they turn to a neutral or pleasant memory or an engrossing activity, highlighting the significant, often underestimated impact of mental and emotional well-being on physical recovery.[29] The applications for everyday use and life are endless.

Again, this isn't emotional prohibition. No one at the children's hospital would say to Sarah to act as if she isn't scared or sad. But that initial feeling, what the Stoics would've called the propatheiai, can be acknowledged without dwelling in the state. Indeed, cognitive reappraisal and cognitive distraction both allow us to recognize our *emotions* so we can strategically respond, rather than automatically react, to challenging situations. The *response* here is what the Stoics would've called the pathe: The more developed emotions that arise when we provide our assent to and evaluate the initial impressions through a cognitive process, thereby converting harmful emotional states into productive ones. By intertwining these advanced cognitive methods with Stoic principles, you can achieve deeper comprehension and control over your emotions, enriching your well-being and resilience.

This conscious shift in focus alleviates emotional turmoil. While the Stoics have long vouched for the mind's capability to rise above disturbances through cognitive reappraisals and distractions, and modern science has proven their impact, this is also another reminder of the similarities between Stoicism and Buddhist mindfulness, wherein counterproductive beliefs and emotions that arise within the course of meditation (or life) are acknowledged without judgment before they're released.

As you improve the ability to cognitively reframe and distract, you'll run against the problem we mentioned earlier in this chapter: How do we strike a balance between adaptive emotional regulation and an accurate understanding of reality? In other words, while modifying perception can be a powerful tool for emotional regulation, it's vital to ensure that this doesn't lead to a consistent distortion of reality. So how do we do that? We can use reality testing, open communication, cognitive flexibility, external feedback, emotional awareness, and therapeutic interventions.

Let's take a look at an example:

Anna, a midlevel manager at a bustling marketing firm, had long aspired to elevate her position within the company. She recognized that to do so, she needed not just to excel at her job but to master the art of navigating workplace dynamics and influencing decision-making processes. However, Anna often found herself sidelined in meetings, her ideas overlooked, and her contributions undervalued. She realized that to change her situation, she needed to employ a strategic approach to emotional regulation and perception.

- *Reality Testing:* Anna first took stock of her interactions at work, objectively analyzing instances where her ideas were dismissed. This led her to recognition that her delivery lacked the assertiveness required to capture her colleagues' attention.
- *Open Communication:* Recognizing the need for clarity, Anna initiated conversations with her colleagues and superiors to solicit feedback on her contributions and how they were perceived. These discussions revealed that her ideas were often lost in her hesitant delivery.
- *Cognitive Flexibility versus Distortion:* Anna worked on distinguishing between her flexible thinking and any negative distortions she might have about her workplace standing. She practiced viewing feedback not as criticism but as constructive advice for personal and professional growth.
- *External Feedback:* Seeking an unbiased perspective, Anna met with a mentor outside her immediate team. The mentor offered insights into effective communication and influence tactics within corporate settings, suggesting that Anna could benefit from more assertively positioning her ideas.

- *Emotional Awareness versus External Impact:* Anna reflected on her emotional responses to workplace dynamics, recognizing that her reluctance to speak up was partly due to fear of rejection. This awareness prompted her to address these fears directly, rather than allowing them to influence her behavior subconsciously. It wasn't, however, all in how she was perceiving it. By looking further, Anna found that there were *some* people in her workplace who felt competitive with her and downplayed her contributions. She determined, based on the workplace dynamics, that she could succeed despite them while utilizing cognitive empathy to slowly gain their trust.
- *Interventions:* To further refine her approach, Anna enrolled in a leadership-development program recommended by her mentor. The program, grounded in principles similar to those of cognitive behavioral therapy (CBT), equipped her with strategies to assert her ideas confidently and influence discussions effectively. Anna also read this book to help her better understand the ways in which empathy and stoicism can work together so that she can influence her colleagues while refining her own self-authority.

Armed with these new strategies and insights, Anna transformed her approach to workplace interactions. She began to present her ideas more assertively, backed by thorough preparation and strategic timing. Her contributions started gaining recognition, and her ability to influence decisions grew. Over time, Anna's enhanced influence and visibility led to her promotion to a senior management position, where she could shape strategic directions for the company.

Like Anna, if we stay grounded in objective evidence, seek external perspectives, and maintain open communication, we can make sure our modified perceptions align closely with reality. Remember that the goal here is to use the tools in this chapter to gain power over our own emotions so as to exercise greater control in our lives. Living in delusions wouldn't achieve that goal.

This chapter shows that although we can't fully control our emotions or the complex ways we react and respond, which can sometimes be overwhelming, we do have some control. We can influence *what* we feel, the *intensity* of our feelings, *when* we experience them, and how we *express* them. Emotions—those nuanced, profound experiences that punctuate our existence—are far from simple reactions to external stimuli. They're deeply interwoven with our cognition, physiology, behavior, motivation, and subjective feelings. While the Stoics paved the initial path toward uncovering the dual nature of emotional reactions, 21st-century neuropsychology broadens this perspective, revealing the multifaceted nature of our emotional being. Current insights don't supersede the Stoic teachings; instead, they enrich them, illustrating the timeless wisdom inherent in ancient philosophies and their congruence with modern science, breaking down our emotional control aspects from mere propatheiai and pathe to these five scientific pillars:

- *Neurophysiological Responses:* Increased heart rate, hormone release, muscle tension, or changes in skin temperature
- *Behavioral Expressions:* Smiling when happy, body language, tone of voice, or even specific actions like slamming a door when angry
- *Motivational Tendencies:* Fear that motivates escape from a situation, or love that might motivate someone to care for another person
- *Subjective Feeling:* The internal, personal experience of the emotion, the warmth of happiness, the burn of anger, or the weight of grief
- *Cognitive Processes:* Thoughts, appraisals, or evaluations; i.e., "I'm being treated unfairly." (Remember, this is also subdivided into the five components Attention, Memories, Beliefs, Perceptions, and Expectations)

I hope I've convinced you that the intricate dance of emotions between mind and body, reason and reaction, isn't something we passively receive but an experience we can shape, influence, and navigate with purpose. Recognizing the profound interplay between the automatic and the cognitive, the physical and the subjective, we become empowered. As Epictetus said in the *Enchiridion* (also known as the *Handbook*) about 2,000 years ago, "Make it your study then to confront every harsh impression with the words, 'You are but an impression and not at all what you seem to be.' Then test it by those rules that you possess; and first by this—the chief test of all—'Is it concerned with what is outside the sphere of choice or inside?' If it is outside, have it to be nothing to you." For Epictetus, we may not dictate the arrival of an emotion (propatheia), but we possess the agency to influence its direction, intensity, and meaning (pathe). He was right about a lot of it, and specially that we must continually challenge and understand our emotional impressions, using the tools of both ancient wisdom and modern science.*

An essential question arises: "Were the Stoics *also* right that we have *no* control over our propatheiai, our initial emotional impulses?"

The modern answer is, "Sort of." We *can* influence our primitively programmed reactive responses, but only in the very long run. Interestingly, despite their propatheiai-pathe distinction, the Stoics would agree, and they would recommend various methods (set out in the upcoming chapters) for this type of control.

There are aspects of the propatheiai that are beyond our control, because they're the result of our limbic system stepping in to ensure survival, a mechanism passed down from our forebears who faced

---

* This ability, however, is no excuse to invent falsehoods about our emotions and deny their existence. In addition, it must live side by side with empathy as set forth throughout this work so that our emotional control doesn't hurt those we care about or society at large. Nor does knowledge of emotional manipulation and distraction justify unethical uses of it against others for political or financial gain. During ancient Roman "bread and circuses," Roman leaders provided free grain and lavish spectacles, like gladiator games, to the populace. This strategy was used to distract from political corruption, economic disparity, and the lack of political rights. Similar strategies are used by corporate and political leaders today. Using external stimuli to distract others from unethical conduct is antithetical to both Stoic ideologies of justice and modern cognitive-psychological methods of healing and isn't the focus of our discussion. This book is for those who want to utilize knowledge of how emotions work to better understand, acknowledge, and enrich their own emotional lives and well-being.

countless dangers. Despite portrayals in media of heroes fearlessly charging into danger, the reality is more nuanced. Everyone experiences fear, or they've been conditioned through extensive training to mitigate its effects. The instinctive reactions are there to protect us. They prompt us to shield ourselves, expand our field of vision, and prepare our bodies to confront or escape threats. We should preserve and embrace this protective instinct.

But some propatheiai don't serve us at all. For instance, consider the impact of unresolved past trauma manifesting as impulsive anger straining your interpersonal intimacies, or a fear of heights rooted in a childhood fall, preventing you from enjoying desired hiking adventures. Similarly, an automatic urge for oral fixation, typical in smokers, poses significant challenges in quitting the habit. Anxiety in social settings, often stemming from prior embarrassing experiences, can hinder the development of leadership qualities. Additionally, emotional distress may lead to overeating or undereating, both of which can adversely affect one's health.

So, what philosophies and doctrines allow us to inhabit the ability to control *these* instincts, the ones that harm us? How can we essentially slow down time so that we respond as an empathic Stoic would within the brief second it takes to in fact respond in these situations? How do we align our instincts with today's world and our own values?

As we develop the skill to regulate our emotions more adeptly and navigate our feelings with intention, we essentially rewire our instinctual responses. This process of emotional regulation doesn't merely change how we react to situations in the moment; it fundamentally alters our emotional landscape. Our instincts, which once might have led us to react in ways that were unhelpful or even detrimental, begin to align more closely with our deliberate, considered responses. Over time, as we consistently apply the principles of both ancient wisdom and modern psychological understanding, we experience a shift, not just in how we manage our emotions, but in the *very nature of those initial impulses*.

Our instincts begin to reflect the person we are striving to become, illustrating a remarkable adaptability of the human psyche. This deep, internal change underscores the power of our agency in shaping not only our emotional responses but also the very instincts that drive those responses, leading us toward a more harmonious and authentic existence.

How do we go about doing this?

Ironically, the answers to going beyond simply understanding how emotions are formed to mastering pathe emotions *and* harnessing our power over our propatheiai lie in Stoicism itself—modernized with a cognitive-behavioral twist, of course. In the next two chapters, we'll discuss methods of daily stoic living that build, over time, an Inner Citadel or mental fortress with the strength to shape our instincts, habits, fears, and everything in between. You'll learn to equip your propatheiai. In this way, we can transform nearly every aspect of our lives, from negotiations and personal relationships to workplace dynamics and conflict resolution, encompassing situations in which we have less relative power.

As we journey toward mastering our emotions and perceptions through the principles of Stoicism, I'll stop to remind us of the empathic applications, remembering that this book is about the power we gain from the intersection of understanding others while controlling ourselves. Strategic empathy, combined with self-regulation, enhances our ability to navigate intricate social interactions ethically and effectively. Integrating these practices not only strengthens our influence and relationships, but also fosters greater empathy and kindness in the world while reinforcing our mental resilience against external pressures.

Chapter 6 Takeaways

In this chapter, we've illuminated the following essential ideas:

- Providing the modern scientific underpinning behind emotional regulation.
- Unraveling the mechanisms behind our ability to consciously influence and manage our emotions, grounded in contemporary psychological and neuroscientific research.

- Offering exercises and tools to move forward with emotional regulation, laying the groundwork for applying Stoic principles effectively in the realm of empathy.

CHAPTER 7

THREE CONCRETE TOOLS OF STOICISM

We suffer more often in imagination than in reality.

— Seneca

In the harsh winter of 1942, Vienna's cobblestone streets, which once echoed Viktor's joyful steps, turned cold and menacing. Viktor, a young and promising psychiatrist, was yanked from the comforting embrace of the life he cherished. Alongside his treasured wife, Tilly, and his aging parents, Gabriel and Elsa, he found himself ensnared by the high walls of the Theresienstadt Ghetto. From there, Viktor was taken to Auschwitz concentration camp, where the formidable gates cast haunting shadows, and piece after piece of devastating news landed like visceral blows. His mother's and brother's lives were cruelly extinguished at Auschwitz. His father's weary heart gave up at Theresienstadt. Later, he'd also learn that Tilly, his anchor, had breathed her last in the cold confines of Bergen-Belsen concentration camp.

Endless days merged into one another, each a torturous cycle of grueling labor, gnawing hunger, the smell of unwashed bodies and chemicals, and the ever-looming specter of death. Yet, amid this suffocating bleakness, Viktor spotted glimmers of defiance. All around him, emaciated bodies somehow sustained a glint in their eyes, clinging tenaciously to life. Flesh was harmed, pain abounded, but the relentless pursuit of meaning persisted.

During the scarce times of respite, Viktor would close his eyes, allowing the memories of Tilly to wash over him. Flashbacks of their shared laughter, whispered dreams, and the gentle touch of her hand became his sanctuary. These vivid recollections, though bittersweet, provided a barrier against the brutal reality that tried to crush his spirit. At times, when despair threatened to overwhelm him, Viktor would find solace in a vision. He saw himself standing before a captivated audience, recounting tales of resilience and the human spirit's unwavering tenacity even in the face of unspeakable horrors. This envisaged purpose guided him through the terrifying nights.

Though shackled, Viktor's healer's spirit remained unbroken. In stolen moments, he would find himself counseling despondent souls, infusing hope with his words and actions. Each day, he strived to find meaning, be it in a reassuring nod to a fellow prisoner, a crust of bread offered selflessly, or a soothing lullaby hummed to ease a troubled mind. A quote by Nietzsche often danced in his thoughts: "He who has a why to live can bear almost any how." This philosophy became Viktor's shield. In the face of anguish, he firmly believed that one's reactions remained a personal choice, and even the deepest pain could be channeled into purpose. As Viktor himself wrote in his book *Man's Search for Meaning*:

> In a last violent protest against the hopelessness of imminent death, I sensed my spirit piercing through the enveloping gloom. I felt it transcend that hopeless, meaningless world, and from somewhere I heard a victorious "Yes" in answer to my question of the existence of an ultimate purpose. At that moment a light was lit in a distant farmhouse, which stood on the horizon as if painted there, in the midst of the miserable grey of a dawning morning in Bavaria. "*Et lux in tenebris lucet*"—and the light shineth in the darkness.[1]

To this day, the legacy of Viktor Frankl illuminates the path for countless souls who have sought light amid their personal darkness. Though he did not necessarily identify as a Stoic, Viktor's suffering and survival underscores these core Stoic tenets: While we can't control everything that happens to us, we can control how we respond to the events around us; and severe suffering and loss underscore the human capacity to find meaning in life even under the most dehumanizing conditions. This human achievement will not eliminate suffering, but we can habituate to unjust anguish, such that we move from merely enduring it to extracting growth from it. Viktor's works and philosophies also shed light on more advanced Stoic concepts; he advocated taking a perspective that minimizes the overwhelming nature of immediate problems and promotes a broader viewpoint, similar to how he saw his own and others' suffering in the context of larger human existence. And awareness of death not as a morbid fascination but as a way to value life and the time we have.

Thus far, our discussion of Stoicism has focused on exercises and methodologies that allow us further control over our emotional state. Now in this and the next chapter, we turn to stoic living and how to develop an Inner Citadel that aligns our primary and automatic emotional responses with the life and values we want for ourselves. The Inner Citadel is a core fortress within your mind that remains untouched by external events and emotions. Developing this strength through internalized core concepts of stoicism allows us to remain calm and rational regardless of what happens around us, while permitting our empathic abilities to reach far and wide, giving us not just internal control but also more power and influence.

Viktor Frankl's journey is a potent beginning to this analysis, because it's an enduring testament to the basic Stoic tenets Dichotomy of Control, Discomfort Embracing, and Habituation. Through the Dichotomy of Control, we learn to distinguish between what is within our power and what lies beyond it, focusing our energy on the former to lead a more fulfilled and less anxious life. Discomfort Embracing encourages us to step out of our comfort zones, cultivating resilience by voluntarily facing life's hardships and uncertainties. Habituation, the third tool, teaches us the value of repetitive exposure to fears and challenges, diminishing their power over us and fostering courage. Together, these practices equip us to construct a resilient core capable of withstanding life's storms while maintaining our composure and integrity. Following this discussion, we'll turn to Chapter 8, where we'll build on this foundation by introducing two advanced Stoic tools: Memento Mori (remembering life's transience, which propels us toward a life marked by deeper connections, meaningful achievements, and a profound appreciation for the present) and Moral Courage (which challenges us to uphold our values and principles, even in the face of adversity, with a steadfast commitment to integrity).

Together, these five tools form a comprehensive strategy for not just enduring life's challenges but thriving amid them, embodying the essence of Stoic resilience and wisdom. As we discuss them, we'll also connect each of these to strategic empathy, discussing how the two can work together to elevate our power in society. We also learn that Stoic techniques can actually enhance our empathic skills and thus, as we learn greater control over ourselves, so too we can better understand others, strengthen relationships, improve our situation, and shift more matters to our sphere of influence while maintaining a strong, value-driven, and ethical code.

Dichotomy of Control: The Borders of Our Sphere of Influence

I spent a couple of months in India as a young law student, studying comparative constitutional law and international human-rights law. We were mostly in Shimla with two weeks spent in Dharamshala. Shimla, a popular honeymoon destination in that area that people often call the "Queen of Hills," is famous for its colonial architecture and historic temples (many of them full of monkeys who would jump on your shoulders and steal your food if you weren't paying close-enough attention) and surrounded by pine, deodar, and oak forests. The most striking component of Shimla was its stunning views of the majestic Himalayas.

I remember stepping off the train from Agra to Shimla with vivid clarity. A group of porters quickly ran to the disembarking passengers, myself included. They were asking to carry our bags. They competed with one another, throwing the heavy luggage on their heads or bending forward with several pieces stacked on their backs, for a tip so small it meant nothing to even those of us putting ourselves through school on loans. A man with leathered skin, a ruffled beard, and a red turban came up to me. He seemed too old to have the job, which he approached with aggressive enthusiasm. He wore these square-shaped glasses, like the kind my father wore. And for a split second, he looked exactly like my father. Under the duress of exhaustion or hunger, I might've even confused the two. Keen to earn his fee, he hardly gave me the chance to say yes. There was a slight smile, forever etched into my memory; then the suitcase was on his back, and I immediately regretted the hefty law books I had brought along.

As learned as I thought myself to be at the time, the paradox of India's democratic successes juxtaposed against its intense struggles overwhelmed my young mind. The thing is, I'd found myself in a country full of wealth, sophistication, innovation, and intoxicating beauty, but one that also has another side to it—the pervasive and undeniable poverty—bearing on its shoulders the weight of *my* bag before *my* very eyes. India is, in this way, not unlike the very world in which we all live: a world where heroes and villains coexist, where disaster sits across the street from triumph. It occurred to me back on that train platform (and hasn't escaped me ever since) that I could, just as easily, have been that porter's daughter instead of the daughter of my own father; that I had done nothing to "deserve" the family I was born into. It wasn't because of anything *I* did as an infant that I had arrived into a home full of love, with parents who knew the significance of the highest expressions of who we are—like poetry. There are many who aren't. It was mere chance that I never went hungry during the postrevolutionary chaos and bloody war of my childhood. There were many who had.

Epictetus, the former slave turned Stoic teacher, opens his *magnum opus*, the *Enchiridion*, by highlighting this very principle. Imagine life as a giant spectrum. On one side, you have aspects that are within your grip: your judgments, values, and intentions. On the other, there are elements beyond your reach: your body's well-being, reputation, and office (employment). To clarify, Stoic philosophy doesn't imply that aspects like your physical well-being, public esteem, and professional life are entirely beyond your influence. The key emphasis here lies in recognizing the dichotomy between what we can influence and what lies beyond our direct command. Regarding your health, reputation, and career, while your actions can significantly shape these areas, ultimately, their outcomes aren't wholly within your sphere of direct management. Even the healthiest body can be struck by disease or a horrific car accident. Your property can be stolen away from you by those inspired by greed or anger. And your reputation can be ruined through incorrect gossip and other people's malicious intent. In other words, what the Stoics mean is that when it comes to health, job, and reputation, is that we don't have *total* control.

Here's what the Stoics believed to be fully within our control, as long as we cultivate the inner life of a Stoic:

- *Judgments:* How we interpret and judge events, situations, and actions, both our own and those of others.
- *Intentions:* The reasons and motivations behind our actions.
- *Desires and Aversions:* What we wish for or try to avoid. Stoics aim to align these with nature and virtue, desiring what is good for the soul and being indifferent to external goods.
- *Reactions:* While we can't control what happens to us, we can control how we respond. For Stoics, this means responding with equanimity, without being overly disturbed by external events.
- *Moral Choices:* Our decisions to act virtuously, to be just, courageous, temperate, and wise.
- *Values:* What we deem important and prioritize in our lives. Stoics prioritize virtue and wisdom over material and external success.

Overall, while the Stoics recognized that many aspects of life are beyond our control, in common with Viktor Frankl, they believed that our power lies in how we perceive, interpret, and respond to those aspects. And, of course, it's precisely these perceptions, interpretations, and responses that further any possible control we *do* have in the other scenarios. That Frankl was placed in a horrific concentration camp, experiencing loss of the sort no human should ever suffer, was no way his *fault* or something he could have prevented. We do *not* have ultimate power over every one of our external circumstances, and those responsible for the evils of this world, whether they inflict these on a single body or entire populations, are not absolved of any responsibility. Concentration camps are objectively horrible places that should not exist for any reason, despite that in Frankl's case, they served as some sort of grotesque test for the power of the human spirit. This, however, doesn't render us entirely powerless. If our focus is on cultivating an inner fortress of virtue and wisdom regardless of external circumstances, our internal and external freedom *will* grow, with the internal side of that liberation being unlimited even while the limitations to the external components persist. Or in the words of Albert Camus, "In the depth of winter, I finally learned that within me there lay an invincible summer."

This is the essence of the dichotomy of control—recognizing what *is* and *is not* within our control, which has some universal aspects (no one can ultimately stop death) and some environmental ones (a person living in a free democracy has far more freedom than a person living under an oppressive dictatorship), but always, *always*, there is *ultimate* control over our own judgments, intentions, desires, reactions, moral choices, and values, all of which impact our feelings.

Imagine that you're seated in a sleek conference room, palms slightly sweaty, heart pounding faster than usual. It's a job interview for your dream position. You've prepped and primped, researched the company and its innovations, looked up who is interviewing you and their accomplishments, and had your best suit cleaned for the occasion. The moment unfolds and your answers begin flowing smoothly, one after the other. The interviewer seems impressed. But then, a difficult question stumps you. Panic seeps in. What if this ruins my chances?

By embracing the Stoic tenet of Dichotomy of Control, you shift your focus *in the moment*. It's not about whether you get the job, but whether you've given it your all. It's not about whether the world sees your worth, but whether you recognize and nurture your own value. This should enable you to regain control over *yourself* (including your thoughts and feelings), which ultimately is your biggest weapon in this interview.

Cicero, a Roman luminary, captured the essence of Dichotomy of Control with an archer's tale. The archer can control the intensity and frequency of practice, their amount of dedication, the choice of bow, and their focus and concentration. They can charm the arrow maker into giving free arrows with which to practice more, appeal to their spouse for more time for archery sessions, and more. There are lots of actions in the archer's control, including and up to the moment of the arrow's release from the bow.

But once the arrow takes flight?

Nature takes over.

Winds may shift. Targets might move. No matter what the archer does, they can't control the arrow beyond this moment in time. Which is why a good archer's worth isn't dictated by how often they hit the bullseye, but by the intention and effort behind every single shot.

We can assess our daily life tests, tasks, negotiations, power plays, and relationships through the archer's lens. When faced with any challenging situation, we can break it down into smaller components, then identify what aspects we can influence or control, remembering the powers of strategic empathy but also being mindful that our biggest sphere of influence is always within ourself.

Let's circle back to that job interview. If you're a stoic empath preparing for the interview, you might sit down the night before (and perhaps again after the interview) and jot down elements you could (or did) control: your preparation, your punctuality, your earnestness. Then list the uncontrollables: the interviewer's mood (maybe he got in a big fight with his wife that morning, but they'll make up tonight, and so tomorrow's interviewees will have a very different experience), unforeseen questions (no matter how much tactical empathy you practice, you aren't God or even a demigod and cannot predict everything), or even technical glitches (the interview is on Zoom, and the interviewer's unstable Internet access is disruptive to the conversation).

This is the dichotomy of control and how our use of it can help us find the internal wisdom of Viktor Frankl, such that we find not only *power* but also *meaning*, no matter where life's twists and turns might take us. Remember that you aren't necessarily alone in this challenging task. You can have open conversations with trusted friends, family members, or a therapist. They can provide valuable perspectives on your responses to different situations and help you recognize areas for growth.

By steering your energy and attention from external outcomes to your internal resolve, you begin to lay a deep structural foundation to your Inner Citadel. You can achieve an inner calm, an unruffled spirit, and, ironically, a higher likelihood of landing those external victories. In essence, understand the boundaries of your control, and you'll find not just tranquility but also empowerment in the midst of life's unpredictable dance.

Significantly, the dichotomy of control also enhances our strategic empathy capabilities by advancing our cognitive and emotional empathic skills. Stoics strive for equanimity—remaining calm and composed regardless of external circumstances. The balanced state of mind that comes along with internalizing the dichotomy of control is crucial in empathetic interactions, as it prevents overreaction to emotional situations. Equanimity allows people to approach others' experiences and emotions with a level of detachment that's necessary for understanding and supporting the other person without becoming overwhelmed or overly emotional themselves. With this balance comes prioritization of virtue and wisdom over material attachments, even at times of great struggle or amid an emotional rise. Moreover, clarity in the limits of our control, both universally and environmentally, instills a sense of humility and acceptance. This awareness helps us to recognize that everyone faces challenges and limitations, some of which are beyond their control. Acknowledging these shared struggles can deepen cognitive and emotional empathy capabilities, as it fosters a sense of shared humanity and an understanding of the diverse challenges people face.

The Stoic goal of developing an internal fortress of virtue and wisdom through the dichotomy of control leads to freedom both internally and externally. Internally, this means cultivating a state of mind that is resilient, adaptable, and compassionate, regardless of external circumstances. Externally, it involves acting in the world in a way that reflects these inner virtues. This dual focus on internal and external aspects reinforces the capacity to empathize, as it emphasizes the importance of maintaining a compassionate stance, no matter the situation.

Discomfort Embracing: Facing Uncomfortable Challenges

Running a marathon barefoot and in shorts in Finland's arctic circle is not a good idea unless you've trained your brain to artificially induce a stress response that helps you resist the effects of cold by releasing opioids and cannabinoids into your body, like Wim Hof. Hof, "the Iceman," has achieved approximately two dozen world records through remarkable displays of physical endurance in conditions that would prove fatal for most. The 59-year-old Dutchman's feats include scaling Mount Everest in Nepal while wearing shorts, holding the Guinness World Record for the longest swim under ice, and running a half-marathon through the Namib Desert without drinking any water.

We know a lot about how Hof's brain works, because his unusual capabilities intrigue neuroscientists enough to study him. For example, Dr. Otto Muzik, a pediatrician in Wayne State University's School of Medicine and his co-authors recently dressed the Iceman in a special bodysuit, put him in an MRI machine, and shot volumes of alternating extremely cold and extremely hot water through the suit in five-minute intervals. In other words, the research team exposed Hof to extreme temperatures while measuring the events in his brain.

Publishing their results in the journal *NeuroImage*, these researchers learned that Hof uses breathing in such a way that it activates a part of the brain that releases opioids and cannabinoids into his body. This release of "happy" chemicals doesn't cause a marijuana or opioid high. This is partly because the body produces cannabinoids and endorphins in smaller quantities than the typical amount in recreational or medicinal marijuana and opioid products, and partly because certain enzymes quickly break these chemicals down after they've carried out their cellular functions. So, they won't get you high. But these components can inhibit the signals responsible for telling the body you're feeling pain or cold and trigger the release of dopamine and serotonin. The result, Dr. Muzik says, is a kind of euphoric effect on the body that lasts for several minutes.[2] This is similar to the effect we call "runners high."[3]

Stoicism's embracing of discomfort is a concept that involves intentionally seeking out and embracing discomfort, challenges, or difficult situations as a means of personal growth, resilience, and self-improvement. It's the act of willingly stepping outside of one's comfort zone to confront experiences that may be unfamiliar, challenging, or even intimidating. When the Stoics embraced this significant tenet of their philosophy, they did not have access to Dr. Muzik's studies or fMRI machines. But they still inherently understood that through self-exposure to adversity and discomfort, we can develop new skills and become more resilient. This is why the Stoics always encouraged people to push their boundaries, take risks, and confront fears in pursuit of personal development and self-discovery. "The impediment to action advances action. What stands in the way becomes the way," said Marcus Aurelius, the "philosopher king."

Discomfort Embracing is a fundamental aspect of Stoic philosophy that emphasizes the development of self-control and fortitude as a means to overcome destructive emotions. Remember that Stoicism, acknowledging that life is full of challenges and adversity beyond our control, focuses on our reactions to these stressors, since those are most within our control. By embracing discomfort, whether physical, emotional, or mental, Stoics believe one can train oneself to remain calm and rational in the face of adversity. This resilience is key to maintaining inner peace. Thus, a notable practice in Stoicism is the concept of voluntary discomfort. This involves intentionally placing oneself in uncomfortable situations to develop discipline and to prepare for unforeseen hardships. The idea is that by becoming accustomed to discomfort, one can reduce the fear and impact of negative events. In this way, embracing discomfort goes hand in hand with the dichotomy of control, and mutually they foster a sense of empowerment and peace.

Significantly, this idea is closely tied with Buddhist ideals of appreciating nonsuffering. Thich Nhat Hanh, a pioneer of "engaged Buddhism," a movement linking mindfulness practice with social action, believed that we should integrate spiritual practice into daily life and use it as a means for addressing social and political injustices. He was a man of acceptance and empathy while still maintaining the significance of action: the space where meaningful and ethical Stoic

Empathy empowerment lies. Thus, he embraced discomfort not as an obstacle, but as a vital part of personal growth. While advocating for "active understanding" in the face of adversity rather than "passive tolerance," he also called for an ongoing state of appreciation for nonsuffering. "When we have a toothache, we know that not having a toothache is happiness," Thich Nhat Hanh famously said, fostering a greater awareness of our everyday experiences and encouraging gratitude for moments of peace and well-being while also recognizing and embracing life's inevitable discomforts as opportunities for deepening our resilience and empathy. In this way, Thich Nhat Hanh demonstrated a form of Buddhist inner peace that is not only compatible but deeply interrelated with external action. Equally important, he reminded us of the impermanence of all things, including pain.

You don't, however, have to be an Iceman or Buddhist monk to practice and receive the benefits of discomfort embracing. Intense exercise of more moderate degrees, or even simply cold exposure or heat therapy, can significantly bolster your physical and mental strength while helping to ground you firmly in Stoic Empathy. Consider, for example, my husband, Stuart.

Stuart lives with severe chronic pain. In the lower region of his lumbar spine, there's an unusual shift and twist in one of the vertebrae. This change causes his spinal canal, the space inside the spinal column where the spinal cord and many nerves are located, to become narrower. Because of this shifted vertebra, the nerves in that area are squeezed, and two of Stuart's discs bulge out. Another one is herniated. Because of this, Stuart has been in constant, daily pain for 30 years. Given the severity of the condition, he shouldn't be able to do much running or other sports. But Stuart, who at the time of this writing is 58 years old, is a triathlete, often competing in triple triathlons in one weekend, and he's still very active in basketball and volleyball.

How can he do this? Through the interconnection between his stoic discipline and ability to withstand the daily discomfort necessary to build a muscular core strong enough to support his misaligned spine. Stuart works out every day, no matter the level of pain with which he wakes. Fueled by the motivation to be an active father and willful participant in his own life and body, he works through aching soreness with the right knowledge of kinesiology and sufficient training in muscular endurance to support his body rather than aggravate his injuries. Back muscles as strong as his cut six-pack thus compensate for his crooked spine. To avoid having muscles so overwhelmed that they stop functioning, effectively resulting in spasms that would land him in bed for days at a time, unable to move, he does 20 minutes of stretching every single day. Every morning, he rolls out of bed with substantial pain, which he works out through his early-morning stretches.

As noted earlier, you can accomplish similar discomfort-embracing effects even through occasional cold or heat therapy. Cold ice baths are a new favorite trend for Silicon Valley CEOs and executive networking retreats, because even just a few minutes a day in an ice bath can increase norepinephrine in the brain, which is associated with focus, attention, and mood. The cold can also activate brown adipose tissue, which can improve metabolism. There's also evidence that cold exposure can stimulate the production of cold-shock proteins, which have neuroprotective effects. Indeed, short-term cold exposure is shown to support human cognitive brain activity.[4]

Personally, I much prefer training myself with the discomfort of a steam sauna or hot tub, otherwise known as heat therapy. Yes, this is a real thing and not just an excuse to blow off the afternoon and head to the spa. These hot treatments can cause your body to make special proteins called "heat-shock proteins," which are beneficial for your health in many ways, including protecting your brain (neuroprotective qualities). Intense heat therapy can also lower blood pressure and make profound reductions in symptoms and clinical biomarkers of heart disease. Recent studies have also shown intense heat to increase the production of capillary blood cells (which can improve blood flow, enhance exercise performance, allow for quicker recovery from injury, and improve general cardiovascular health).[5]

Discomfort-embracing techniques aren't limited to physical strain. As Seneca said, "Difficulties strengthen the mind, as labor does the body." Confronting and working through difficult emotions, such as fear, anxiety, or grief, are also important ways to build resilience. In the world right now, there's one man who stands out in this respect, and he's actually known as the "happiest man in the world." He is Yongey Mingyur Rinpoche, a Tibetan monk with a kind, round face and thick, dark eyebrows. Mingyur Rinpoche's brain has been studied for over 20 years and cited more than 1,100 times in scientific literature throughout the world. It all began when Harvard neuroscientist Richie Davidson met the Dalai Lama back in 1992, at which time the political and spiritual leader in exile asked Dr. Davidson to study the effects of meditation on the human brain. Dr. Davidson didn't begin his most famous research involving ECG and fMRI readings of brains in meditations of senior monks, however, until 2002, when he was inspired to take a closer look at the brain of a monk he'd met decades earlier at a meditation retreat, Mingyur Rinpoche. Coincidentally, 2002 was the same year I had a private audience with the Dalai Lama myself (more on this later).

Dr. Davidson's original studies began with Mingyur Rinpoche but then extended to many more senior meditation-practicing monks, hooking them to EEG machines and measuring their brains with what looks like a surrealist art piece: a shower cap extruding a spaghetti of wires. This specially designed cap holds 256 thin wires in place, each leading to a sensor pasted to a precise location on the scalp. Tight connection between the sensor and the scalp makes all the difference between recording usable data about the brain's electrical activity and having the electrode simply be an antenna for noise. With stunning results the likes of which Dr. Davidson had not even dreamed, he and his team began to study these brains amid meditation inside fMRI machines. Having learned of the impact of meditation as a remarkably effective neuroplasticity tool, Dr. Davidson went on to specifically confirm through his widely circulated published works that meditation can advance nearly all of our social and emotional skills. Even beyond that, in an 18-year-long longitudinal study, meditation appears to slow down the aging process (the brains of these practiced monks were as much as 10 years younger than those of their control group counterparts).[6]

You don't need to devote your life to meditation as a Buddhist monk to see some of these effects. Increasing emotional resilience at all is a very helpful tool in Stoic practices, because it furthers our ability to understand and process emotions. Even more moderate amounts of meditation can *physically* change the brain by thickening the cortical areas of the brain.[7]

Cortical areas are distinct regions within the cerebral cortex, the outermost layer of the brain. The cerebral cortex is responsible for many higher-order brain functions such as perception, reasoning, decision-making, and language. Thus, mindfulness meditation can benefit brain areas responsible for attention, emotional regulation, and self-awareness.[8] This review delves into the neuroscientific mechanisms and benefits of mindfulness meditation. It covers a wide range of studies and provides a comprehensive overview of the current understanding of how meditation affects the brain.

The ability of meditation to physically affect and enhance our brains also extends to its changes to the gray-matter density in the brain. This study found that participation in an eight-week mindfulness-based stress reduction (MBSR) program can lead to changes in gray-matter concentration in brain regions involved in learning and memory processes, emotion regulation, self-referential processing, and perspective-taking. Meditation can also increase pain tolerance. Meditation is, in its own way, a kind of superpower.[9]

Naturally, the link between discomfort embracing and improved cognitive and emotional empathic skills is solid. Regular practice of mindfulness and meditation enhances self-awareness and the ability to observe one's thoughts and feelings without judgment, core components of empathy. In addition, when we practice embracing discomfort, we develop a deeper appreciation of struggle, pain, and adversity. This understanding makes us more attuned to the discomforts and sufferings of others. Even by regularly challenging ourselves and stepping outside our comfort zones, we can better relate to others who face challenges, be they physical, emotional, or psychological. This experiential knowledge fosters a deeper sense of compassion.

Therefore, discomfort embracing, rooted in the belief that growth often occurs outside of our comfort zone, isn't just a central tenet of daily stoic living but also an advanced method of improving our empathy skills. By willingly facing discomfort and adversity, we can develop resilience, adaptability, and a greater sense of self-awareness. It's a principle often associated with personal development, self-improvement, and the pursuit of one's full potential. Learning to tolerate and embrace physical discomfort develops patience and a deeper understanding of struggle, which are vital in empathizing with others. In addition, practices like intermittent fasting and high-intensity exercise improve not only physical health but also emotional stability. Better emotional regulation is key in empathetic interactions, as it enables one to remain calm and supportive, even in emotionally intense situations.

EXERCISES

Incorporating this concept—embracing discomfort to overcome anxiety—involves exercises that push us slightly and progressively beyond our comfort zones, allowing us to develop resilience and adaptability. Here are exercises tailored to addressing anxieties related to work or school deadlines, social rejection, and global events.

Exercise: Using Discomfort Embracing to Overcome Anxiety Related to Work or School Deadlines

Objective: To build resilience toward deadline-related stress through gradual exposure to time management and organizational discomfort.

Identify Your Stress Patterns: Start by noting the specific aspects of deadlines that trigger your anxiety. Is it the fear of not having enough time, the pressure of expectations, or something else?

Set Incremental Deadlines: Break down your project into smaller tasks and set mini-deadlines for each. These should be slightly tighter than comfortable, pushing you to adapt to a more disciplined schedule without overwhelming stress.

Practice Voluntary Discomfort: Intentionally schedule one of your tasks to be done in a more challenging environment than you're used to—perhaps in a public library or a busy café, if you usually work in quiet spaces. The aim isn't to impair your work but to accustom yourself to maintaining focus amid distractions.

Reflect and Adjust: After each mini-deadline, reflect on your emotional and mental state. How did the discomfort affect you? What did you learn about your capacity to handle stress? Adjust your approach based on these reflections for the next task.

Exercise: Using Discomfort Embracing to Overcome Fear of Social Rejection

Objective: To gradually desensitize yourself to the fear of social rejection by intentionally engaging in low-risk social interactions.

Take Small-Talk Challenges: Begin with the goal of initiating small talk in low-stakes environments, such as asking a cashier how their day is going or complimenting a stranger. The idea is to get comfortable with initiating interactions, even with the risk of being ignored or receiving a nonengaged response.

Express an Unpopular Opinion: In a safe, respectful setting, share an opinion that may not be widely accepted or is minorly controversial among friends or in a discussion group. This should be done in a manner that invites conversation, not conflict, allowing you to experience and navigate differing viewpoints.

Seek Constructive Feedback: Approach someone you trust and ask for honest feedback on an aspect of yourself you're working to improve. This practice opens you to potential critique, helping you find value in others' perspectives without taking it as personal rejection.

Reflect on the Social Challenge: After each activity, reflect on what the experience felt like, what was challenging, and how you managed your feelings of anxiety. Over time, these reflections will help you see your growth and resilience.

Exercise: Using Discomfort Embracing to Overcome Anger

Objective: To build resilience toward anger triggers through gradual exposure and mindful practice, allowing for better emotional regulation and empathetic interactions.

Identify Anger Triggers: Reflect on situations or individuals that typically trigger your anger. It could be during discussions, certain topics, or specific environments.

Simulate a Confrontation: In a safe and controlled environment, simulate a mild confrontation with a friend or a coach. You should do this respectfully and with agreed-upon boundaries to ensure it remains a learning experience.

Breathe Mindfully and Set a Time Delay: During the simulation, practice mindful breathing techniques to remain calm and focused. Deep breaths can help manage physiological responses to anger. To amplify the effects of breathing, set a rule for yourself to wait for a short period, such as 10 seconds to a minute, before responding. This delay gives you time to process your emotions.

Reflect and Adjust: After each simulation, reflect on your emotional responses and identify what triggered your anger and how you managed it. Adjust your approach in subsequent simulations based on these reflections.

Exercise: Using Discomfort Embracing to Overcome Fear Regarding Global Events

Objective: To cultivate a balanced perspective on global events, reducing anxiety by engaging with discomfort in a controlled, informed manner.

Get Informed Exposure: Choose one global issue that makes you afraid. Dedicate a short, set amount of time each day (e.g., 15 minutes) to read about it from reputable sources. This controlled exposure helps prevent the overwhelm of constant news while keeping you informed.

Take an Actionable Step: Identify one small, actionable step you can take to positively contribute to the issue at hand, such as participating in a community cleanup for environmental concerns. This provides a sense of agency, transforming anxiety into action.

Practice Mindfulness and Acceptance: Incorporate a daily mindfulness practice focused on accepting what is within your control and releasing what is not. This could involve meditation, journaling, or another reflective practice that helps you process your feelings about global events.

Engage in Community: Engage in discussions with a community or support group that shares your concerns about global events. This can provide a sense of solidarity and shared purpose, reducing feelings of isolation and helplessness.

Each of these exercises incorporates the Stoic practice of embracing discomfort as a means of personal growth. By gradually exposing yourself to the sources of your anxiety in a controlled and mindful manner, you can build resilience, develop a more balanced perspective, and enhance your emotional well-being.

Habituation: Reducing Resistance with Repeated Exposure

In his insightful quote "Practice yourself, for heaven's sake in little things, and then proceed to greater," Epictetus offers valuable guidance for dealing with life's challenges. He advises starting with mastery over small, seemingly minor tasks before moving on to bigger and more complex ones. This principle carries significant weight in many areas of life, from personal development to professional achievement. By focusing first on the smaller tasks, we establish a solid foundation for tackling future challenges, hone our abilities, foster self-assurance, and cultivate an attitude geared toward growth and improvement. Building on Epictetus's wisdom, this approach aligns remarkably well with modern psychological practices such as systematic desensitization or exposure therapy, or what this book refers to as *habituation*. These techniques are grounded in the idea of gradually exposing oneself to the object or situation that causes anxiety or distress so as to learn to gain stoic control over distressful or anxious stimuli. Just as Epictetus suggests starting with small tasks and progressing to greater ones, systematic desensitization involves beginning with less challenging stimuli and slowly moving toward more challenging ones. This method helps us to incrementally build up our tolerance and resilience, reducing fear and anxiety in the process. By applying this gradual approach to both personal and professional challenges, we can effectively manage and overcome our apprehensions and limitations. Thus, the Stoic practice of focusing on small, manageable tasks first can be seen as an early form of this therapeutic concept, highlighting the enduring relevance and practicality of Stoic principles in contemporary life.

Research has found systematic desensitization quite effective for many phobias and anxiety disorders. By gradually facing the feared object or situation in a controlled and structured manner, each of us can reduce or even eliminate our anxiety response over time.[10]

Let's use the example of public-speaking anxiety, which is quite common in corporate settings. Below is a template exercise on how to overcome fear of public speaking using habituation.

EXERCISES

Exercise: Using Habituation to Overcome Fears of Public Speaking

A Step-by-Step Guide to Conquering Stage Fright: You're not alone in your fear of public speaking. Many of us tremble at the thought of standing before an audience. But fear not, for within these pages lies a path to confidence and calmness. Let's embark on this journey together, using time-tested methods to overcome our shared apprehension.

Begin with Tranquility: Before facing the crowd, let's learn to face our inner turmoil. Practice deep breathing exercises, engage in progressive muscle relaxation, and visualize serene landscapes. These techniques aren't just prespeech rituals; they're tools to steady your heartbeat whenever anxiety tries to take the stage.

Craft Your Ladder of Confidence: Imagine a ladder, each rung a step toward your goal. Start with the lowest, least-frightening rung—perhaps it's speaking to your reflection. Progress might lead you to a friendly audience of close friends or family. Gradually, you'll climb higher, facing larger and less familiar groups. Remember, every step up is a victory.

Embrace Gradual Exposure: Progress isn't a race. Spend a week, maybe two, getting comfortable with each rung on your ladder. Begin where you're most at ease. Maybe it's reciting a speech to your cat; then, perhaps, a small gathering in your living room. With each step, the once-daunting crowd will seem more like an audience of old friends.

Practice Relaxation in Action: As you climb, keep your relaxation tools at hand. When nerves arise, as they naturally will, return to your breathing, feel each muscle relax, and recall the peace of your inner sanctum. These techniques are the safety net beneath your high-wire act.

Go from Practice to Performance: Eventually, your practice will lead you to real stages—community centers, boardrooms, or even larger venues. Embrace these opportunities to test your newfound skills. Each real-world experience is a chance to refine your abilities and to prove to yourself that you can do this.

Continue Your Journey: Your journey doesn't end with the last page of this book. The world is filled with stages awaiting your voice. Take your ladder with you, climb it at your pace, and know that with each speech, you're not just speaking; you're also listening to the quieting of your fears.

Exercise: Using Habituation to Overcome Envy

Objective: To reduce feelings of envy by gradually exposing yourself to situations that trigger envy and developing a more balanced and appreciative perspective.

Identify Envy Triggers: Start with some self-reflection to identify specific situations or people that trigger your feelings of envy. Is it a colleague's success, a friend's lifestyle, or someone's possessions? Note down these triggers to understand the sources of your envy.

Construct Your Gratitude Ladder: Create a list of positive aspects of your life that you're grateful for. Start with small, easily appreciable things, such as a supportive friend or a recent accomplishment.

Gain Gradual Exposure: Spend a few minutes each day looking at the social-media profiles of those who trigger your envy. Initially, focus on appreciating one positive aspect of their posts without comparing yourself.

Interact and Compliment Others: In real-life interactions, make a conscious effort to compliment those who trigger your envy. This could be praising a colleague's work or validating a friend's achievement. This practice helps shift your mindset from envy to appreciation.

Reflect and Adjust: After each exposure to an envy-triggering situation, reflect on your feelings and responses in a journal. Note any positive changes in your perspective and areas that need further work.

Lead Yourself to Empathy: Engage in role-playing exercises where you imagine being in the shoes of the person you envy. Consider their challenges and struggles to develop empathy and reduce envy.

Practice Mindfulness and Acceptance: Incorporate mindfulness exercises such as meditation or deep breathing, focusing on accepting your feelings of envy without judgment. This helps in managing and gradually reducing these emotions.

Embrace Greater Challenges: Actively participate in events or activities where you're likely to encounter those you envy. For example, attend networking events or social gatherings. Use these opportunities to practice gratitude and positive interaction.

See Your Evolution: Over time, you'll notice a shift in your perspective. Envy will diminish as you develop a more balanced and appreciative outlook on your life and the achievements of others.

Exercise: Using Habituation to Overcome Dread of Confrontation

Transform Apprehension into Assertiveness: If the thought of negotiating your salary fills you with dread, you're not alone. Many of us find the prospect daunting. Yet, there's a pathway from fear to empowerment, a journey that transforms apprehension into assertive confidence.

Find Your Inner Calm: Negotiation, especially when it concerns your livelihood, can seem overwhelming. The first step is to find your calm amid this anxiety. Techniques like deep breathing, guided imagery, and progressive muscle relaxation aren't just prenegotiation rituals; they're lifelines to steady your nerves and clear your mind.

Construct Your Confidence Ladder: Imagine a ladder, each rung a step toward your goal. Start simple—perhaps role-playing negotiations with a friend or colleague. As you become more comfortable, the scenarios can become more complex, simulating the real-life challenge of a salary negotiation. This gradual progression builds your skills and confidence in a controlled, manageable way.

Practice Leading to Performance: Begin in the safety of practice, with role-playing exercises that mirror potential negotiation scenarios. This is your training ground, where feedback and reflection refine your approach. As confidence builds, you'll find these simulated negotiations progressively resembling the real thing.

Keep Calm in the Heat of Negotiation: As you step into actual salary negotiations, keep your relaxation techniques close at hand. Visualize a successful outcome before each discussion to set a positive tone. If anxiety spikes, return to your breathing, finding peace and clarity amid the stress.

Embrace Greater Challenges: With each negotiation, no matter how small, seek out opportunities to stretch your abilities. Attend workshops, seek feedback, and constantly refine your approach. Each challenge is a chance to grow.

See Your Evolution: Over time, you'll notice a shift. What once seemed insurmountable will become manageable, then routine. Your salary negotiations will transform from a source of stress to a demonstration of your value and skills.

Overcoming fears such as public speaking, confrontation, and general anxiety is akin to unlocking new realms of personal power and influence in your life. When you conquer the fear of public speaking, you open doors to express your ideas more effectively, inspiring and persuading others with your words. This skill is invaluable, whether in leadership roles, team collaborations, or social settings. Similarly, mastering the art of confrontation, not as a combative tool but as a means of constructive communication, empowers you to address issues head-on, negotiate better, and advocate for yourself and others. This assertiveness fosters respect and credibility among peers and superiors alike. Last, reducing general anxiety enhances your decision-making abilities, resilience, and overall mental clarity. When you're not hindered by undue stress, you're more capable of strategic thinking and innovation, qualities essential for leadership and influence. In essence, overcoming these fears doesn't just alleviate personal discomfort; it cultivates a stronger, more confident persona capable of shaping your environment rather than being shaped by it. This transformation not only brings a profound sense of control over your own life but also significantly amplifies your impact and influence in the wider world.

Relating this all back to our empathic practice, consider how fusing strategic empathy with habituation-based techniques for overcoming fears creates a potent formula for personal empowerment. When you combine empathy with the confidence you gain from overcoming fears such as public speaking or confrontation, it allows for more impactful and influential interactions. Habituation methods reduce fear responses, freeing you to focus more on the emotional and psychological states of those you are engaging with. This deeper understanding enables you to tailor your communication in a way that resonates more profoundly with others, whether in negotiations, leadership, or collaborative endeavors.

Integrating Dichotomy of Control, Discomfort Embracing, and Habituation with Strategic Empathy

The integration of the foundational Stoic tools—Dichotomy of Control, Discomfort Embracing, and Habituation—with strategic empathy forms a comprehensive strategy for personal and interpersonal development, enhancing our ability to navigate complex social dynamics with confidence, insight, and influence. The easiest way to make this connection is to think back to our friend the terrifying tarantula, back in Chapter 3's discussion of Affect Labeling. Recall what Dr. Lieberman and his team reported in *Psychological Science* in 2012: that *telling* the spider you're afraid of it *while* being exposed to it is the best way to conquer your fear of spiders. You can even come close to touching the tarantula through this combined method. Looking back, you can see the impact of affect labeling ("You're terrifying, spider!") quadrupled through dichotomy of control ("I can't control what the spider does"), embracing discomfort ("I will go another step forward"), and of course, habituation ("The more exposure, the better").

In addition to strategic-empathy tools strengthening the impact of Stoic methods, the reverse is true: Stoicism amplifies empathic abilities.

By embracing the Dichotomy of Control, for example, we cultivate self-awareness and emotional regulation, enabling us to differentiate between what we can change and what we must accept. This awareness allows us to approach interactions with intentionality, maintaining equanimity in the face of external circumstances and deepening our connections through a shared understanding of human vulnerability.

Discomfort Embracing pushes us beyond our comfort zones, encouraging us to confront and adapt to a broad spectrum of emotional states. This deliberate exposure fosters resilience, enabling us to support others in distress with empathy and understanding without succumbing to avoidance or emotional overload. It challenges us to engage with the discomforts of others, leading to more profound connections and a richer awareness of their experiences. When combined with empathy, this approach not only strengthens our capacity to endure hardships but also deepens our ability to connect with, understand, and support others. This synergy between embracing discomfort and practicing empathy has a transformative impact across various aspects of our lives, enhancing our personal power, leadership abilities, relational dynamics, and conflict-resolution skills. Let's explore how this powerful combination empowers us in work contexts, negotiations, personal relationships, and beyond:

- *Empowerment in Work Contexts:* In professional settings, embracing discomfort propels us to take on challenging projects, speak up in meetings, and step out of our comfort zones, fostering innovation and growth. This proactive stance, coupled with empathy, enables us to understand and address the concerns and motivations of our colleagues and clients more effectively. By willingly facing discomfort and showing genuine concern for others, we build trust and credibility, establishing ourselves as compassionate, resilient leaders who inspire teams and drive positive change within organizations.
- *Amplifying Influence in Negotiations:* Negotiation scenarios often involve a degree of tension and discomfort. By leaning in to these feelings, we learn to navigate negotiations with a calm and focused presence, viewing challenges as opportunities for growth and collaboration rather than threats. Empathy allows us to genuinely understand and consider the needs and perspectives of the other party, facilitating solutions that are mutually beneficial. This approach not only leads to more successful negotiation outcomes but also enhances our reputation as fair and effective negotiators.
- *Strengthening Personal Relationships:* Embracing discomfort in personal bonds involves being open to difficult conversations, acknowledging and working through conflicts, and stepping into the shoes of others to understand their feelings and perspectives. This vulnerability, when paired with empathy, fosters deeper bonds, trust, and mutual respect. It encourages us to grow alongside our partners, friends, and family, enhancing the quality of our connections to others and our overall emotional well-being.
- *Resolving Conflicts with Empathy and Courage:* Conflict resolution benefits immensely from the combination

of embracing discomfort and practicing empathy. Facing conflicts directly, rather than avoiding them, requires courage and a willingness to engage with uncomfortable emotions. Empathy allows us to appreciate the other person's perspective, facilitating a more compassionate and effective resolution process. This balanced approach ensures that both parties feel heard and respected, leading to solutions that address the needs of all involved.

- *Broadening Our Influence:* The practice of embracing discomfort, enriched by empathy, broadens our influence by challenging us to grow, adapt, and respond to life's challenges with grace and understanding. This dynamic enhances our leadership qualities, making us more relatable, approachable, and impactful. We become capable of inspiring positive change, not only in our own lives but also in the lives of those around us, embodying the ideals of courage, compassion, and resilience.

Similarly, habituation, through repeated exposure to fears and stressors, diminishes their emotional impact, strengthening our emotional resilience and capacity for calm, collected responses. This process not only prevents empathy collapse but also enriches our empathetic engagements, making them more sustainable and grounded. By reducing fear responses, habituation allows us to focus more on the emotional and psychological states of those we engage with, tailoring our communication to resonate more deeply, whether in negotiations, leadership, or collaborative efforts. Incorporating the mastery of habituation and strategic empathy into our personal and professional lives offers a transformative pathway to enhancing our personal power. This synthesis not only equips us to navigate our fears and anxieties with grace but also significantly bolsters our ability to connect, lead, and influence across various spheres of life. By delving into how this integrated approach can amplify our effectiveness in work contexts, negotiations, personal relationships, and conflict resolution, we uncover the profound impact of combining self-regulation with empathetic engagement. Let's take a closer look at how habituation, within the context of dichotomy of control, combines with empathy to empower us.

- *Enhancing Personal Power in Work Contexts:* In the workplace, mastering habituation to overcome personal fears such as public speaking or confronting challenging tasks allows us to step into leadership roles with confidence. This newfound self-assurance, coupled with the ability to engage empathetically with colleagues, superiors, and subordinates, enhances our leadership presence. By projecting confidence and demonstrating understanding, we can inspire trust and motivate teams, increasing our influence and personal power within organizational structures. Strategic empathy enables us to navigate office politics more effectively, recognize unspoken needs and concerns, and craft solutions that address these issues, thereby solidifying our role as indispensable leaders.
- *Amplifying Influence in Negotiations:* Negotiations, whether they're about salaries, contracts, or business deals, often stir anxiety and fear of rejection or failure. Habituation teaches us to approach these situations with a calm, steady mindset, reducing the emotional charge and allowing us to focus on the negotiation itself. When we combine this with strategic empathy—clarifying the motivations, fears, and desires of the other party—we unlock a powerful tool for influence. This dual approach enables us to craft proposals that not only meet our needs but also appeal to the interests of others, thereby increasing the likelihood of successful outcomes. Our ability to remain composed and empathetic positions us as strong, persuasive negotiators who wield significant personal power.
- *Strengthening Personal Relationships:* The principles of habituation and strategic empathy have

profound implications for our personal lives and relationships. By confronting and managing our fears, we open ourselves to deeper, more meaningful connections. This process fosters a strong sense of self, which is attractive and compelling in personal interactions. Furthermore, practicing empathy allows us to understand and meet the emotional needs of our partners, friends, and family members more effectively. This deepened understanding and mutual respect amplify our personal power by fostering relationships based on trust, respect, and mutual growth.

- *Resolving Conflicts with Compassion and Assertiveness:* Conflict resolution is another area where the combination of habituation and strategic empathy proves invaluable. Facing conflicts head-on, without the paralyzing effect of fear, enables us to address issues directly and constructively. Strategic empathy allows us to see the conflict from the other party's perspective, acknowledging their feelings and viewpoints without necessarily agreeing with them. This approach not only facilitates a more compassionate resolution but also ensures that our own needs and boundaries are respected. By balancing assertiveness with empathy, we can navigate conflicts in a way that strengthens relationships rather than eroding them, enhancing our personal power through our ability to resolve disputes effectively and ethically.
- *Broadening Our Influence:* Ultimately, the synergy between overcoming personal fears through habituation and enhancing empathetic engagement broadens our influence across all areas of life. This integrated approach empowers us to lead with integrity, negotiate with confidence, build stronger alliances, and resolve conflicts with compassion and assertiveness. It aligns closely with the Stoic ideal of

> living a life of virtue and wisdom, where personal power isn't wielded through dominance but through strength of character, depth of understanding, and the ability to inspire and influence others positively.

By embracing this holistic approach to personal development, we not only enhance our own lives but also contribute to the betterment of our communities and workplaces. The combination of personal empowerment and empathetic engagement truly amplifies our impact in the world, turning challenges into opportunities for growth and leadership into an act of service. Central to this empowerment is the Stoic principle of the dichotomy of control, reminding us to discern between what is within our power to change and what is not. This wisdom adds a profound layer of strength to our endeavors, guiding us to invest our energies wisely, focus on our responses to external circumstances, and maintain inner peace amid life's uncertainties. Understanding and applying this principle in conjunction with embracing discomfort and practicing empathy enhances our personal power by teaching us the value of responding with intentionality and purpose, rather than reacting to things beyond our control. This insightful integration of ancient wisdom and modern practice offers a robust framework for personal growth and leadership, grounding our actions and interactions in a deep sense of purpose and control.

Consider Charles Darwin's famous finding, that it's not the strongest of the species that survive, nor the most intelligent, but the ones most responsive to change.

More effective emotional regulation helps maintain a balanced and adaptable emotional state that embraces rather than fears change, essential for providing empathetic responses that are supportive without being overwhelmed. Indeed, even power and influence themselves can be uncomfortable—that is, until we embrace that discomfort and habituate ourselves to it. You can be more mindful and considered in your responses even to triggering issues and questions, a crucial tool in sensitive empathetic interactions. In this way, we become better leaders of our own lives and more effective at managing ourselves.

Together, these Stoic tools enhance our strategic empathy, enabling us to read and respond to the thoughts and emotions of others more effectively. This fusion of empathy with Stoic practices empowers us to maintain a calm and confident demeanor, positioning us as leaders admired for both our strength and our insight. It encourages us to seek diverse experiences and interactions, fostering a more inclusive empathy that comprehends the varied backgrounds and challenges people face. This holistic approach not only enriches our interpersonal relationships but also bolsters our influence and decision-making, propelling us to new heights of personal and professional success. In embracing these Stoic principles, we develop a balanced and adaptable emotional state that's receptive to change, enhancing our empathetic responses and leadership capabilities, ultimately cultivating an Inner Citadel of resilience, wisdom, and compassion.

We walk away from this chapter having begun building our fortress. We now turn to the building blocks of Memento Mori and Moral Courage.

Chapter 7 Takeaways

In this chapter, we've outlined the following three critical tools of Stoicism:

- *Dichotomy of Control:* Differentiating between what we can control and what we can't, teaching us to channel our energy and efforts wisely.
- *Discomfort Embracing:* Viewing discomfort as an opportunity for growth and resilience, helping us face challenges head-on and navigate difficult or uncomfortable scenarios.
- *Habituation:* Forming positive habits through consistent practice and integrating empathic responses into our daily interactions, thereby shaping our character and natural reactions over time.

CHAPTER 8

ADVANCED STOICISM TOOLS: MEMENTO MORI AND MORAL COURAGE

If you think clearly about it, it makes no sense to think you're seeking happiness, if you do nothing to restrain angry, spiteful, and malicious thoughts and emotions.

— The Dalai Lama

I first wrote my own obituary when I was 25 years old. The idea came to me as I was signing the divorce papers ending a relationship with a good man with whom I shouldn't have remained but who contributed greatly to shaping the person I am today. Emerging from that growth and inspired by both *Tuesdays with Morrie* and the *Meditations*, which I'd recently read, I decided to write not what my obituary *would* say if I were to die that day but what I *wanted* it to say. I wanted to embrace the certainty of death not with fear, but as a catalyst for fuller involvement in life.

It wasn't easy, leaving that marriage. Besides the conventional issues facing me as a member of the Iranian community and its seeming refusal to accept my decision here, I was also losing my best friend. We'd been sweethearts since I was 16 years old, and he was the only man I'd ever *known* known—you know, in the biblical sense of the word. He was intertwined with my entire family, almost like the son my father never had. And I was scared. I was a divorcée at 25, on my third country, and about to enter a world of law and power the likes of which I'd scarcely seen outside the portrayal of television dramas, with a bagful of debt, amid the aftermath of 9/11 that labeled Iran as a member of the "Axis of Evil," by extension entangling all Americans of Iranian decent as its descendants. And I was alone. Without my parents. Without my sisters. My Iranian community was still back in Canada. My new American friends had known me for a year or two, and they were all as broke as I was (like attracts like, I suppose—why couldn't have I made more rich and connected kid friends?). I'd never worked full time. I was asked questions to help determine whether I was a "security threat" when applying for law-firm jobs, based only on my national heritage and nothing else, and sometimes told to "go back to where I came from."

Not easy. But thrilling! I was *alone* and making all of my own decisions. After going from my father's house to my husband's house, I had a house of my own. My car was mine. My apartment was stacked floor to ceiling with books and displayed Persian *termeh* tapestries on the walls. My shoes were bright-colored stilettos. Every morning, I walked into an office so fancy it made me squeal with delight. After work, I could go to the Art Institute and sit with my favorite painting (*Resting*, by Antonio Mancini) for as long as I wanted, take extension courses in whatever subject I wanted to learn (How to Appreciate Great Opera and The Joy of Mathematics), and party until whenever I wanted (I was 25, and Crowbar in Chicago was in its heyday!). I'd had the benefit of loving and educated parents who sacrificed everything to bring me to this side of the world. But I'd also earned it. Worked and scraped and walked upright when others shamed my polyester suit or divorced status or darker skin tone.

I was ready for life to happen. For love to find me. For success to greet me. And every year, on my birthday, I was writing my obituary: always thinking back to that moment when this practice started, life-changing divorce papers in my hands waiting to be executed, noting the massive transformational and candidly terrifying changes and risks necessary for me to be all of the person I wanted to be. I began using my awareness of mortality as an integrated tool to deepen my engagement with life. I'd always prioritized relationships, but this life-pattern enhancement would allow me to find an authenticity and depth of meaning that I'd barely tapped into. So, this is how I came to write my obituary every year, usually on my birthday, for approximately a quarter of a century.

My practice helped me maintain focus and courage in facing challenges while embracing life's opportunities. By annually reflecting on my desired legacy, I deepened my understanding of mortality and found greater meaning in my journey. Now, in Chapter 8: Advanced Stoicism Tools, I invite you to explore the power of Memento Mori (death acceptance) and Moral Courage. Together, they can guide us toward a life of purpose, balance, and authenticity.

As you read these pages, I encourage you to think more broadly about everything we've discussed in this book thus far. We discussed emotional versus cognitive empathy; tools like affect labeling, silence, active listening, mirroring and repeating, and probing questions—all techniques for empathetic interactions, to understand better how to connect with and better understand others. Then, we strategically used that awareness to gain power in daily dynamics, routine negotiations, and big life events. The astute use of empathy requires emotional regulation, so we went on to discuss ancient Stoic teachings and modern neuroscience studies, which help us manage ourselves even in the most challenging of circumstances. We learned the mechanics behind emotional control through better understanding how feelings are experienced and displayed. We discussed powerful mechanisms to help us build our Inner Citadel and extend our control beyond our pathe to include guiding our instinctual propatheiai, the core of personal strength, resilience, and autonomy: the dichotomy of control, discomfort embracing, habituation, and now, death acceptance and moral courage. You've surely already begun thinking about the throughlines in these teachings and how they all connect.

Memento Mori (Death Acceptance)

Emperor Aurelius likely never imagined that his private journal, the work we now know as the *Meditations*, would be preserved through handwritten copies and brought to global renown with the eventual invention of the printing press nearly 1,300 years after the emperor's death. As plague and political intrigue swept across Rome, Marcus Aurelius was embracing and writing about Memento Mori, a constant reminder of life's fragility and the inevitability of death. Among his writings about this was the profound realization: "You could leave life right now. Let that determine what you do and say and think." A philosophy not born out of fear, but out of a deep understanding that life's impermanence should be a guide to living with purpose, integrity, and urgency. When death finally came for Marcus Aurelius in A.D. 180, he faced it not as an emperor losing his kingdom, but as a philosopher embracing the natural conclusion of life's journey.

Memento Mori, from a Latin phrase that translates to "remember you must die," is an ancient philosophy that threads through human history, reminding us of the inevitability of death as a means to value and enrich life. While rooted in Stoicism and referenced in Marcus Aurelius, Memento Mori was later adopted in various cultural and religious contexts, serving as a poignant reminder to live with purpose, mindfulness, and authenticity. It's not intended to evoke fear or morbidity; rather, Memento Mori encourages a profound appreciation for the present moment and a reevaluation of what truly matters. It invites us to reflect on our own lives and consider the legacy we wish to leave behind. Accepting the inevitability of death also reminds us of our shared human experience and vulnerability. By consciously remembering that life is transient, we're inspired to make the most of each day, prioritize genuine connections and meaningful pursuits, ponder deeply on the legacy we wish to leave behind, and live in a way that leaves no room for regret. In addition, recognizing our own mortality leads to a deeper appreciation for the struggles and triumphs of others, thus expanding our empathic prowess.

Time is finite and thus a precious resource not to be squandered in actions that don't add value to our legacy. Stoic Memento Mori thus urges a transformation in behavior—where understanding, strength, power, and generosity become the cornerstones of our interactions.

Memento Mori and Delayed Gratification

Neurotransmitters like dopamine and endorphins are crucial in our experiences of pleasure and pain. Dopamine, the pleasure hormone, slowly enhances mood and is linked to activities like sex, exercise, and music, triggering enjoyment and satisfaction. Endorphins, on the other hand, quickly relieve pain and stress, notably during exercise, leading to a feeling similar to a "runner's high." These neurotransmitters are central to the concepts of instant gratification. Instant gratification results in a swift release of dopamine and endorphins, offering immediate but short-lived happiness from pleasurable activities.

Delayed gratification, however, is more intricate. It requires forgoing immediate pleasures for greater, long-term rewards and involves different brain processes and neurotransmitters like serotonin, oxytocin, and norepinephrine. The prefrontal cortex plays a key role here, focusing on decision-making and self-control. Serotonin, associated with mood regulation, increases with long-term goals, contributing to well-being. Oxytocin, the "bonding hormone," is released in activities involving trust and is essential for long-term bonds. Norepinephrine aids focus and motivation, crucial for achieving long-term objectives.

Memento Mori, a meditation on the inevitability of death, imparts a sense of urgency and perspective on the value of time. It reminds us that life is finite and each moment is precious. This awareness naturally steers one toward delayed gratification, a technique where immediate pleasures are postponed in favor of more substantial, long-term rewards. The Stoics believed that true satisfaction comes from virtuous living and achieving meaningful goals, which often requires forgoing short-term desires.

In the practice of delayed gratification, the brain's reward system is recalibrated. The prefrontal cortex, responsible for decision-making and self-control, becomes more engaged. This aligns with the Stoic virtue of discipline and the conscious choice to resist immediate temptations for greater future gains, and Memento Mori encourages us to set and pursue such goals, knowing our time is limited. Oxytocin, the bonding hormone, is released through meaningful social interactions and long-term relationships, again reflecting the Stoic value of community and deep connections over fleeting pleasures.

Norepinephrine, vital for focus and attention, becomes particularly important in the pursuit of long-term objectives. This aligns with the Stoic emphasis on perseverance and resilience. Through the lens of Memento Mori, we are reminded to maintain focus on our ultimate goals, undistracted by short-lived pleasures.

In integrating Memento Mori into our lives, we find a powerful ally in the practice of delayed gratification. This Stoic reminder not only imbues our actions with a sense of purpose and urgency but also fortifies our resolve to choose paths that lead to more enduring and meaningful rewards. It's a call to balance the ephemeral joys of life with the pursuit of lasting fulfillment, keeping in mind the finite nature of our existence.

EXERCISE: WRITING AN OBITUARY TO HIGHLIGHT THE MEANINGS OF LIFE

This exercise encourages you to write the obituary you desire, helping you envision the life you want to lead. Inspired by the concept of Memento Mori, this work prompts a self-audit to set clear goals, maintain motivation, prioritize life choices, and ensure authentic living.

To begin, consider your core values, your proudest achievements, the way you want to be remembered, and the goals you still wish to achieve. Then, write an obituary that captures these elements, focusing on personal qualities, relationships, and impacts rather than material success. This is your "Ideal" obituary.

Next, write an obituary reflecting your present life realistically. What it might actually look like if something were to happen to you on this very day. Although you're very much alive if you're reading this book, we'll call this your "Actual" obituary.

Compare the two—the "Actual" and the "Ideal."

Look at areas for growth and alignment.

Based on your insights, set specific, achievable goals to bridge the gap between your current and ideal self. You'll note that some of the Actual-to-Ideal gaps can be filled right away. For example, if you decide to tell your estranged childhood friend you still love her, you can meet that goal with reasonable haste. Other Actual-to-Ideal gaps will take longer and require short- and mid-term goal setting.

For full instructions and a reflection page you can print or download, visit my website www.sherminkruse.com. This exercise will help you gain a clearer vision of the life you want to lead and take meaningful steps toward achieving it.

As you embark on this journey of reflection and goal setting, it's vital to approach it with honesty and deep introspection. Remember, this exercise is for your benefit, a personal exploration to align your life's path with your truest aspirations. It's not about creating an image for others or meeting external expectations, but rather about understanding and shaping your own narrative.

By engaging in this process, you're doing much more than simply planning for the future. You are taking proactive steps to live more consciously and meaningfully in the present. This exercise is a tool to bring clarity to your values and priorities, helping you to make decisions and take actions that resonate with your core being. It's an invitation to live authentically, in a way that honors your deepest desires and aspirations. Each step you take, each goal you set, brings you closer to a life that is not only fulfilling in the future but also rich and meaningful in the here and now. Allow yourself the space to be honest, to dream, and to plan with a vision that truly reflects who you are and whom you wish to become. This is your story to write, your life to shape. Embrace this opportunity to craft a life that resonates with your truest self, both today and in all your tomorrows. As Morrie Schwartz said, "There's a better approach. To know you're going to die, and to be prepared for it at any time. That way, you can actually be more involved in your life while you're living."[1]

Moral Courage: Strength of Character, Virtue, and Reason

Do you know the tale of Maximus Decimus Meridius, the central figure of Ridley Scott's epic, *Gladiator* (2000)? It's one of my all-time favorites. It's a story of bravery, honor, and vengeance set against the grand backdrop of the Roman Empire. How could I *not* love a film that begins with some really terrific scenes of Marcus Aurelius come to life as the philosopher emperor himself, played brilliantly by Richard Harris (of Dumbledore fame). Then there's Joaquin Phoenix, who perfectly portrays the emperor's jealous and villainous son, Commodus. But the hero of the movie is a completely fictional character: Maximus—Russell Crowe at his best—a once-favored general whom the envious Commodus betrays. Maximus's life is shattered, his family cruelly taken from him and his status stripped away. Escaping his death sentence, Maximus ends up reduced to a gladiator slave who can win his freedom only through combat. Maximus, our once-just philosopher, is set on a path of vengeance for his family's murder and the corruption that Commodus seeped into the heart of Rome.

In the arena, Maximus's courage is undeniable. He faces down ferocious gladiators, wild beasts, and ultimately, the treacherous Commodus himself. Each battle, each victory, is a step closer to avenging his family and fulfilling his promise of retribution. The audience is swept up in the spectacle, the raw physicality, and the sheer will of Maximus as he fights not just for survival, but for his cause. There is very little in cinematic history more satisfying than when he announces to the entire arena, as Commodus has no choice but to sit and watch:

> My name is Maximus Decimus Meridius, commander of the Armies of the North, general of the Felix Legions. Loyal servant to the true emperor, Marcus Aurelius. Father to a murdered son. Husband to a murdered wife. And I will have my vengeance, in this life or the next.

I get chills just thinking about it!

Yet, compelling as it is, Maximus's tale of courage diverges from the path of moral courage as the Stoics understood it.

Remember that Stoicism emphasizes virtue, wisdom, and the mastery of oneself. It views courage not just as a matter of facing physical danger but as the resolve to act rightly and justly—guided by moral principles, *not* personal vendetta or emotional turmoil. The Stoics would argue that true courage is found not in the heat of battle or the quest for revenge, but in the quiet, daily decisions to live with integrity, to stand up for justice, and to maintain one's ethical principles even when it's most challenging. It's about the internal struggle, the battle within, to choose the right path, even when it leads away from personal desires or the allure of retribution.

Gladiator presents us with a form of courage that thrills and inspires: true grandiose heroism that is a testament to the human spirit's resilience. Yet, it invites us to reflect on the nature of true courage—the Stoic ideal—that lies not in the external display of valor but in the steadfast adherence to one's principles. Maximus cared about Rome, which is why Marcus Aurelius's character preferred him, but in the movie, he is far more driven by vengeance and retribution. Rome is only secondary.

Gladiator is *such* a great movie, and I'll forever be a huge fan. And it's also a reminder that the most profound battles we face are often *not* against external enemies, but within ourselves, as we strive to live according to our highest ideals, regardless of the personal cost.

In our modern world, there aren't any gladiator arenas, but "arenas" surround us everywhere—political arenas, corporate arenas, even interpersonal arenas. Sometimes, it does seem as though you'd have to slit a few throats to make partner, win that election, or capture the heart of the person you love.

And maybe you do.

It's just not what Stoic Moral Courage is.

For adherents of Stoicism, the concept of Moral Courage isn't a mere abstraction but a vital, lived virtue that demands the moral fortitude to act justly and make decisions that align with the highest ethical standards. This brand of courage is deeply rooted in the Stoic commitment to virtue, requiring an individual to uphold their integrity even when confronted with the most daunting moral challenges.

It's about steadfastly placing ethics and principled action at the forefront, far outweighing any personal inclinations toward revenge or retribution. This prioritization of ethical integrity over personal vendettas is what sets moral courage apart from mere bravery or boldness.

Moral courage, as envisioned by the Stoics, is propelled by an unwavering conscience and a profound sense of moral duty. It's this inner compass that guides individuals to choose the path of righteousness, even when such choices come at a significant personal cost. The true test of moral courage arises not in moments of clear-cut decision-making but in the nuanced complexities of real-world situations, where the right course of action is obscured by conflicting interests, societal pressures, or personal desires for success—where you know, according to your own values, what that "right action" is, but it's risky or too scary, and you know the "wrong action" can get you the win. It's not always hard, the right path, but sometimes it is. It is precisely in such challenging times that the essence of moral courage becomes most vital, *not* in the moments that demand less of us. Plato defines *courage* as "the state of the soul which is unmoved by fear; . . . self-restraint in the soul about what is fearful and terrible; being intrepid in the face of death; the state which stands on guard over correct thinking in dangerous situations; . . . force of fortitude in respect of virtue; [and] calm in the soul about what correct thinking takes to be frightening or encouraging things." Or as Nelson Mandela said, "I learned that courage was not the absence of fear, but the triumph over it. The brave man is not he who does not feel afraid, but he who conquers that fear."

In practicing moral courage, we engage in a deliberate process of self-examination and reflection, constantly questioning not just the actions we must take but the motivations behind them. It's a courage that demands honesty with ourselves, the courage to confront our own flaws and biases, and the resilience to amend them in pursuit of a more virtuous life. This introspective journey is critical to developing the kind of moral courage that can withstand the tests of external circumstances, societal pressures, and internal conflicts.

Significantly, however, Stoic Moral Courage *doesn't require* moral perfection, because that wouldn't be possible for any human.

In my own half century of life, even despite all of the profound joy I've experienced, there have also been days when I've awakened to a world so heavy that pulling aside the covers to rise in the morning seemed nearly impossible. In a very physical way, it felt as though there was a sinking ship on my head and ensnarled around my body, and by moving my body, I also had to move that whole ship with me. I carried its unbalanced hull as I lifted myself out of bed, maneuvered around its stern and bow as I pulled up my socks, bore the musty smell of its interior, and fought with my eyes and mind to gain clarity as I tried to see the world through portholes. We can call this depression, anxiety, or just the weight of trauma being borne not just on my shoulders but on every inch of my insides. I suppose we could also just call it a very bad day. For days like those, though they were few and far between, simply to get dressed and offer a kind smile to my children as they pitter-pattered down the stairs for breakfast, took moral courage.

Maybe you've never had that experience. Or maybe you've had a lot more ships on and around you in the mornings than I have. Either way, you've most likely known what it is to look back at a relatively routine day and wonder how you got through it.

In other words, there are times when the bleakness of the world is so profound that for some of us, for many of us, "*even to live,* is an act of courage" (Seneca). This statement, simple yet powerful, encapsulates a fundamental Stoic principle and an existential truth: that there is intrinsic value and strength in the act of living, especially amid life's many adversities. To wake up in the morning and choose to *live* can be, in and of itself, the act of courage you need for that day as you build up your resilience, work on controlling your judgments and thoughts, release the need to control the external, embrace discomfort, habituate to fears, and thank Death for not being at your door that day. Thus, living becomes and can *always* be more than a passive state of existence.

The Stoic philosophers of ancient Greece and Rome placed significant emphasis on moral courage. They viewed it not as an isolated virtue but as an integral component of a virtuous life, deeply intertwined with wisdom and self-discipline. For Stoics like Seneca and Marcus Aurelius, true courage was less about enduring physical hardships and more about maintaining moral integrity in the face of life's trials. It's the foundation of strong character, resistance to being swayed by unjust or harmful temptations, and the ultimate cultivation of managing fear and desire without allowing our judgment to be compromised. It enhances our inner peace and stability and, most essentially to the purpose of this book, allows us to positively influence those around us.

And as Epictetus reminds us, we should carefully consider the cost at which we compromise our integrity. He implores, "Consider at what price you sell your integrity; but please, for God's sake, don't sell it cheap." This underscores the value of maintaining moral principles and cautions against undervaluing one's ethical standards. Or, as my favorite investor, Warren Buffett, said, "Somebody once said that in looking for people to hire, you look for three qualities: integrity, intelligence, and energy. And if you don't have the first, the other two will kill you."[2] Because without the first, that very same intelligence and energy can destroy any enterprise, whether it be a company or a family. The quote reflects Buffett's broader business philosophy, which focuses not only on financial metrics but also on the character of the people running the companies he invests in. He understands that long-term success is built on a foundation of ethical behavior and responsible decision-making. This perspective has been a key part of his investment strategy and advice on leadership and hiring practices.

Grand acts of heroism and death-defying stunts are neither required nor sufficient for a life of power and purpose. Building resilience in the face of adversity with moral courage and mindful empathy is challenging in this complex world, as the final chapter of this book discusses further. Moral courage, however, is what ties the Stoic tools and methods that we've described together, permitting for profound reflection of and growth in our human spirit. The Stoic concept of moral courage remains profoundly relevant in the modern world. In a society often characterized by ethical ambiguity and moral relativism, the Stoic call to uphold virtue and integrity is both challenging and necessary. Whether it's in confronting social injustices, making ethical decisions in the workplace, or maintaining personal integrity in everyday life, the Stoic virtue of moral courage continues to offer guidance.

This is even more difficult in today's world in some ways that Plato could not have even imagined. Amid the fast-paced currents of social media, Jameela Jamil's story stands as a testament to moral courage in resisting cancel culture. An actress known for her activism and her award-winning role in the hit TV show *The Good Place*, Jamil faced backlash for using crass language and allegedly overinflating her health issues. Instead of retreating, she engaged in dialogue, distinguishing between being "called out" and truly "canceled," noting that real cancellation involves losing jobs and platforms. "That mostly happens to civilians, not celebrities," Jameela said to the *Harvard Gazette*'s Jill Radsken in September 2020. "I got canceled 45 times in February. All of my shows got recommissioned, I landed a huge campaign, and my book deal remains. I'm [expletive] fine."[3] As Jamil later said on a 2024 episode of the BBC's *Woman's Hour*, rather than allowing herself to be pressured into silence, her online behavior has changed to show more "grace and empathy" than she had in the past.

By choosing engagement over avoidance, Jameela promoted a more nuanced and compassionate approach to public discourse, showing that constructive engagement and resilience can turn criticism into growth opportunities.

Social media has redefined how we communicate and perceive the world. While it offers unparalleled opportunities for connection and awareness, it also presents significant challenges to moral courage. Platforms can amplify herd mentality, where popular opinion often drowns out minority voices. The fear of criticism or online harassment can discourage individuals from expressing their true beliefs or standing against the tide. Practicing moral courage in this digital age involves being true to one's convictions and expressing them respectfully, even when they go against the popular narrative. It also means critically evaluating the information one consumes and shares, resisting the temptation to engage in or endorse cancel culture, and nurturing a digital environment conducive to healthy, open dialogue.

True power lies not in silencing criticism but in our capacity to engage with it constructively, fostering a culture of empathy, understanding, and, ultimately, resilience against the divisive tendencies of our times.

Such enduring courage is essential not only to live a just life, but also for our society to advance. Barry Marshall's story is a good example of this resilience within the scientific community. After earning his medical degree in 1974, Marshall started working at Royal Perth Hospital, where he met pathologist Robin Warren. They proposed that it wasn't stress but actually the bacteria *Helicobacter pylori* that caused peptic ulcers and stomach cancer. Barry was ridiculed by the scientific community, which was steadfast in its belief that bacteria couldn't survive in the stomach's acidic environment and therefore couldn't possibly cause ulcers or cancer. Despite this, Barry remained committed. In 1984, frustrated by his inability to convince other doctors of his hypothesis without solid experimental evidence, he took a bold step: he drank a petri dish of *H. pylori* bacteria, actually *trying* and *hoping* to give himself an ulcer.

Barry explained to *Nature* in October 2014, "I was becoming increasingly frustrated because I was successfully treating stomach-ulcer patients with antibiotics but couldn't convince other doctors to use this approach without solid experimental evidence . . . Without data proving that I could reproduce an ulcer by infecting an animal with *H. pylori*, a human experiment was the only option."[4] The human being experimented on, of course, was himself. Expecting to develop an ulcer over a few years, he was surprised when symptoms appeared within days. A report of his subsequent illness and recovery, published in 1985, confirmed his hypothesis, proving that a microorganism, not stress, causes most peptic ulcers.

The groundbreaking work of Barry (and his co-researcher, Robin Warren) not only earned them the 2005 Nobel Prize in Physiology or Medicine but also revolutionized the treatment of peptic ulcers, helping millions of patients worldwide. This example highlights the importance of challenging established norms and the power of moral courage in advancing scientific knowledge.

Think back to times in your own life when you or others you know have embodied the Stoic virtues of wisdom and courage, demonstrating that even in the face of widespread condemnation, it's possible to respond with integrity and a commitment to higher principles. Maybe things didn't end as well some of those times as they did for Jameela Jamil and Barry Marshall, but the real takeaway isn't the specific result of a particular act of moral courage. Rather, it's the importance of living courageously regardless of the result. Life inevitably brings both victories and defeats. As Rudyard Kipling wisely puts it:

> If you can dream—and not make dreams your master;
> If you can think—and not make thoughts your aim;
> If you can meet with Triumph and Disaster
> And treat those two impostors just the same;[5]

Then you'll discover your true self. Our identity remains intact and separate from the events, whether good or bad, that happen to us. Ultimately, it's our response to these events that defines us.

In today's digital landscape, these principles are more important than ever. The online world tends to segregate people into ideological echo chambers, reinforcing existing beliefs and creating an environment where opposing views are seldom heard or considered. This polarization can hinder the development of a well-rounded perspective essential for moral courage. To cultivate this virtue in such an environment, we must actively seek dissenting viewpoints, engage in open and respectful conversations with those who disagree, and resist the urge to retreat into comfortable but limited worldviews.

Moral courage here *also* involves the willingness to challenge our own beliefs, to listen and learn from others, and to foster a culture of understanding amid diversity. This is particularly challenging in this time of rapid information overload. Back in the early 1990s, shortly after I'd moved to Canada and as a member of the Iranian expat community, I developed a deep admiration for an Iranian British journalist—the remarkable Christiane Amanpour. She was chief international correspondent for CNN at the time. I remember following her career with whatever broken English I had as she was on the ground in Sarajevo during one of the most violent and complex times in European history. The Bosnian War raged on, reminding me of my own past, and I watched on TV as Amanpour inserted herself at the heart of the conflict, determined to uncover the truth amid the chaos.

Sarajevo, once a city known for its cultural diversity and harmony, was a war zone in the '90s. The sounds of gunfire and explosions echoed through the streets, and the sight of destroyed buildings and fleeing civilians was a daily reality. Amid breaking news and fast media updates, Amanpour felt the responsibility to report the truth in an era of information overload. While colleagues often rushed to publish first, sometimes sacrificing accuracy, Amanpour was determined to navigate with moral courage, which included a commitment to disciplined journalism and a rigorous fact-checking process. Her reporting from the besieged city wasn't just about capturing the violence on camera but about telling the stories of those who were suffering. To do this, Amanpour had to navigate a labyrinth of misinformation and propaganda. The conflicting narratives from various factions made it a daunting task to separate fact from fiction.

This was decades ago, long before social media was a reality. But even then, "first to publish" was the goal for most journalists, and misleading headlines prevailed.

Not for Amanpour. In the midst of the siege, Amanpour was often seen speaking with residents, aid workers, and soldiers, meticulously cross-referencing their accounts. She would spend hours verifying details from multiple sources, ensuring that her reports were accurate. This was not without risk; moving through the city was dangerous, with snipers and shelling a constant threat. Her commitment to truth-telling exposed her to significant physical danger, as journalists were often targeted in such volatile environments.

The international community was initially skeptical of the scale of the atrocity, and her reporting drew ire from those who preferred their actions remain hidden, but Amanpour's relentless pursuit of the truth helped bring global attention to the genocide. She faced accusations of bias and threats to her safety, yet she remained steadfast in her mission.

Looking back at Amanpour's resistance to rapid information overload in an era where quick news bites often overshadow comprehensive reporting, I see that her high standard for journalists *extends* to those who consume the news—like all of us. Moral courage doesn't require physical danger and war correspondence. We can embody it every day as we aim to inform ourselves, read the news, scroll social media, and consume media. We do it every time we choose what story to share on our platforms, what tales to tell in the office breakroom, and how we talk about our own community and friendships. Each of us can make sure to take the time necessary to form a well-considered, ethical response to the events around us. This, too, is Stoic Moral Courage.

EXERCISES

Building on the foundation of modern challenges and the stories of those who exemplify moral courage, we now turn to practical application. The following section introduces practical exercises and daily practices designed to cultivate moral courage in our lives. Rooted in both ancient wisdom and contemporary psychology, these exercises include negative visualization, ethical-dilemma discussion, volunteering, journaling, mindfulness meditation, and practicing gratitude. Each exercise helps us navigate moral decisions, manage emotions, and embody moral courage in meaningful ways. Let's explore these practices to integrate them into our routines and foster moral clarity and courage.

Exercise: Negative Visualization (Premeditatio Malorum) and Ethical-Dilemma Discussion

Purpose: To prepare you for facing difficult situations; to enhance your ability to navigate complex moral decisions.

Exercise: Imagine a scenario where you need to make a tough moral choice. Visualize the potential challenges and consequences, and think about how you would respond. Engage in discussions about the ethical dilemmas with friends, family, or colleagues. Consider dilemmas from news stories, books, or movies. Discussing these situations can sharpen your moral reasoning and decision-making skills.

(Also try Role-Playing Different Perspectives: Choose a current ethical dilemma or moral issue. Write or discuss how people with different perspectives might view the issue.)

This Stoic exercise helps to reduce fear and anxiety about adverse outcomes. It can also broaden your understanding and tolerance of diverse moral viewpoints.

Exercise: Volunteering and Community Service

Purpose: To put your moral values into action.

Exercise: Regularly engage in volunteer work or community service. This hands-on approach allows you to confront real-world moral challenges and practice courage in a supportive environment.

Exercise: Daily Journaling for Self-Reflection

Purpose: To encourage introspection and clarity in your values and actions.

Exercise: Each day, write about a moral decision you faced and how you handled it. Reflect on what influenced your decision, how you felt, and what you might do differently in the future.

Exercise: Mindfulness Meditation for Emotional Regulation

Purpose: To help you manage your emotions and reactions, which is essential for moral courage.

Exercise: Spend 10 to 15 minutes each day in mindfulness meditation, focusing on your breath and observing your thoughts and feelings without judgment. This practice can increase your ability to remain calm and composed during challenging moral situations.

Exercise: Gratitude Practice

Purpose: To foster a positive and empathetic outlook.

Exercise: At the end of each day, write down three things you're grateful for. This practice can help maintain a positive mindset, which is crucial for facing moral challenges with a clear and compassionate perspective.

Integrating Memento Mori and Moral Courage with Strategic Empathy

Integrating the advanced Stoic tools of Chapter 8—Memento Mori and Moral Courage—with strategic empathy provides a profound framework for deepening our empathetic engagements and enhancing our personal integrity and influence. This integration not only enriches our strategic empathy abilities but also fortifies our capacity for meaningful connections and ethical leadership in the face of life's inevitable challenges.

Think back to our discussions of strategic empathy.

Let's begin first by fully integrating Memento Mori and the practice of deliberate empathy, observing how they intertwine in ways that enhance personal growth and power in terms of emotional intelligence and interpersonal relationships. Deliberate empathy goes beyond mere understanding of another person's feelings; it involves a thoughtful approach to connecting with others on a deeper emotional level. When we engage with others through the lens of empathy, a profound camaraderie with our shared mortality colors our interactions.

Memento Mori encourages an awareness of the inevitability of death, which can foster a deeper understanding of the transient nature of life. This awareness can lead to a greater capacity for cognitive empathy—the ability to understand and consider the perspectives and feelings of others. Recognizing the brevity of life can make us more inclined to understand and appreciate the experiences and challenges of others, as we are all sharing this common, finite journey.

The mutual recognition of life's transience fosters more genuine, compassionate, and considerate interactions. In the face of life's inevitable end, trivial conflicts lose their grip, a space is created for more meaningful and authentic connections, and creative solutions arise. We become more attuned to the needs, feelings, and perspectives of others, recognizing that, like us, they too are navigating the complexities of a finite existence. And with that attunement, we see ethical paths to power and control previously blurred by the fog of the moment's minutiae.

Engaging with others from a place of mutual mortality also brings to light the shared journey of humanity. Everyone faces the unknown, contends with fears, and harbors dreams. In this shared journey, everyone deserves compassion and empathy. Tactical empathy, fueled by the awareness of Memento Mori, encourages us to approach each interaction with a sense of shared vulnerability and common destiny.

The blend of Memento Mori and strategic use of empathy thus becomes a profound approach to life. It's not just about acknowledging our mortality but also about using that knowledge to enrich our interactions and relationships. We begin to see others not just as characters in our story, but as fellow travelers in life's journey, each with their own tales, struggles, and aspirations. This perspective shift is transformative, both for ourselves and for those we interact with, as it cultivates a legacy of understanding, compassion, and meaningful connections.

Valuing Relationships and Empathetic Connection

Reflecting on mortality often leads to a reevaluation of what is truly important in life. For many, relationships with others take on heightened significance. This shift in priorities can drive a person to engage more deeply in empathetic processes, striving to understand and connect with others on a meaningful level. This not only enriches personal attachments but also enhances one's ability to navigate social and professional interactions effectively.

Coping with Hardships and Offering Support

The contemplation of mortality can instill a sense of resilience and a more nuanced grasp of life's challenges. When one develops the ability to empathize cognitively with others, this can lead to being a more effective supporter and confidant during others' hardships. By understanding that life is fragile and often challenging, one might be better equipped to offer genuine support, which can be empowering for both the giver and receiver of empathy.

Ethical Decision-Making and Leadership

The realization that life is finite and the ability to understand others' viewpoints can contribute to more ethical and considerate decision-making. In leadership positions, this combination of self-awareness and empathy can lead to more humane and responsible choices, garnering respect and trust, which are essential components of influential and effective leadership.

Emotional Intelligence and Personal Growth

Regular contemplation of one's mortality, coupled with the practice of cognitive empathy, can lead to increased emotional intelligence. Recognizing the temporality of life can make one more attuned to the emotions and needs of others, fostering a more empathetic and emotionally aware approach to interactions. This heightened emotional intelligence is a form of power that can enhance personal and professional relationships.

More on Moral Courage and Strategic Empathy

While moral courage empowers us to stand firm in our ethical convictions, strategic empathy equips us with the understanding and insight necessary to navigate the complex terrain of human emotions and relationships. It's at the confluence of these virtues that we find the true strength of Stoic philosophy for the modern world.

Moral courage isn't merely about bravery in the face of physical danger but encompasses the resilience and fortitude required to uphold one's principles despite external pressures and temptations. It calls for action that's aligned with virtue, even when such actions might lead to personal disadvantage or societal disapproval. However, to effectively enact moral courage, one must first understand the perspectives, emotions, and motivations of others. This is where strategic empathy comes into play.

Strategic empathy goes beyond mere emotional contagion or the capacity to feel what another person is feeling. It's a deliberate and thoughtful approach to engaging with others, whereby one seeks to understand their viewpoints, emotions, and underlying motivations. This form of empathy is strategic in that it informs how we can best communicate and act in ways that are both effective and ethically sound. By understanding others, we can tailor our actions and words in a manner that respects their humanity while still standing firm in our moral convictions.

The synergy between moral courage and strategic empathy enables us to navigate complex social dynamics with grace and integrity. For instance, when faced with a situation that demands speaking out against injustice, strategic empathy allows us to consider the most effective way to convey our message so that it resonates with our audience. Simultaneously, moral courage gives us the strength to voice our convictions, even in the face of potential backlash.

Moreover, strategic empathy enhances moral courage by reminding us that our actions and decisions impact others. It fosters a sense of connectedness and shared humanity, which in turn reinforces our commitment to act courageously in defense of virtue and the common good. This interconnectedness ensures that our practice of Stoicism isn't a solitary endeavor but a communal one, where the cultivation of personal virtues contributes to the well-being of society as a whole.

In essence, moral courage and strategic empathy aren't isolated virtues but complementary forces that, when combined, enable us to live more fully in accordance with Stoic principles. They allow us to engage with the world in a way that's both courageous and compassionate, asserting our values while understanding and respecting the values of others. This dynamic interplay is what equips us to lead lives of purpose, balance, and profound impact, embodying the Stoic ideal of living in harmony with both our inner selves and the world around us.

By fostering both moral courage and strategic empathy, we build bridges between our Inner Citadel and the external world, ensuring that our actions aren't only principled but also effective and compassionate. This holistic approach to Stoicism offers a powerful framework for navigating the challenges of modern life, empowering us to make a meaningful difference in our own lives and the lives of others.

The integration of Memento Mori and Moral Courage with strategic empathy offers a powerful approach to living and leading with integrity, compassion, and purpose. By embracing the finite nature of our existence, we are inspired to engage more deeply and meaningfully with others, enriching our empathetic connections with a sense of urgency and significance. Simultaneously, the cultivation of Moral Courage ensures that our empathetic engagements are guided by a strong ethical compass, empowering us to take bold actions that reflect our deepest values and convictions. Together, these Stoic tools enhance our strategic empathy, enabling us to navigate the complexities of human relationships with wisdom, compassion, and moral fortitude. This holistic approach not only strengthens our personal and professional synergies but also fosters a legacy of positive impact and ethical leadership, making a lasting difference in the lives of those we touch.

As we transition from Chapter 8's deep dive into the practices of Memento Mori and Moral Courage, we stand at the precipice of the Inner Citadel. This book's final chapter, Chapter 9, builds on the foundational understanding we've cultivated, guiding us through the ethical implications of our newfound Stoic Empathy skills and meeting the complexities of modern life head-on.

Chapter 8 Takeaways

In this chapter, we explored two advanced Stoic tools:

- *Memento Mori (death acceptance):* Emphasizing life's impermanence encourages us to live fully in the present. It enhances empathic interactions by reminding us of the value and fleeting nature of each human connection.
- *Moral Courage:* This tool advocates for living ethically and courageously, standing firm in our principles. In empathic interactions, it guides us to ensure that our engagements aren't only empathetic but also align with ethical and moral standards.

* * *

In the first eight chapters of this book, we've dissected empathy and Stoicism as standalone philosophies while also harmonizing them into a holistic framework aimed at adeptly navigating human intricacies with moral clarity and tactical acumen. As we move forward to conclude the book, let's carry with us the insights and skills honed through this exploration, applying them with power and control, but also clarity and integrity, the subject matter of Chapter 9, because no discussion of pathways to influence is complete without also evaluating the ethical dimensions of wielding such influence. In doing so, we'll explore the fascinating work of expanding Stoic Empathy from an individual empowerment context to applying it on the broader ethical landscape of societal power and influence, focusing on how this method of gaining power is compatible with staying true to our own values. This evolution underscores the transformative potential of Stoic Empathy, not just as a philosophy for personal growth but as a cornerstone for ethical leadership and meaningful social change. The principles we've delved into serve as a beacon, guiding us through the complexities of human interaction with grace and moral clarity.

CHAPTER 9

ETHICS, FAIRNESS, AND THE BIG WHY

With great power comes great responsibility.

— THE BIBLE, VOLTAIRE, THE HADITH, AND SPIDER-MAN'S UNCLE BEN, AMONG OTHERS

When I was 23 years old, I met the Dalai Lama.

This was not at a book reading or among many adoring fans at a community meditation, but in a private room in his sanctuary in Dharamshala. I spoke with him, shook his hand. He blessed my scarf, signed my book, and agreed to answer some questions. I mean—I was a big nobody, and here I was, talking with one of the most influential humans who perhaps has ever lived; certainly, a universally notable sage. With me were about 15 other law students and a handful of professors. We were in India in the summer following my first year of law school to study comparative constitutional law and international human-rights law. Most of the time, we were poring through various international declarations and treaties while also analyzing the constitutions of the United States, India, and South Africa. But on this day, over the echo of meditation chants, I stood with a man revered by millions the world over. The mist of cinnamon and cardamom incense favored by Tibetan nuns transposed me all the way back to my mother's kitchen: a childhood scarred by war, oppression, and lost family . . . a new world of promise.

We had landed earlier that same day. When I say "landed," I mean that the military helicopter we had chartered to fly us through the foothills of the Himalayas so we could get from Shimla to Dharamshala on time for this once-in-a-lifetime opportunity touched down in the small town in North India that's the seat of the Tibetan government in exile. As the chopper set down, a group of children surrounded us, asking for rupees and motioning toward their empty bellies and dry mouths. At this point in my life, I hadn't yet traveled the world, but I had lived in the Middle East, Canada, and the U.S. I'd seen the ocean once—when my first husband took me to Jamaica for our honeymoon. I didn't know anyone important or famous or rich. I had no real ties to power in America, Canada, Iran, India, or anywhere. I don't think I've ever been as broke as I was on that day, with a ledger of law school loans and credit card debts now a little longer because I'd charged my share of that chopper ride to an accommodating, albeit scratched-up Visa card. I was meeting the Dalai Lama because one of the professors in my group knew his head of security, who had arranged for the meeting before the lama flew to the United States to appear on *Larry King Live*—serendipity at its finest, for me. Not for the sea of hungry kids around me. I gave one of them whatever change I had as the others grabbed my sleeves to redirect me to them.

I've never subscribed to a religious doctrine. I wouldn't even say I'm spiritual. Yet, when standing next to the lama, I could sense him exuding an energetic presence that overwhelmed me: a fortress of strength and empathic resilience that the outside world hasn't been able to crumble. Though that wasn't very surprising—you'd expect a global leader of any kind to be energetic, charismatic, and dynamic, a true politician. They'd have to be, to lead and guide an entire people. What did surprise me was, first, how warm he was toward everyone, and second, how sharp his eyes looked, as if they could see 360 degrees around him and somehow beyond. I saw that day what the Inner Citadel *really* looks like. It wasn't the image of a stoney castle I'd had in mind before. The strength was there, certainly. You could sense it. The man could not be tackled. But he was of flesh and beamed vitality. His hands were soft. At 62 years old, his skin was unwrinkled (and even today, he still looks a good 25 years younger than his age). His words, though likely spoken many times before, didn't seem rehearsed.

My mind buzzed with a million questions, but I knew that our time with him was less than an hour, that everyone else wanted to ask questions too, and that he had already imparted much wisdom through his books and sermons. Most of my student colleagues asked him about anger and gratitude, about meditation and suffering, about hatred and kindness. So, I asked something they didn't; I asked him about international diplomacy and how he's able to productively engage with other world leaders given his situation. After all, *his* government convenes in exile in India without an army to protect them or official trade capabilities, while the Chinese government, along with its military and economy, control Tibet geographically. Tibetans are severely restricted in practicing Buddhism, facing restrictions of religious sites and gatherings. Monks and nuns inside Tibet are subject to political indoctrination, "reeducation centers," prison, and even torture because of their religion. The Dalai Lama's external governmental functions haven't been able to "Free Tibet" despite what the T-shirts say.

"In other words," I asked, "is your pacifism succeeding?"

I meant no disrespect when I asked him my question. It's just that while I stood next to a sacred man, I also was speaking with a political leader. The blend of spiritual and political, the weight and gifts of both, weighed him down and lifted him up at the same time. I wanted to see what passivity meant to this renowned Buddhist, for certainly it didn't mean to do nothing and just accept fate.

Thankfully, he wasn't offended. I'll never forget his tone and the sparkle of tenacity with wings of spirituality in his eyes. While his exact words escape me, I remember that he told me the journey was not finished; nor had it just begun . . . that we were participating in the cycle of universe creation, destruction, and re-creation amid infinite time. He discussed the significance of every moment, and that seeking traditional corporeal notions of freedom and control aren't as powerful as the authentic freedom and meaningful autonomy always within our grasp.

On that day, I didn't know that I understood what he meant. Not really. It's only now, decades later, that it's revealing itself to me.

Empathy isn't weakness.

Acceptance isn't passive.

The Inner Citadel isn't best achieved through defensive armies and tall, unshatterable walls—not if you want to be fulfilled in your life and have meaningful relationships.

Cognitive reframing can control the very pace of time as we experience it.

The ability to listen, inquire, mirror, articulate, and understand others—this is power.

No, we cannot control everything simply by willing it, but neither are we ever entirely helpless.

We can rise to tolerate the uncomfortable.

By accepting the end, we can welcome life, and do it all with integrity.

Stoic Empathy, when we apply it with intentionality and purpose, can allow us to navigate the intricate dance of geopolitical complexities with compassion and strategic depth, helping us find meaningful singularity within a vast infinity.

The Dalai Lama's approach mirrors the core thesis of this book: that true power and meaningful influence are born from an unwavering commitment to ethical principles deeply rooted in empathy and fortified by resilience. In other words, the power we gain with Stoic Empathy is far more likely to align with our moral virtues than power without it. First, with strategic empathy, we not only understand the perspectives and emotions of others, but also the power we hold over them and how our actions affect them. This awareness is crucial for making ethical decisions that consider the impact on those around us. Stoicism, on the other hand, teaches us to focus on our internal responses and what we can control, enhancing our ability to make reasoned decisions by tempering our impulsive reactions. This enables us to consider ethical implications more thoroughly, fostering conscientious behavior toward others.

With Stoic Empathy we can isolate those moments immediately following or preceding the stimuli of external life—the moments before anticipation or response, the time within which our power lies. And then, incredibly, Stoic Empathy tells us how to use that power with wisdom and compassion. The overwhelming truth is that so much of life's beauty lies in those very split seconds. It certainly has for me.

That tickling stillness before my husband's lips touched mine for the very first time. The eerie silence that followed the explosive thuds of missile attacks coming into Tehran. The anticipatory hush in a concert hall just before the first note is played. The warm, comforting aroma of turmeric and cinnamon swirling through my mother's kitchen in the midafternoon. The pitter-patter sound of my children's feet rousing me from deep sleep before I cognitively recognize the cuddles I'm about to get. The fraction of a second when I realize I've made a huge mistake and my heart sinks before the consequences start to unfold. The joyful laughter as my friends and I played soccer within the enclosed walls of our apartment building's courtyard in brief periods of calm amid the chaos of war. The expectant pause in a conversation when I know my best friend is about to share important news. The painful release of awareness before my mother would turn off the radio, stopping the news of yet more conflict. The fleeting moment of stillness when I reach the top of a hike, just before I view the landscape. The hushed, fearful crack of time spent piling with my sisters and parents under our bedroom doorframes during unexpected night raids. The quiet rustle of pages vibrating through the kitchen before my 13-year-old becomes fully immersed in her newest fantasy book. The suspended time when my paintbrush hovers over a canvas, just before it makes its first stroke. The peaceful midafternoon, watching the sunset from a Tehran rooftop as pans of sour fruit dry into snacks. The spark of reflection in my youngest child's eyes just before he breaks into a belly laugh. The instant of disbelieving stillness when I've received life-altering news.

With Stoic Empathy, you can extend that moment, the one between stimulus and response, the one where you exercise your free will—that portion between environment and response that is purely you—while also advancing your ability to cognitively, justly, and empathically use reason in that exertion. Your life will emulate a pro athlete's career progression; a pivotal shift where the game seems to slow down for you, elevating your performance to a level where you can appear to possess an almost supernatural grasp of the sport of life. Like the Tom Brady of power dynamics, Stoic Empathy imparts a profound discernment of yourself and those around you, granting you the extraordinary ability to slow the game of life to your advantage. In this state, reminiscent of Neo's bullet-time sequences in *The Matrix*, the rapid pace of existence momentarily eases, affording you a vast realm of contemplation and choice. Within this suspended reality, you find yourself endowed with the capacity to deliberate your responses with the precision of a seasoned athlete, carefully considering each move with wisdom and compassion. As the chaos of the world seems to decelerate, we gain clarity to transcend immediate impulses and align our actions with our deepest values and ethical principles.

In this heightened awareness, it becomes easier to acknowledge the profound influence we hold over our interactions and the well-being of others and thus navigate life's complexities with the resilience of a champion and the integrity of a true sportsman. Moreover, as we immerse ourselves in this expanded space, we discover the profound potential for fostering meaningful connections with teammates who seamlessly anticipate each other's moves on the field. With each deliberate choice made from a place of empathic understanding and stoic resolve, we not only enrich our own lives but also contribute to the collective experience of human existence, fostering a more compassionate and ethically grounded society.

To illustrate the impact of Stoic Empathy on our moral resolve, I have selected 10 ethical pillars to support our life today. These pillars were chosen for their universal relevance, transcending cultural boundaries to highlight fundamental principles of a morally guided life. Let's review how Stoic Empathy fosters each of these 10 essential pillars:

Ten Pillars of Ethical Living

1. Truth without Cruelty

In power dynamics, negotiations, leadership scenarios, and interpersonal relationships, integrity is rooted in honesty, not only in conveying accurate information but also in ensuring our messages don't obscure the truth deliberately or entail unnecessary cruelty. One distinguished researcher in this area, Dr. Emma Levine, a behavioral scientist at the University of Chicago, conducted a stream of studies investigating the tension between honesty and benevolence. Her work echoes that of others demonstrating that the so-called inherent conflict between honesty and kindness is far exaggerated, and that it is very possible to be both truthful and benevolent. This is not to say that we should give false hope or avoid difficult conversations to be nice. Rather, that we can be honest *and* employ strategies designed to make sure that honesty leads to long-term positive change for both parties involved and/or the parties' relationship. As Dr. Levine says, "rather than attempting to resolve the honesty-benevolence dilemma via communication strategies that focus narrowly on the short-term conflict between honesty and emotional harm, we recommend that communicators instead invoke communication strategies that integrate and maximize both honesty and benevolence to ensure that difficult conversations lead to long-term welfare improvements for targets."[1] We can do this by making benevolent intentions clear, providing resources or solutions, and utilizing Stoic Empathy. Stoic Empathy plays a pivotal role in upholding this ethical guideline by cultivating:

- Self-awareness and emotional regulation, enabling us to communicate with clarity and composure, avoiding the temptation to resort to cruelty.
- Active Listening to understand the perspectives and concerns of others in power dynamics, negotiations, and leadership scenarios; and to tailor our communication with constructive intent.
- Dichotomy of Control to focus on being truthful and transparent in our communication, regardless of how others may react or perceive it.
- Discomfort Embracing to use Silence more strategically and frequently, allowing the other side to reveal more information; and permitting moments of silence so we may reflect on the impact of our words and actions in interpersonal relationships. Dr. Levine's

work in the psychology lab has actually shown that the strategic empathy tool of silence, or as she puts it, "no words at all," can be an excellent way to be benevolent but honest.

- Mirroring and Repeating and Habituation to ensure that our messages are conveyed clearly and respectfully and that we develop the habit of speaking truthfully without causing harm, even in challenging or confrontational situations.
- Probing Questions and Affect Labeling to deepen our understanding of the motivations behind our communication and consider the potential impact on others, as well as recognize and manage our own and others' emotions, especially when faced with difficult conversations where honesty is crucial.
- Moral Courage to speak truthfully even when it may be challenging or unpopular, standing firm in our commitment to integrity and respect for others' dignity.

Thus, Stoic Empathy allows us to foster a culture of openness, kindness, and integrity that respects each person's dignity.

2. Resisting Group Pressure

Group dynamics can lead to conformity, diluting individual moral responsibility. Ethical integrity sometimes requires resisting the tide of popular opinion or group consensus, especially when it conflicts with core moral principles. But this is not always an easy task; as Friedrich Nietzsche said, "The individual has always had to struggle to keep from being overwhelmed by the tribe." Stoic Empathy fosters our courage to stand alone by allowing us to:

- Engage in self-awareness and emotional regulation using Stoic practices such as mindfulness, contemplation of values, meditation, and cognitive reframing so we can better recognize when group dynamics are influencing our actions rather than having our own moral principles empower us to make autonomous decisions aligned with our values amid group pressure. By cultivating emotional resilience, we can maintain composure and clarity of thought, allowing us to resist the emotional sway of the group and stay true to our ethical convictions.

- Strategically empathize with the perspectives of others while remaining steadfast in our ethical convictions, fostering the courage to stand alone when necessary for upholding moral principles.
- Utilize tools such as Active Listening and Dichotomy of Control to understand the perspectives of others within the group, maintain a clear understanding of our own moral principles, and focus on our individual responsibility to act in accordance with our values, regardless of group consensus.
- Use Silence and Discomfort Embracing to resist the urge to conform to group pressure prematurely, acknowledging any discomfort that arises from going against the group, and remain steadfast in our commitment to ethical integrity.
- Lean in to Mirroring and Repeating to ensure our concerns and principles are clearly communicated within the group, while Habituating ourselves to expressing our viewpoints confidently, even in the face of opposition or disagreement.
- Use Probing Questions to encourage critical thinking within the group and challenge assumptions that may lead to unethical behavior, while reflecting on Memento Mori as a reminder of the transient nature of social pressures, reinforcing our commitment to moral principles.

- Utilize tools such as Affect Labeling and Moral Courage to manage any emotional discomfort that arises from going against the group and stand firm in our convictions, even in the face of social pressure, and advocate for ethical behavior with integrity and resilience.

In the face of group pressure, maintaining ethical integrity is a challenging yet essential task. By leveraging Stoic Empathy and its practices, we equip ourselves with the tools to stand firm in our convictions, navigate the complexities of group dynamics, and ultimately act in alignment with our core moral principles.

3. Honoring Our Promises

In the early days of the Roman Republic, around 458 B.C.E., Rome faced a grave threat from the Aequi, a neighboring tribe that had laid siege to a Roman army. The situation was dire, and the Senate decided to appoint a dictator, a temporary position granted full authority to deal with emergencies. They chose Lucius Quinctius Cincinnatus, a retired general who had returned to his modest farm to live a quiet life. When the envoys from the Senate arrived to inform Cincinnatus of his appointment, they found him plowing his field. Without hesitation, Cincinnatus left his plow, donned his toga, and set out for Rome to assume his new role.

As dictator, Cincinnatus swiftly organized the Roman forces and led them to a decisive victory over the Aequi. His strategic brilliance and leadership not only saved the besieged Roman army but also secured peace for the Republic. However, Cincinnatus's commitment to his promise did not end with the military victory.

True to his word and exemplifying the Stoic values of duty and humility, Cincinnatus resigned from his dictatorial powers just 15 days after his appointment, once the crisis was resolved. He returned to his farm, resuming his life as a humble farmer. His actions stood in stark contrast to the potential for power to corrupt, demonstrating his dedication to the Roman Republic and his personal integrity.

Cincinnatus's story had a profound impact on Roman history and culture. He became a symbol of civic virtue, selflessness, and the ideal Roman citizen who placed the needs of the Republic above personal ambition. His legacy influenced the values of Roman leadership and continued to be celebrated throughout the history of the Republic and the Empire.

The story of Cincinnatus also had a lasting influence beyond Rome. In the 18th century, George Washington, the first president of the United States, was often compared to (and many say inspired by) Cincinnatus for his similar virtues. Washington's decision to step down from the presidency after two terms was seen as an embodiment of the same commitment to public service and humility. By stepping down, Washington helped set a precedent for the peaceful transition of power, a cornerstone of American democracy. His actions reinforced the principle that leadership is a temporary trust, and that the welfare of the nation should always take precedence over personal power or ambition.

Cincinnatus's honoring of his promises and his dedication to duty exemplify how the actions of a single individual, guided by integrity and a sense of responsibility, can resonate through history and inspire future generations. His story reminds us that true leadership lies not in the pursuit of power but in the commitment to serve and uphold the principles of justice and virtue.

Reliability and trustworthiness are built on our ability to keep our word. This commitment reflects our respect for others and the seriousness with which we approach our obligations. It also speaks to our self-discipline in only making promises we are prepared and able to keep. Unfortunately, it's not always easy, particularly when we're overwhelmed with life's many, multifaceted, and sometimes conflicting commitments. Stoicism and empathy both play crucial roles in upholding the ethic of honoring promises. Stoicism teaches the importance of duty, integrity, and self-control, helping individuals stay true to their commitments even in the face of challenges. Empathy, on the other hand, fosters a deep understanding of others' perspectives and the impact of our actions on them. By combining these philosophies, we can cultivate the moral strength and compassion needed to honor our promises, ensuring that our actions align with our values and contribute positively to the lives of others.

Stoic Empathy fosters this ethic through:

- Self-awareness and emotional regulation, which are essential for appreciating the impact of our commitments on others, managing conflicting obligations effectively, and extending our capacity for self-discipline in fulfilling our obligations.
- Affect Labeling to recognize and manage our emotions when faced with overwhelming commitments. By identifying and labeling feelings of stress or anxiety, we can address them more effectively, allowing us to approach our promises with a clearer and calmer mindset.
- A practice of active listening to understand the expectations and needs of others when making promises, while applying the Dichotomy of Control to increase awareness of what we can and cannot control and make realistic commitments aligned with our values and capacities.
- Probing Questions to clarify expectations and potential obstacles associated with fulfilling promises. Then we gradually habituate ourselves to making only promises that align with our values and capacities, avoiding overcommitment. This ensures that our promises are reliable and achievable. By repeatedly honoring our promises and committing to our responsibilities, we strengthen our capacity for reliability and trustworthiness over time, making it easier for others to trust us even in challenging circumstances.
- A practice of Memento Mori and Moral Courage to remind ourselves of the fleeting nature of time as well as the importance of fulfilling promises promptly

and upholding commitments even in challenging circumstances, demonstrating integrity and reliability.

In combining these Stoic and empathetic principles, we not only honor our promises but also set a powerful example for others, fostering a culture of trust, integrity, and ethical behavior.

4. Respecting Relationships

The Harvard Study of Adult Development, often referred to as the Harvard Grant Study, is one of the longest-running studies on human development. It found that the single biggest predictor of happiness and health is the quality of our relationships. Spanning over 85 years, this study has followed 724 men from adolescence to old age, demonstrating that strong, supportive connections are more crucial to a long and happy life than factors such as wealth, social class, or IQ. The findings indicate that individuals with robust relationships are generally happier, healthier, and live longer than those with weaker social ties. These results underscore the profound impact that meaningful connections have on our overall well-being, emphasizing the importance of social fitness—the ability to build and maintain strong relationships—as a key component of a fulfilling life.[2]

Therefore, it follows that advancing and respecting relationships is a core human ethic. Winning at the cost of damaging trust or goodwill often proves to be a hollow victory. Ethical decision-making weighs immediate gains against the enduring health of personal and professional relationships. Stoic Empathy promotes the ethical principle of respecting connections with others by fostering:

- Attunement to the emotions and needs of those we interact with, using Active Listening to understand the perspectives and emotions of others, and Mirroring and Repeating to validate the emotions and experiences of others and to defuse negative emotions.
- The application of the Dichotomy of Control to focus on aspects of a relationship that we can influence and nurture, rather than worrying about external

factors beyond our control. Recognize the control we have over our own responses, prioritizing our own ethical conduct and intentions while respecting the autonomy and agency of others. All the while, we cultivate Moral Courage to stand up for what is right within the relationship, even if it involves confronting difficult truths or challenging situations.

- Habituation and Memento Mori to value long-term health and delayed gratification within a relationship over short-term gains, to weigh the consequences of our actions on the bonds we share with others, and to remind ourselves of the fleeting nature of life and the importance of cherishing meaningful ties to others while recognizing the ones that don't serve us.
- The employment of Probing Questions to uncover underlying issues and concerns within the relationship, fostering open communication and trust. We practice Silence to create space for thoughtful reflection on the potential impact of our actions on relationships, and we practice Discomfort Embracing by acknowledging any discomfort that may arise from difficult conversations, decisions within the relationship, or even the silence itself.

Fostering and nurturing relationships isn't just about achieving personal happiness; it represents a fundamental ethical principle that emphasizes the importance of trust, respect, and empathy. Stoic Empathy, with its focus on understanding and connecting with others, aligns perfectly with this principle by promoting thoughtful, compassionate, and ethical interactions. Embracing these practices not only enhances personal well-being but also contributes to a more harmonious and interconnected society.

5. Cultural Competence

Understanding cultural differences is crucial in our interconnected world. Cultural competence involves more than just awareness; it's about actively seeking to understand others' perspectives and experiences and letting this understanding inform our actions and decisions. Sometimes this awareness comes easily—for example, when you've lived in or married into a different culture that grounded you in that culture's nuances. But often, particularly when our past interactions with people of a culture are limited, discerning that culture can be a challenge. Stoic Empathy advances cultural competence, for instance, by promoting:

- Deeply appreciating cultural differences through self-awareness and empathic attunement. For instance, we can use Active Listening and Dichotomy of Control to fully understand and appreciate the perspectives and experiences of individuals from different cultures and focus on aspects of cultural cognition that we can influence and actively seek to learn about rather than becoming overwhelmed by factors beyond our control.
- More interactions with diverse cultures and approaching each of them with humility, curiosity, and a genuine desire to bridge cultural divides. In this way, we can Embrace Discomfort with and Habituate ourselves to the uneasiness that can come with interactions with unfamiliar cultural nuances or practices.
- Mirroring and Repeating to peel back the layers of understanding while validating the perspectives and experience of others, fostering connection. This is a particularly powerful tool in communications with those from other cultures or linguistic backgrounds. It allows us to recognize our own cultural biases and limitations while remaining open to learning from others, allowing their cultural perspectives to inform our actions and decisions.

- The use of Probing Questions to inquire without judgment about cultural practices, traditions, and perspectives, fostering genuine curiosity and clarity. In doing so, we can also use Memento Mori to remind ourselves of the shared mortality, humanity, and interconnectedness among individuals from diverse cultural backgrounds.
- Affect Labeling to defuse negative reactions from any misunderstandings and cultural clashes while cultivating Moral Courage to challenge stereotypes, prejudices, and discriminatory practices, promoting fairness, inclusion, and cultural sensitivity.

In our interconnected world, appreciating cultural differences is more than just a business necessity—it's a crucial skill for fostering meaningful connections and collaboration, and maybe even the easiest way to preserve our shared human history. As internationally prominent cellist Yo-Yo Ma said, "In the end we will conserve only what we love. We love only what we understand, and we will understand only what we are taught. We must learn about other cultures in order to understand, in order to love, and in order to preserve our common world heritage."

Cultural competence involves actively seeking to understand others' perspectives and experiences, allowing this understanding to guide our actions and decisions. Stoic Empathy advances cultural competence by promoting self-awareness, empathic attunement, and genuine curiosity about cultural differences.

6. Seeking Counsel

No one has all the answers, and ethical dilemmas can often benefit from diverse perspectives. Seeking advice from trusted mentors, colleagues, or friends can provide new insights, challenge our assumptions, and help us avoid ethical blind spots. It's a recognition that wisdom often comes from collective understanding. Stoic Empathy facilitates asking for help when we need it by encouraging us to:

- Use the Dichotomy of Control to embrace humility and recognize the limitations of our own perspectives and abilities. In this way, we can develop a keener awareness of our emotions and biases, allowing us to approach ethical dilemmas with an open mind and a willingness to consider alternative viewpoints.
- Cultivate Moral Courage by being willing to ask for help, even in the face of pride or discomfort, and Habituate ourselves to view having people around us we can rely on as an asset, not a weakness.
- Foster a spirit of collaboration and collective wisdom, acknowledging that ethical decision-making is enriched by the contributions of others and ultimately strengthens our ability to navigate complex moral dilemmas with integrity and discernment.

Seeking diverse perspectives is a cornerstone of ethical decision-making, as complex dilemmas often require the collective wisdom and varied experiences of others. This practice not only broadens our horizons but also deepens our empathy, enabling us to consider the multifaceted impacts of our decisions. By integrating the principles of Stoic Empathy, we learn to value humility and recognize our own limitations. This mindset fosters an environment where seeking help becomes a strength, enhancing our moral courage and our ability to act with integrity. Additionally, embracing collaboration and collective wisdom ensures that we approach ethical dilemmas with a well-rounded perspective, ultimately leading to more thoughtful and just outcomes. In doing so, we build a robust framework for ethical leadership and even profound innovation grounded in empathy, humility, and the pursuit of shared understanding.

7. Commitment to Continuous Learning

Ethical understanding is not static; it evolves with new experiences and insights. A commitment to ongoing learning about ethical principles, societal changes, and the complex contexts of our actions ensures that our ethical framework remains robust and relevant. Stoic Empathy nurtures continuous learning and has since its founding. Socrates, for example, renowned for his contribution to the foundation of Western philosophy, was a firm believer in continuous learning and self-examination. His approach to philosophy, known as the Socratic method, involved asking probing questions to stimulate critical thinking and illuminate ideas. This method was not about providing answers but about fostering deeper insight through continuous questioning and dialogue. Stoic Empathy can cultivate this ethic of ongoing learning in various ways. For example, it advocates for:

- Fostering curiosity, humility, and adaptability in our approach to ethical understanding. We can utilize tools such as Active Listening to absorb information about ethical principles, societal changes, and contextual factors that influence decision-making, Silence to allow the "other" to teach us something we may not already know, and Mirroring and Repeating key concepts or insights that others share during learning experiences to encourage expansion and reinforce our understanding.
- Having us use the Dichotomy of Control to recognize that ethical principles are dynamic and subject to interpretation and that they require ongoing exploration and reflection for us to deepen our grasp of them. This practice can also shift our learning efforts toward aspects within our control.
- Showing empathy toward *ourselves*, allowing us to acknowledge and address the internal conflicts and pressures that may lead us astray from our values, using tools such as Probing Questions on *ourselves*. This enables us to delve deeper into our own values and motivations, uncovering the underlying reasons behind our actions. By asking ourselves probing questions such as "How does this decision align with my core principles?" we can gain a deeper clarity of

our values and strengthen our resolve to uphold them in all aspects of our lives.

- Encouraging Discomfort Embracing as a natural part of the learning process as we recognize that growth often occurs when we challenge our existing beliefs and assumptions, remaining open to new experiences, insights, and perspectives and thus cultivate a growth mindset that values learning as a means of refining our ethical framework and responding effectively to evolving societal challenges.

Therefore, by integrating the principles of Stoic Empathy, we can consistently evolve and refine our ethical frameworks, ensuring they remain relevant and effective in addressing new challenges. This ongoing commitment to learning fosters a deeper connection to our values, promoting integrity and wisdom in our actions.

8. Transparency in Decision-Making

In 2008, the global financial crisis sent shockwaves through economies worldwide, and Starbucks, a beloved coffee giant, was not immune to the economic downturn. Sales plummeted, stores closed, and the company's stock price nosedived. Recognizing the dire situation, Howard Schultz, the former CEO who had stepped down in 2000, returned to steer the company through its darkest hours. His leadership style, characterized by an unwavering commitment to transparency, empathy, and Stoic principles, would prove pivotal.

From the outset, Schultz understood that restoring trust and morale among Starbucks employees was crucial. Embracing Stoic values of duty and resilience, he initiated a series of open forums and town hall meetings, inviting employees from all levels to participate. These gatherings were candid discussions about the company's financial struggles and the steps needed for recovery. Schultz's transparency, a hallmark of his empathetic leadership, was not about sugarcoating the situation but about fostering a sense of collective responsibility and resilience.

Employees, instead of feeling left in the dark, felt informed and included in the recovery process. This openness helped build trust and maintain morale during tough times. Schultz's willingness to engage directly with employees, listen to their concerns, and incorporate their feedback into the company's strategy reflected the principles of Stoic Empathy. His approach not only motivated the workforce but also reinforced a shared commitment to Starbucks's mission and values.

Beyond communication, Schultz implemented strategic initiatives to revitalize Starbucks. He focused on enhancing the customer experience, revamping food offerings, and investing in store renovations. One notable move was the decision to close all U.S. Starbucks stores for a few hours to retrain baristas in the art of making espresso, emphasizing quality and signaling dedication to the best coffee experience.[3]

Schultz's transparent approach and decisive actions ultimately paid off. By 2010, Starbucks had weathered the financial storm and emerged stronger. The company's stock price rebounded and sales began to climb. Schultz's leadership during this period solidified his reputation as one of the most effective and inspirational leaders in the business world.

Being open about how we make decisions fosters an environment of trust and accountability. It involves explaining the rationale behind decisions, especially those that affect others, and being willing to discuss and defend these choices. Stoic Empathy promotes this transparency by encouraging us to:

- Utilize strategic empathy to consider the feelings of those around us without empathy collapse to rationally weigh their reactions, consider potential responses to them, and view them in light of the overall objectives.
- Use Active Listening to understand the perspectives of all stakeholders involved in decision-making processes. We apply the Dichotomy of Control to focus on aspects within our control, such as clearly communicating the rationale behind our decisions and actively listening to feedback.

- Embrace Discomfort by acknowledging any ethical dilemmas or conflicting interests that may arise during the decision-making process, encouraging honest and transparent communication.
- Use Probing Questions to encourage open dialogue and critical reflection on the decision-making process and Affect Labeling to acknowledge and address any emotions or concerns that may arise.
- Cultivate Moral Courage by being willing to disclose relevant information, even when it may be uncomfortable or challenging, ultimately contributing to a culture of transparency and accountability.

Embracing transparency in decision-making enables leaders and organizations to navigate challenges with integrity and create a more engaged and resilient community.

9. Advocating for Justice

Ethical action involves advocating for fairness and justice beyond personal integrity, out into the broader community. This means standing up against injustice, inequality, and exploitation, and working toward creating a more equitable society. With Stoic Empathy, we can advance this ethic by various means. For example:

- Cultivating a deep understanding of others' experiences and promoting empathy-driven action to address systemic issues of injustice and inequality and how they affect marginalized communities, using Active Listening to understand their experiences and perspectives. We can also use Discomfort Embracing in confronting the uncomfortable truths about systemic oppression and committing to take action despite the challenges involved.

- Recognizing the importance of standing up against oppression and exploitation, cultivating Moral Courage by speaking out against injustice, even in the face of opposition or personal risk, and advocating for systemic changes that promote justice and equality for all members of society.
- Applying the Dichotomy of Control to focus on taking action where we can make a meaningful difference, such as advocating for policy changes or supporting grassroots movements. We can also reflect on the Stoic concept of Memento Mori as a reminder of the fleeting nature of life and the urgency of taking action to address systemic injustices before it's too late.

By integrating these principles into our lives, we not only uphold our personal integrity but also contribute to a more just and compassionate world, embodying the true spirit of Stoic Empathy.

This brings us to the 10th ethical pillar. It is placed last not because it is the most or least important, but because, for many, it is the most challenging to realize. This final pillar, made possible through Stoic Empathy, enables us to achieve a higher level of ethical conduct, demanding deep introspection, unwavering commitment, and the courage to act with utmost integrity.

10. Control Body Language and Tone to Reflect Your Values

At the time of this writing, I've produced almost 80 TED and TEDx talks, performances, and activations, culminating in a total of millions of views by people around the world. I work with the speakers for months in advance of filming to curate ideas, revise scripts, help speakers memorize their talks, and perhaps most important, rehearse with the speakers so they present their talks in the most impactful manner. In this capacity, I've worked with every kind of leader you can imagine, helping all of them to find their "idea worth spreading." For most if not all the speakers, their time on my stage is the pinnacle of their professional and even personal life. It's what they've been working toward for as long as they can remember. And what they say, how they say it, and how others perceive it will frame their life's missions going forward.

Over the more than 30 years that I've been training to understand my audience, build influence, advocate for an idea, and maintain control over my own actions, words, tone, demeanor, and even thoughts and emotions—whether as a litigator or as a TEDx speaker and producer—I've picked up three very important insights into nonverbal communication and its impact on our attempts to build leverage through empathy and emotional regulation.

The first is that every speaker gets nervous *and* shows they're nervous when they're on the red TED dot with cameras, lights, and an audience glued to them, just like every lawyer gets anxious about addressing a courtroom. A lot of my speakers, even the seasoned ones, sway from side to side when they're on stage. People literally rock themselves as a soothing mechanism, visibly, in public, and in a manner they wouldn't want to be perceived by others (until they're coached out of it). I know a founder of a multi-billion-dollar company whose knee sometimes shakes when he addresses the boardroom; a unicorn start-up leader who looks up while giving speeches as if trying to remember what she's going to say next; and a high-level appointed politician who overuses the word *like* when addressing her team as if she were back in high school.

The second trend I've observed through my years of persuasion training is that looking nervous makes speakers seem unsure to their audience, and therefore less compelling. Worse, the audience isn't just underwhelmed by the anxious uncertainty; sometimes they're led to question the very truth of what the speaker is saying.

The third pattern I've seen is that while most people who make it to the TEDx stage have received some form of body language training or coaching, almost no one has received *tonal* training. The reality is that so often it's not what you say, but *how* you say it, that counts. Think, for example, of agent 007's famous line: "My name is Bond. James Bond." The line was delivered with a confident, downward tone, which conveyed authority and finality. Now imagine it spoken with a rising, questioning tone: "My name is Bond? James Bond?"

The difference would be dramatic—much more open and welcoming, far less authoritative and strong.

When Epictetus remarked, "Don't explain your philosophy. Embody it," he was emphasizing a concept that transcends mere verbal expression, incorporating not just the subtleties of tone and body language but indeed making them integral components of that embodiment. Epictetus's assertion suggests that philosophy is not just to be articulated but lived, with every nuance of our demeanor and nonverbal cues playing a critical role in its expression.

This is where the 7/38/55 Rule comes in. Derived from the pioneering research of Albert Mehrabian in the 1960s—some 1,875 years after the lifetime of Epictetus—the 7/38/55 Rule posits that in face-to-face communication, approximately 7 percent of the message is conveyed through words, 38 percent through tone of voice, and a significant 55 percent through body language.

It's important to recognize that these percentages aren't precise. The diversity in individual communication styles and the complexity of human interaction mean that the exact contribution of words, tone, and body language varies from one situation to another. Moreover, cultural differences, personal idiosyncrasies, and the context of the communication itself can all influence how we convey and interpret messages. Nonetheless, the 7/38/55 breakdown—not a rule as much as a guiding principle—underscores the impact of nonverbal cues in our interactions and gives us a framework to consider *all* facets of communication in understanding and connecting with others. It suggests that a significant portion of what we understand from others comes not from their words, but from their tone and body language. Significantly, it follows that this is also how *others* understand *us*.

This insight alone enhances our ability to regulate our emotions and respond to others with tact and composure. But Stoic Empathy takes us so much further than mere insight—it gives us greater control. Stoicism and empathy together empower us to control our body language and tonal variations, ensuring our communication aligns with our intentions and values.

When we practice Stoic principles, we learn to regulate our emotions and responses, preventing our tone from being dictated by fleeting feelings of anger, frustration, or anxiety. We can maintain a steady, calm, and confident tone, even in challenging situations. We can communicate our intentions clearly and consistently, reducing the risk of misunderstandings and conveying a sense of reliability and trustworthiness. We can use a well-modulated tone that reflects our inner stability and commitment to ethical conduct, ensuring that our spoken words match our values and intentions.

Practicing empathy, on the other hand, enhances our understanding of others' feelings and perspectives, enabling us to respond appropriately and authentically. Our heightened awareness of others' reactions to what we're saying and doing allows us to adjust our nonverbal cues in real time. For instance, if we notice signs of discomfort or misunderstanding in our listeners, empathy encourages us to adopt more open and reassuring body language, maintaining eye contact, nodding, or using affirmative gestures—not only making our communication more effective but also demonstrating our sensitivity to others' feelings.

When we convey our messages with congruence between our words, tone, and body language, we are reinforcing our commitment to ethical behavior. We're fostering trust and respect in our interactions. We're also ensuring that we consistently embody the values we espouse, thereby strengthening one of the most important ethical pillars—acting with integrity and authenticity.

Remember that the goal here isn't perfection. You will make mistakes. We all do. Rather, the goal is to live with intention, embrace growth, and continuously strive to become better versions of ourselves.

Chapter 10 Takeaways

Stoic Empathy not only equips us to live a life of strength and influence but also surpasses other methods of gaining influence by helping us live such a life ethically. It highlights the value of meaningful relationships and enables us to remain true to ourselves as we climb peak after peak.

AFTERWORD

At 11 years old, against the backdrop of a nation in turmoil, I was learning lessons beyond my years. The gatherings at our home were more than just social events scented with saffron and parsley; they were a microcosm of the world outside, brimming with laughter, sorrow, music, and whispered truths. Each guest brought with them not just dishes of aromatic food but also their fears, hopes, and resilience. Observing them was to intuitively understand the power of strategic empathy; to see beyond my own experiences, understand the struggles and joys of others, and open a window to a world both complex and interconnected. My family, friends, and neighbors, each navigating their own challenges, taught me to listen, to observe, and to understand the intricacies of human emotions and relationships. This ability to connect and empathize strategically was not just an act of compassion. This means of survival, of navigating the tumultuous waters of reality, followed me across the world and to dimensions of influence beyond my imagination, despite hostile measures always in my path.

As for Stoicism, a philosophy I would only come to name later in life, I see it now embodied in the very fabric of my existence. The war, the uncertainty, the ever-present danger—these were elements outside my family's control. Yet within the walls of our home, amid the music, dance, and poetry, there was a collective strength, a stoic resolve. We celebrated, mourned, and expressed ourselves in ways that defied the chaos outside. We found joy in the small moments: a spoonful of saffron rosewater rice pudding, the laughter of children, and the comfort of familiar melodies. In these clips of time, Stoicism was not just a philosophical concept, but a lived experience. It was about focusing on what we could control—our responses, our attitudes, and our choices, to find joy and solidarity in the face of adversity.

This thought and action process shaped me. It taught me that while I can't control the world, I can control my reactions to it. I learned to navigate life with a heart that understands and feels deeply for others, yet with a mind that remains focused and resilient amid challenges.

Combining strategic empathy with Stoicism has given me a powerful framework for ethically navigating power dynamics in our complex world. But more than that, it has taught me to freeze the time between stimulus and response. In that space is where life stands—because it's where willpower thrives. The opportunity to anticipate and respond to catalysts with wisdom and empathy—this is where human will sits. It's where character grows, where strength thrives, and where control is the most unfettered.

As I look back on my life now, I see that the lessons of how to exercise my power within these moments were my inheritance, passed down not in words but through the lived experiences of those around me. In my patchwork of memories from childhood in Iran in the late '80s, long before I went into the world as an adult, I see the early threads of strategic empathy and Stoicism.

My lessons came not just from science and facts, but from stories and experiences.

My mom navigating the potentially perilous encounter with the morality police in the bazaar . . . Joel Braunold's empathic work in peacebuilding . . . Seneca's observation that we suffer more in imagination than reality . . . James Bond's powerful tonal inflections . . . Lily's dances of defiance during parties back in our tiny apartment in Tehran . . . Epictetus's path from slavery to advisor to the emperor . . . the ravages of war and bullying in my childhood . . . Marcus Aurelius's meditations and memento mori . . . Viktor Frankl's persistent spirit against all odds . . . Barry Marshall giving himself a petri dish of bacteria to cure millions . . . ancient ideas of propatheiai and pathe . . . Hof the Iceman running the marathon in his underwear in the arctic . . . and Mingyur Rinpoche's brain full of Buddhist insights . . .

They are all my teachers, and now yours too.

They show us that true strength isn't about being impervious to external pressures, but about upholding ethical integrity and remaining steadfast amid life's challenges. The key lesson here is that real power doesn't come from denying vulnerability, but from embracing it with compassion and understanding.

True and ethical resilience—whether in the face of authority or in international diplomacy—isn't about hardening ourselves against the world. Instead, it's about engaging with it fully and intentionally, living a life filled with kindness. Stoic Empathy teaches us that our greatest strength lies in empathetic engagement with the world. As we navigate the ethical challenges of our era, from the digital divide to striving for fairness in an unequal world, we must remember that our true strength is not in the walls we build around ourselves, but in the bridges we build to others.

These lessons resonate deeply, reminding us that even in the most trying times, we have the power to choose our path—a path defined by clarity, resilience, and the quiet strength of the human spirit.

May your journey with Stoic Empathy take you far and keep you grounded.

ENDNOTES

Chapter 2

1. Giacomo Rizzolatti and Laila Craighero, "The Mirror-Neuron System," *Annual Review of Neuroscience* 27 (2004): 169–92, https://doi.org/10.1146/annurev.neuro.27.070203.144230.

2. Schmidt et al., "The Human Mirror Neuron System—A Common Neural Basis for Social Cognition?" *Psychophysiology* 58, no. 5 (May 2021): e13781, https://doi.org/ 10.1111/psyp.13781.

3. Selen Atasoy, Isaac Donnelly, and Joel Pearson, "Human Brain Networks Function in Connectome-Specific Harmonic Waves," *Nature Communications* 7 (January 21, 2016): 10340, https://doi.org/ 10.1038/ncomms10340.

4. Fan et al., "Is There a Core Neural Network in Empathy? An fMRI Based Quantitative Meta-Analysis," *Neuroscience and Biobehavioral Reviews* 35, no. 3 (January 2011): 903–11, https://doi.org/10.1016/j.neubiorev.2010.10.009.

Chapter 3

1. Arash Javanbakht and Linda Saab, "What Happens in the Brain When We Feel Fear and Why Some of Us Just Can't Get Enough of It," *Smithsonian Magazine*, October 27, 2017, https://www.smithsonianmag.com/science-nature/what-happens-brain-feel-fear-180966992/; Adam Rowden, "What to Know about Amygdala Hijack," *Medical News Today*, April 19, 2021, https://www.medicalnewstoday.com/articles/amygdala-hijack.

2. Diane Musho Hamilton, "Calming Your Brain During Conflict," *Harvard Business Review*, December 22, 2015, https://hbr.org/2015/12/calming-your-brain-during-conflict.

3. David S. Jessop, "The Power of Positive Stress and a Research Roadmap," *Stress* 22, no. 5 (September 2019): 521–3, https://doi.org/10.1080/10253890.2019.1593365.

4. Lieberman et al., "Putting Feelings into Words: Affect Labeling Disrupts Amygdala Activity in Response to Affective Stimuli," *Psychological Science* 18, no. 5 (May 2007): 421–8, https://doi.org/10.1111/j.1467-9280.2007.01916.x.

5. Katharina Kircanski, Matthew D. Lieberman, and Michelle G. Craske, "Feelings into Words: Contributions of Language to Exposure Therapy," *Psychological Science* 23, no. 10 (October 1, 2012): 1086–91, https://doi.org/10.1177/0956797612443830.

6. Valeriia V. Vlasenko, Emma G. Rogers, and Christian E. Waugh, "Affect Labelling Increases the Intensity of Positive Emotions," *Cognition and Emotions* 35, no. 7 (October 2021): 1350–64, https://doi.org/10.1080/02699931.2021.1959302.

7. Alisa Yu, Justin M. Berg, and Julian J. Zlatev, "Emotional Acknowledgment: How Verbalizing Others' Emotions Fosters Interpersonal Trust," *Organizational Behavior and Human Decision Processes* 164 (May 2021), 116–35, https://doi.org/10.1016/j.obhdp.2021.02.002.

8. Valeriia V. Vlasenko, Emma G. Rogers, and Christian E. Waugh, "Affect Labelling Increases the Intensity of Positive Emotions."

9. Margaret C. Stewart, Maria Atilano, and Christa L. Arnold, "Improving Customer Relations with Social Listening: A Case Study of an American Academic Library," *International Journal of Customer Relationship Marketing and Management* 8, no. 1 (January–March 2017), 49–63, https://scholars.unf.edu/ws/portalfiles/portal/39750717/Improving+Customer+Relations+with+Social+Listening%3A+A+Case+Study.pdf.

10. Ashish Agarwal, "How 'Listening' to Their Customers Made These Companies So Big," *Medium*, June 25, 2020, https://toashishagarwal.medium.com/how-listening-to-their-customers-made-these-companies-so-big-ece5d4eb3c24. *See also*: Amanda O'Bryan, "How to Practice Active Listening: 16 Examples and Techniques," *PositivePsychology.com*, last modifed May 24, 2024, https://positivepsychology.com/active-listening-techniques/; Listening case studies: Suzan Last, "Case Study: The Cost of Poor Communication," in *Technical Writing Essentials: Introduction to Professional Communications in the Technical Fields* (Pressbooks, 2019), https://pressbooks.bccampus.ca/technicalwriting/chapter/casestudy-costpoorcommunication/; Steward, Atilano, and Arnold, "Improving Customer Relations."

11. Steli Efti, "How Keeping Quiet Saved Our Startup $225K," *TechCrunch*, Dec. 28, 2014, https://techcrunch.com/2014/12/28/how-shutting-up-saved-our-startup-225k/.

Chapter 4

1. van Baaren et al., "Mimicry for Money: Behavioral Consequences of Imitation," *Journal of Experimental Social Psychology* 39, no. 4 (2003), 393–8, https://doi.org/10.1016/S0022-1031(03)00014-3.

2. Jacob et al., "Retail Salespeople's Mimicry of Customers: Effects on Consumer Behavior," *Journal of Retailing and Consumer Services* 18, no. 5 (September 2011): 381–8, https://doi.org/10.1016/j.jretconser.2010.11.006.

3. Nicolas Guéguen, "Mimicry and Seduction: An Evaluation in a Courtship Context," *Social Influence* 4, no. 4 (October 2009): 249–55, https://doi.org/10.1080/15534510802628173.

4. Vanessa Van Edwards, "Mirroring Body Language: 4 Steps to Successfully Mirror Others," *Science of People*, July 2, 2024, https://www.scienceofpeople.com/mirroring/.

5. Travis Bradberry, "12 Mind Tricks That Make You Likeable and Help You Get Ahead," *Inc.*, January 13, 2016, https://www.inc.com/travis-bradberry/12-mind-tricks-that-make-people-like-you-and-help-you-get-ahead.html.

6. Susan C. Young, *The Art of Body Language: 8 Ways to Optimize Non-Verbal Communication for Positive Impact* (Renew You Ventures, 2017).

Chapter 5

1. Tim Hagemann, Robert W. Levenson, and James J. Gross, "Expressive Suppression during an Acoustic Startle," *Psychophysiology* 43, no. 1 (January 2006): 104–12, https://doi.org/10.1111/j.1469-8986.2006.00382.x; Jackson et al., "Suppression and Enhancement of Emotional Responses to Unpleasant Pictures," *Psychophysiology* 37, no. 4 (July 2000): 515–22, https://doi.org/10.1017/s0048577200990401; Ute Kunzmann, Cenita S. Kupperbusch, and Robert W. Levenson, "Behavioral Inhibition and Amplification during Emotional Arousal: A Comparison of Two Age Groups," *Psychology and Aging* 20, no. 1 (March 2005): 144–58, https://doi.org/10.1037/0882-7974.20.1.144; James J. Gross and Robert W. Levenson, "Emotional Suppression: Physiology, Self-Report, and Expressive Behavior," *Journal of Personality and Social Psychology* 64, no. 6 (June 1993): 970–86, https://doi.org/10.1037//0022-3514.64.6.970.

2. Brackett et al. (2012) demonstrated the significance of emotional regulation in school settings, finding that students with better emotional skills performed better academically and had more positive social interactions. According to a meta-analysis by O'Boyle et al., emotional intelligence is consistently linked with better job performance across various professions. *See also*: Abraham Carmeli, Meyrav Yitzhak-Halevy, and Jacob Weisberg, "The Relationship between Emotional Intelligence and Psychological Wellbeing," *Journal of Managerial Psychology* 24, no. 1 (2009): 66–78, https://doi.org/10.1108/02683940910922546; Peter Salovey and John D. Mayer, "Emotional intelligence," *Imagination, Cognition, and Personality* 9, no. 3 (March 1990): 185–211, https://doi.org/10.2190/DUGG-P24E-52WK-6CDG; Brackett et al., "Enhancing Academic Performance and Social and Emotional Competence with the RULER Feeling Words Curriculum," *Learning and Individual Differences* 22, no. 2 (April 2012): 218–24, https://doi.org/10.1016/j.lindif.2010.10.002; O'Boyle et al., "The Relation between Emotional Intelligence and Job Performance: A Meta-Analysis," *Journal of Organizational Behavior* 32, no. 5 (2011): 788–818, https://doi.org/10.1002/job.714. More broadly, Stéphane Côté, Anett Gyurak, and Robert W. Levenson, "The Ability to Regulate Emotion Is Associated with Greater Well-Being, Income, and

Socioeconomic Status," *Emotion* 10, no. 6 (December 2010): 923–33, https://doi.org/10.1037/a0021156.

3. A study by English et al. (2012) found that habitual emotional suppression can lead to increased stress, poorer relationships, and even health problems over time. This is due to the cognitive load required to consistently suppress emotional responses. Another study by Butler et al. (2007) suggested that while emotional suppression might be beneficial in the short term in certain stressful situations, it's not a healthy long-term strategy, often leading to decreased memory recall and increased physiological responses. *See also:* Tammy English, Oliver P. John, and James J. Gross, "Emotion Regulation in Close Relationships," in *Oxford Handbook of Close Relationships* ed. Jeffry A. Simpson and Lorne Campbell (Oxford: Oxford University Press, 2013), 500–13, https://doi.org/10.1093/oxfordhb/9780195398694.013.0022; Butler et al., "The social consequences of expressive suppression," *Emotion* 3, no. 1 (March 2003): 48–67, https://doi.org/10.1037/1528-3542.3.1.48. Damasio's (1994) work on patients with damage to the ventromedial prefrontal cortex, a region involved in processing emotions, found that while these patients retained their cognitive faculties, their inability to experience emotions made decision-making challenging. This suggests emotions play a pivotal role in effective reasoning. *See also:* Young et al., "Damage to Ventromedial Prefrontal Cortex Impairs Judgment of Harmful Intent," *Neuron* 65, no. 6 (March 2010): 845–51, https://doi.org/10.1016/j.neuron.2010.03.003.

Chapter 6

1. J. E. LeDoux, "Emotion Circuits in the Brain," *Annual Review of Neuroscience* 23 (2000): 155–84, https://doi.org/10.1146/annurev.neuro.23.1.155; Ralph Adolphs, "What Does the Amygdala Contribute to Social Cognition?" *Annals of the New York Academy of Sciences* 1191, no. 1 (March 2010): 42–61, https://doi.org/10.1111/j.1749-6632.2010.05445.x.

2. Sylvia D. Kreibig, "Autonomic Nervous System Activity in Emotion: A Review," *Biological Psychology* 84, no. 3 (July 2010): 394–421, https://doi.org/10.1016/j.biopsycho.2010.03.010.

3. Marian Joëls and Tallie Z. Baram, "The Neuro-Symphony of Stress," *Nature Reviews Neuroscience* 10, no. 6 (June 2009): 459–66, https://doi.org/10.1038/nrn2632; Bruce S. McEwen, "Physiology and Neurobiology of Stress and Adaptation: Central Role of the Brain," *Physiological Reviews* 87, no. 3 (July 2007): 873–904, https://doi.org/10.1152/physrev.00041.2006.

4. Ulf Lundberg, "Psychophysiology of Work: Stress, Gender, Endocrine Response, and Work-Related Upper Extremity Disorders," *American Journal of Industrial Medicine* 41, no. 5 (May 2002): 383–92, https://doi.org/10.1002/ajim.10038.

5. Wolfram Boucsein, *Electrodermal Activity*, 2nd ed. (Springer Science & Business Media, 2012).

6. This is because meditation activates the anterior cingulate cortex, a part of the brain involved in various cognitive and emotional processes, including attention; it also impacts fronto-limbic networks (including areas such as the prefrontal cortex, and limbic structures including the amygdala and hippocampus), which are crucial in regulating emotions, stress responses, decision-making, and social interactions. *See also:* Tang, Hölzel, and Posner, "The Neuroscience of Mindfulness Meditation." Other studies demonstrate that mindfulness meditation reduces our blood pressure. For example, in a 2019 study published in the *Journal of Human Hypertension*, the mindfulness group showed significantly lower blood pressure readings and improvements in mental health markers compared to the control group after just eight weeks of meditation. *See also:* Márquez et al., "Benefits of Mindfulness Meditation in Reducing Blood Pressure and Stress in Patients with Arterial Hypertension," *Journal of Human Hypertension* 33, no. 3 (March 2019): 237–47, https://doi.org/10.1038/s41371-018-0130-6.

7. P. Salmon, "Effects of Physical Exercise on Anxiety, Depression, and Sensitivity to Stress: A Unifying Theory," *Clinical Psychology Review* 21, no. 1 (February 2002): 33–61, https://doi.org/10.1016/s0272-7358(99)00032-x; Rosenbaum et al., "Physical Activity Interventions for People with Mental Illness: A Systematic Review and Meta-Analysis, *Journal of Clinical Psychiatry* 75, no. 9 (September 2014): 964–74, https://doi.org/10.4088/JCP.13r08765.

8. Ansgar Conrad and Walton T. Roth, "Muscle Relaxation Therapy for Anxiety Disorders: It Works but How?" *Journal of Anxiety Disorders* 21, no. 3 (2007): 243–64, https://doi.org/10.1016/j.janxdis.2006.08.001.

9. Triscoli et al., "Touch between Romantic Partners: Being Stroked Is More Pleasant Than Stroking and Decelerates Heart Rate," *Physiology and Behavior* 1 (August 2017): 169–75, https://doi.org/10.1016/j.physbeh.2017.05.006; Kelley J. Robinson, Lisa B. Hoplock, and Jessica J. Cameron, "When in Doubt, Reach Out: Touch Is a Covert but Effective Mode of Soliciting and Providing Social Support," *Social Psychological and Personality Science* 6, no. 7 (September 2015): 831–9; Mazza et al., "Pain Perception and Physiological Responses Are Modulated by Active Support from a Romantic Partner," *Psychophysiology* 60, no. 8 (September 2023): e14299, https://doi.org/10.1111/psyp.14299. Note that touch can have a positive or a negative valence depending on, for example, the speed and body's area in which the touch occurs, socio-cultural norms, context, gender, interpersonal relationship, identity of the person providing the touch, and nonverbal visual cues. For our purposes, we'll discuss *affective* touch, or welcomed touch in a comforting relationship.

10. "Does Dunking Your Head in Water Ease Anxiety? Ask This Professor's Diving Mice," *UVAToday*, October 16, 2023, Research and Discovery, https://news.virginia.edu/content/does-dunking-your-head-water-ease-anxiety-ask-professors-diving-mice.

11. Coles et al., "A Multi-Lab Test of the Facial Feedback Hypothesis by the Many Smiles Collaboration," *Nature Human Behaviour* 6, no. 12 (December 2022): 1731–42, https://doi.org/10.1038/s41562-022-01458-9.

12. Giacomo Rizzolatti and Laila Craighero, "The Mirror-Neuron System," *Annual Review of Neuroscience* 27 (2004): 169–92, https://doi.org/10.1146/annurev.neuro.27.070203.144230 (Mirror neurons are in several regions of the brain, including the premotor cortex and the inferior parietal cortex, the portions of the frontal lobe responsible for motor planning and integrating sensory information with parts of the body); a study by Nummenmaa, Glerean, Hari, & Hietanen (2014) published in the journal *Proceedings of the National Academy of Sciences of the United States of America* looked into the brain networks involved in emotional contagion. Their results suggest that both affective and motoric body-related information contribute to emotional contagion (Nummenmaa et al., "Bodily Maps of Emotions," *Proceedings of the National Academy of Sciences of the United States of America* 111, no. 2 (January 14, 2014): 646–51, https://doi.org/10.1073/pnas.1321664111).

13. Adam D. I. Kramer, Jamie E. Guillory, and Jeffrey T. Hancock, "Experimental Evidence of Massive-Scale Emotional Contagion through Social Networks," *Proceedings of the National Academy of Sciences of the United States of America* 111, no. 24 (June 2, 2014): 8788-90, https://doi.org/10.1073/pnas.1320040111.

14. Vittorio Gallese, Christian Keysers, and Giacomo Rizzolatti, "A Unifying View of the Basis of Social Cognition," *Trends in Cognitive Sciences* 8, no. 9 (September 2004): 396–403, https://doi.org/10.1016/j.tics.2004.07.002 (highlighting the role of mirror neurons in understanding others' actions and the emotions tied to those actions); Marco L. Loggia, Jeffrey S. Mogil, and M. Catherine Bushnell, "Empathy Hurts: Compassion for Another Increases Both Sensory and Affective Components of Pain Perception," *Pain* 136, no. 1–2 (May 2008): 168–76, https://doi.org/10.1016/j.pain.2007.07.017. *See also:* Jeremy Sutton, "Mirror Neurons and the Neuroscience of Empathy," PositivePsychology.com, September 7, 2023, https://positivepsychology.com/mirror-neurons/ explaining how mirror neurons facilitate learning, empathy, and social understanding by allowing individuals to simulate observed actions and emotions, with implications for education, therapy, and trauma research; the article incorporates numerous references and studies ranging from the late 1990s to as recent as 2022 to support its findings.

15. *See also:* Edward L. Deci and Richard M. Ryan, "The 'What' and 'Why' of Goal Pursuits: Human Needs and the Self-Determination of Behavior," *Psychological Inquiry* 11, no. 4 (October 2000): 227–68, https://doi.org/10.1207/s15327965pli1104_01.

16. More relevant here is the emergence of positive psychology, championed by scholars like Martin Seligman, which has brought forth new concepts that intersect with motivation—such as grit, flow, and character strengths. *See:* Martin E. P. Seligman, *Flourish: The New Positive Psychology and the Search for Well-Being* (New York: Free Press, 2011); Angela Duckworth, *Grit: The Power of Passion and Perseverance* (New York: Scribner, 2016). These constructs offer additional layers to understanding the forces driving human behavior, providing a more comprehensive and nuanced view of what propels individuals toward various life goals and personal development paths. Importantly, they demonstrate that emotions can both result from and influence our motivations.

17. Richard M. Ryan and Edward L. Deci, "Intrinsic and Extrinsic Motivations: Classic Definitions and New Directions," *Contemporary Educational Psychology* 25, no. 1 (January 2000): 54–67, https://doi.org/10.1006/ceps.1999.1020.

18. Josh M. Cisler and Ernst H.W. Koster, "Mechanisms of Attentional Biases towards Threat in Anxiety Disorders: An Integrative Review," *Clinical Psychology Review* 30, no. 2 (March 2010): 203–16, https://doi.org/10.1016/j.cpr.2009.11.003; Sonia J. Bishop, "Neurocognitive Mechanisms of Anxiety: An Integrative Account," *Trends in Cognitive Sciences* 11, no. 7 (July 2007): 307–16, https://doi.org/10.1016/j.tics.2007.05.008; Bar-Haim et al., "Threat-Related Attentional Bias in Anxious and Nonanxious Individuals: A Meta-Analytic Study," *Psychological Bulletin* 133, no. 1 (January 2007): 1–24, https://doi.org/10.1037/0033-2909.133.1.1; Andrew D. Peckham, R. Kathryn McHugh, and Michael W. Otto, "A Meta-Analysis of the Magnitude of Biased Attention in Depression," *Depression and Anxiety* 27, no. 12 (November 3, 2010): 1135–42, https://doi.org/10.1002/da.20755; Christopher M. Janelle, Robert N. Singer, and A. Mark Williams, "External Distraction and Attentional Narrowing: Visual Search Evidence," *Journal of Sport and Exercise Psychology* 21, no. 1 (March 1, 1999): 70–91, https://doi.org/10.1123/jsep.21.1.70.

19. Schiller and colleagues (2010) summarize this research in "Emotional Memory: Chapters and Articles," *ScienceDirect*, https://www.sciencedirect.com/topics/social-sciences/emotional-memory. *See also:* Maureen Ritchey, Laura A. Libby, and Charan Ranganath, "Cortico-Hippocampal Systems Involved in Memory and Cognition: The PMAT Framework," *Progress in Brain Research* 219 (2015): 45–64, https://doi.org/ 10.1016/bs.pbr.2015.04.001; and Elizabeth A. Phelps, "Human Emotion and Memory: Interactions of the Amygdala and Hippocampal Complex," *Current Opinion in Neurobiology* 14, no. 2 (April 2004): 198–202, https://doi.org/10.1016/j.conb.2004.03.015.

20. Both Phelps (2004) and Ritchey, Libby, and Ranganath (2015) indicate that emotions can enhance memory encoding, with certain locales or stimuli triggering strong emotional reactions based on past experiences.

21. Lisa Feldman Barrett, Kristen A. Lindquist, and Maria Gendron, "Language as Context for the Perception of Emotion," *Trends in Cognitive Sciences* 11, no. 8 (August 2007): 327–32, https://doi.org/10.1016/j.tics.2007.06.003. *See also:* Lindquist, K. A., MacCormack, J. K., & Shablack, H. (2015), "The Role of Language in Emotion: Predictions from Psychological Constructionism," *Frontiers in Psychology*, 6, 444, https://doi.org/10.3389/fpsyg.2015.00444. Brooks, J. A., Shablack, H., Gendron, M., Satpute, A. B., Parrish, M. H., & Lindquist, K. A. (2017), "The Role of Language in the Experience and Perception of Emotion: A Neuroimaging Meta-analysis," *Social Cognitive and Affective Neuroscience* 12(2), 169-183, https://doi.org/10.1093/scan/nsw121.

22. Douglas S. Mennin and David M. Fresco, "Emotion Regulation Therapy," in *Handbook of Emotion Regulation*, ed. J. J. Gross (New York: Guilford Press); 469–90. This chapter touches upon how beliefs and cognitive patterns can be targeted to treat emotional disorders in the context of emotion regulation therapy.

23. *See also:* E. Tory Higgins, *Beyond Pleasure and Pain: How Motivation Works* (Oxford: Oxford University Press, 2011); Andreas Kappes and Gabriele Oettingen, "The Emergence of Goal Pursuit: Mental Contrasting Connects Future and Reality," *Journal of Experimental Social Psychology* 54 (September 2014): 25–39, https://doi.org/10.1016/j.jesp.2014.03.014.

24. Studies by Shepperd et al. (2002) and Ma et al. (2017) delve into the impact of expectations on emotional well-being. *See:* Shepperd et al., "A Primer on Unrealistic Optimism," *Current Directions in Psychological Science* 24, no. 3 (June 10, 2015): 232–37, https://doi.org/10.1177/0963721414568341; Lawrence K. Ma, Richard J. Tunney, and Eamonn Ferguson, "Does Gratitude Enhance Prosociality?: A Meta-Analytic Review.," *Psychological Bulletin* 143, no. 6 (June 2017): 601–35, https://doi.org/10.1037/bul0000103.

25. Hofmann et al., "How to Handle Anxiety: The Effects of Reappraisal, Acceptance, and Suppression Strategies on Anxious Arousal," *Behaviour Research and Therapy* 47, no. 5 (May 2009): 389–94, https://doi.org/10.1016/j.brat.2009.02.010.

26. See *Outsmarting Implicit Bias,* a project at Harvard University ("Make Stress Work for You" Module).

27. Jeremy Sutton, "Socratic Questioning in Psychology: Examples and Techniques," *PositivePsychology.com*, July 12, 2024, https://positivepsychology.com/socratic-questioning/.

28. Gavin I. Clark and Sarah J. Egan, "The Socratic Method in Cognitive Behavioural Therapy: A Narrative Review," *Cognitive Therapy and Research* 39, no. 6 (2015): 863–879, https://doi.org/10.1007/s10608-015-9707-3; Jeffrey E. Young, Janet S. Klosko, and Marjorie E. Weishaar, *Schema Therapy: A Practitioner's Guide* (New York: Guilford Press, 2006); "The Schema Therapy Model," Schema Therapy Society e.V. (ISST) - Schema Therapy Central Concepts, n.d., https://www.schematherapysociety.org/Schema-Therapy..

29. "Lurie Children's Offers Kids Virtual Escape from Intensive Care Unit," Ann and Robert H. Lurie Children's Hospital of Chicago, March 27, 2019, https://www.luriechildrens.org/en/news-stories/lurie-childrens-offers-kids-virtual-escape-from-intensive-care-unit/.

Chapter 7

1. Viktor E. Frankl, *Man's Search for Meaning* (Boston, MA: Beacon Press, 2015).

2. Otto Muzik, Kaice T. Reilly, and Vaibhav A. Diwadkar, "'Brain over Body'—A Study on the Willful Regulation of Autonomic Function during Cold Exposure," *NeuroImage* 172 (May 15, 2018): 632–41, https://doi.org/10.1016/j.neuroimage.2018.01.067.

3. Desai et al., "A Systematic Review and Meta-Analysis on the Effects of Exercise on the Endocannabinoid System," *Cannabis and Cannabinoid Research* 7, no. 4

(August 2022): 388–408, https://doi.org/10.1089/can.2021.0113. Also note that high-intensity exercise like robust workouts or long endurance training can increase the levels of a special substance in the brain called brain-derived neurotrophic factor. This substance is crucial for keeping the brain flexible (neuroplasticity) and helping with thinking and learning abilities. Carl W. Cotman and Nicole C. Berchtold, "Exercise: A Behavioral Intervention to Enhance Brain Health and Plasticity," *Trends in Neurosciences* 25, no. 6 (June 2002): 295–301, https://doi.org/10.1016/s0166-2236(02)02143-4; Kristin L. Szuhany, Matteo Bugatti, and Michael W. Otto, "A Meta-Analytic Review of the Effects of Exercise on Brain-Derived Neurotrophic Factor," *Journal of Psychiatric Research* 60 (January 2015): 56–64, https://doi.org/10.1016/j.jpsychires.2014.10.003.

4. Didrik Espeland, Louis de Weerd, and James B. Mercer, "Health Effects of Voluntary Exposure to Cold Water – a Continuing Subject of Debate," *International Journal of Circumpolar Health* 81, no. 1 (September 22, 2022), https://doi.org/10.1080/22423982.2022.2111789.

5. *See* Kuhlenhoelter et al., "Heat Therapy Promotes the Expression of Angiogenic Regulators in Human Skeletal Muscle," *American Journal of Physiology: Regulatory, Integrative, and Comparative Physiology* 311, no. 2 (August 2016): R377–91, https://doi.org/10.1152/ajpregu.00134.2016; Vienna E. Brunt and Christopher T. Minson, "Heat Therapy: Mechanistic Underpinnings and Applications to Cardiovascular Health," *Journal of Applied Physiology* 130, no. 6 (June 2021): 1684–1704, https://doi.org/ 10.1152/japplphysiol.00141.2020; and Kevin C. Kregel, "Heat Shock Proteins: Modifying Factors in Physiological Stress Responses and Acquired Thermotolerance," *Journal of Applied Physiology* 92, no. 5 (May 2002): 2177–86, https://doi.org/10.1152/japplphysiol.01267.2001.

6. Adluru et al., "BrainAGE and Regional Volumetric Analysis of a Buddhist Monk: a Longitudinal MRI Case Study," *Neurocase* 26, no. 2 (April 2020): 79–90, https://doi.org/10.1080/13554794.2020.1731553.

7. Lazar et al., "Meditation Experience Is Associated with Increased Cortical Thickness," *Neuroreport* 16, no. 17 (November 28, 2005): 1893–7, https://doi.org/10.1097/01.wnr.0000186598.66243.19.

8. Yi-Yuan Tang, Britta K. Hölzel, and Michael L. Posner, "The Neuroscience of Mindfulness Meditation," *Nature Reviews Neuroscience* 16, no. 4 (March 18, 2015): 213–25, https://doi.org/10.1038/nrn3916.

9. Hölzel et al., "Mindfulness Practice Leads to Increases in Regional Brain Gray Matter Density," *Psychiatry Research* 191, no. 1 (January 20, 2011): 36–43, https://doi.org/10.1016/j.pscychresns.2010.08.006; Zeidan et al., "Brain Mechanisms Supporting the Modulation of Pain by Mindfulness Meditation," *Journal of Neuroscience* 31, no. 14 (April 6, 2011): 5540–8, https://doi.org/10.1523/JNEUROSCI.5791-10.2011; Doll et al., "Mindful Attention to Breath Regulates Emotions via Increased Amygdala–Prefrontal Cortex Connectivity," *NeuroImage* 134 (July 1, 2016): 305–13, https://doi.org/10.1016/j.neuroimage.2016.03.041.

10. In an era where technology continually reshapes our lives, therapists are using virtual-reality exposure therapy (VRET) to help patients overcome fears and phobias. *See also:* Shiban et al. (2020), "Treatment Effect on Biases in Size Estimation in Spider Phobia," *Biological Psychology* 121, Part B (December 2016): 146–52, https://doi.org/10.1016/j.biopsycho.2016.03.005; Cleare et al., "Adverse Childhood Experiences and Hospital-Treated Self-Harm," *International Journal of Environmental Research and Public Health* 15, no. 6 (June 11, 2018): 1235, https://doi.org/10.3390/ijerph15061235; and Navarro-Haro et al., "Evaluation of a Mindfulness-Based Intervention with and without Virtual Reality Dialectical Behavior Therapy Mindfulness Skills Training for the Treatment of Generalized Anxiety Disorder in Primary Care: A Pilot Study," *Frontiers in Psychology* 10 (2019): 55, 10.3389/fpsyg.2019.00055.

Chapter 8

1. Mitch Albom, *Tuesdays with Morrie: An Old Man, a Young Man, and Life's Greatest Lesson* (New York: Broadway Books, 2007).

2. Marcel Schwantes, "Warren Buffett Says Integrity Is the Most Important Trait to Hire For. Ask These 12 Questions to Find It," *Inc.*, February 13, 2018, https://www.inc.com/marcel-schwantes/first-90-days-warren-buffetts-advice-for-hiring-based-on-3-traits.html.

3. Jill Radsken, "Jameela Jamil Is in a Good Place," *Harvard Gazette*, September 22, 2020, https://news.harvard.edu/gazette/story/2020/09/jameela-jamil-talks-cancel-culture-in-hollywood/.

4. Meghan Azad, "Q&A: Barry Marshall," *Nature* 514 (2014): S6–7, https://doi.org/10.1038/514S6a.

5. Rudyard Kipling, "If," in *Rewards and Fairies* (London: Macmillan, 1910).

Chapter 9

1. Emma E. Levine, Annabelle R. Roberts, and Taya R. Cohen, "Difficult Conversations: Navigating the Tension between Honesty and Benevolence," *Current Opinion in Psychology* 31 (February 2020): 38–43, https://doi.org/10.1016/j.copsyc.2019.07.034.

2. Harvard Second Generation Study, n.d., https://www.adultdevelopmentstudy.org/; Robert J. Waldinger and Marc S. Schulz, *The Good Life: Lessons from the World's Longest Scientific Study of Happiness* (New York: Simon & Schuster, 2023).

3. "Starbucks to Close All U.S. Stores for Training," NBCNews.com, February 26, 2008, https://www.nbcnews.com/id/wbna23351151.

INDEX

T

U

V

W

Y

Z

ACKNOWLEDGMENTS

I'm grateful to acknowledge:

My mother, Nahid, who wakes up every morning with thoughts of how she can create something beautiful or be of service to those she loves.

My father, Amir, who spends his days focused on self-improvement and gratitude for every breath.

My editor and friend, Anne, to whose wisdom and trust I owe much of this book.

My husband, Stuart; my sisters, Atessa and Mahsa; my children, Cole, Amara, Pierce, and Zeeba; my first round of readers, including June, Ghazal, Maaike, Rachel, Lisa, and Joan; and all my wonderful friends and family for their unwavering support, encouragement, and advice.

My agent, Erin, for believing in me.

And the privileges that the freedoms and security my life has afforded me, making it possible to recover from trauma, accept suffering, maximize joy, and further my mind.

ABOUT THE AUTHOR

Shermin Kruse is a globally recognized negotiation consultant, law professor, author, and TEDx producer whose transformative work in empathy, stoicism, and complex negotiation has influenced audiences from corporate boardrooms to university classrooms and international stages. Born in Tehran during a period of profound social and political upheaval, Shermin began her writing journey at the age of 10, penning poetry in Farsi as a means of processing life under the intense pressures of war and governmental oppression. Her family later emigrated to Canada with little more than a few suitcases, marking the beginning of a journey that would see Shermin rise from a young immigrant to a celebrated thought leader and influential global voice.

With a background in philosophy and neuropsychology from the University of Toronto and a law degree from the University of Michigan Law School, Shermin launched her legal career with a specialty in international business law. As a partner at the prestigious law firm Barack Ferrazzano, she spent 17 years representing Fortune 500 clients, including giants like LVMH, Google, and Walmart. Her legal practice, grounded in resolution-oriented strategies, provided her with in-depth expertise in high-stakes negotiations, cross-border transactions, and corporate management. This experience became a foundation for her approach to tactical empathy, a method she pioneered that combines cognitive empathy with strategic action to create lasting impact and positive change.

Shermin is also the author of the critically acclaimed novel *Butterfly Stitching*, which interweaves her family's experiences in Iran with themes of resilience, love, and survival under oppression. The novel has resonated with readers around the world for its poignant and authentic storytelling, painting a rich tapestry of life and love amidst the Iranian revolution's turmoil. Beyond fiction, her work as a writer includes the textbook *Global Transactions and Regulation*, an essential resource for law students and business professionals alike, which provides insights into the ethical, political, and legal dimensions of cross-border commercial activities.

As the founder and executive producer of TEDxWrigleyville, Shermin has produced and scripted over 60 TEDx talks and performances, many of which have been featured on TED.com and garnered millions of views across 40 countries. These talks, often centered on resilience, cultural understanding, and the transformative power of empathy, reflect her dedication to curating ideas that promote social change. Shermin has also given TEDx talks herself, including her popular 2022 talk on "Negotiating from a Place of Weakness Using Cognitive Empathy," which has been viewed by hundreds of thousands worldwide.

In addition to her role as a professor at Northwestern University Pritzker School of Law, where she teaches complex negotiation, leadership, and global transactions, Shermin frequently speaks on tactical empathy, leadership, and stoicism, sharing her expertise at academic conferences, at corporate events, and through media outlets such as NPR, PBS, and numerous influential podcasts. Her recent engagements include talks for the David Axelrod Institute for Politics, NPR's Illinois Public Media, and keynotes at prominent women's leadership events.

Shermin's impact extends beyond the academic and corporate worlds to the nonprofit sector, where she has founded multiple NGOs and serves on the boards of organizations such as the ACLU and RefuSHE. Her humanitarian work has earned her accolades including the annual Woman Extraordinaire award from the International Women Associates, recognition as one of the nation's top 100 "Women to Watch" by *BizWomen* magazine, and numerous other honors that celebrate her dedication to fostering empathy, justice, and human rights.

In *Stoic Empathy*, Shermin offers a powerful paradigm for navigating life's complexities by blending cognitive empathy with the resilience of stoic principles. Drawing on neuroscience, philosophy, and her own personal journey, she provides readers with actionable insights into cultivating influence, self-leadership, and emotional regulation. Whether you're a corporate leader, educator, or parent, or simply seeking tools to navigate personal and professional challenges with integrity, *Stoic Empathy* is a road map for achieving success through balance, compassion, and strength.

Shermin lives in Chicago with her four children.

www.sherminkruse.com

Hay House Titles of Related Interest

THE SHIFT, the movie,
starring Dr. Wayne W. Dyer
(available as an online streaming video)
www.hayhouse.com/the-shift-movie

***

HIGH PERFORMANCE HABITS: How Extraordinary People Become That Way, by Brendon Burchard

BE THE CALM OR BE THE STORM: Leadership Lessons from a Woman at the Helm, by Captain Sandy Yawn

THE GAP AND THE GAIN: The High Achievers' Guide to Happiness, Confidence, and Success, by Dan Sullivan with Dr. Benjamin Hardy

GRAVITAS: The 8 Strengths That Redefine Confidence, by Lisa Sun

INTENTIONALITY: A Groundbreaking Guide to Breath, Consciousness, and Radical Self-Transformation, by Finnian Kelly

SOVEREIGN: Reclaim Your Freedom, Energy, and Power in a Time of Distraction, Uncertainty, and Chaos, by Emma Seppälä, Ph.D.

All of the above are available at your local bookstore or may be ordered by visiting:

Hay House USA: www.hayhouse.com®
Hay House Australia: www.hayhouse.com.au
Hay House UK: www.hayhouse.co.uk
Hay House India: www.hayhouse.co.in

***

We hope you enjoyed this Hay House book. If you'd like to receive our online catalog featuring additional information on Hay House books and products, or if you'd like to find out more about the Hay Foundation, please contact:

HAY HOUSE

Hay House Publishers (India) Pvt Ltd
Muskaan Complex, Plot No. 3,
B-2, Vasant Kunj, New Delhi 110 070
Phone: +91 11 41761620
www.hayhouse.co.in

—

Published in the United States by:
Hay House LLC, P.O. Box 5100, Carlsbad, CA 92018-5100
(760) 31-7695 or (800) 654-5126
www.hayhouse.com® • www.hayfoundation.org

Published in Australia by:
Hay House Australia Publishing Pty Ltd
18/36 Ralph St., Alexandria NSW 2015
Phone: +61 (02) 9669 4299
www.hayhouse.com.au

Published in the United Kingdom by:
Hay House UK Ltd
1st Floor, Crawford Corner,
91–93 Baker Street, London W1U 6QQ
Phone: +44 (0)20 3927 7290
www.hayhouse.co.uk

—

CONNECT WITH

HAY HOUSE

ONLINE

hayhouse.co.in

@hayhouseindia

@hayhouseindia

@hayhouseindia

'The gateways to wisdom and knowledge are always open.'

Louise Hay